CIVIL WAR II

AMAZING SPIDER-MAN

CIVIL WAR II: AMAZING SPIDER-MAN. Contains material originally published in magazine form as CIVIL WAR II: AMAZING SPIDER-MAN #1-4 and AMAZING SPIDER-MAN #7-8. First printing 2016. ISBN# 978-1-302-90250-6. Published by MARVEL WORLDWIDE, INC., a subsidiary of MARVEL ENTERTAINMENT, LLC. OFFICE OF PUBLICATION: 135 West 50th Street, New York, NY 10020. Copyright © 2016 MARVEL No similarity between any of the names, characters, persons, and/or institutions in this magazine with those of any living or dead person or institution is intended, and any such similarity which may exist is purely coincidental. **Printed in Canada.** ALAN FINE, President, Marvel Entertainment; DAN BUCKLEY, President, TV, Publishing & Brand Management; JOE QUESADA, Chief Creative Officer; TOM BREVOORT, SVP of Publishing; DAVID BOGART, SVP of Business Affairs & Operations, Publishing & Partnership; C.B. CEBULSKI, VP of Brand Management & Development, Asia; DAVID GABRIEL, SVP of Sales & Marketing, Publishing; JEFF YOUNGQUIST, VP of Production & Special Projects; DAN CARR, Executive Director of Publishing Technology; ALEX MORALES, Director of Publishing Operations; SUSAN CRESPI, Production Manager; STAN LEE, Chairman Emeritus. For information regarding advertising in Marvel Comics or on Marvel.com, please contact Vit DeBellis, Integrated Sales Manager, at vdebellis@marvel.com. For Marvel subscription inquiries, please call 888-511-5480. **Manufactured between 9/9/2016 and 10/17/2016 by SOLISCO PRINTERS, SCOTT, QC, CANADA.**

10 9 8 7 6 5 4 3 2 1

CIVIL WAR II

AMAZING SPIDER-MAN

WHEN SCIENCE GEEK PETER PARKER WAS BITTEN BY A RADIOACTIVE SPIDER, HE GAINED THE PROPORTIONAL SPEED, STRENGTH AND AGILITY OF A SPIDER; ADHESIVE FINGERTIPS AND TOES; AND THE UNIQUE AWARENESS OF DANGER CALLED "SPIDER-SENSE." AFTER YEARS OF BARELY GETTING BY AND MOONLIGHTING AS SPIDER-MAN, PETER HAS LIVED UP TO HIS POTENTIAL AND FORMED HIS OWN COMPANY, PARKER INDUSTRIES, WITH OFFICES AROUND THE WORLD.

RECENTLY, SPIDER-MAN AND THE REST OF THE SUPER HERO COMMUNITY TURNED BACK AN ALIEN INVASION THANKS TO THE PRECOGNITIVE VISION OF A NEW INHUMAN NAMED ULYSSES. BUT LITTLE IS KNOWN ABOUT ULYSSES AND A DEBATE IS FORMING REGARDING WHETHER OR NOT HIS VISIONS SHOULD BE TRUSTED AND USED.

WRITER
CHRISTOS GAGE

ARTIST
TRAVEL FOREMAN

COLOR ARTIST
RAIN BEREDO

LETTERER
VC's JOE CARAMAGNA

COVER ARTISTS
KHARY RANDOLPH & EMILIO LOPEZ (#1)
AND
TRAVEL FOREMAN & JASON KEITH (#2-4)

ASSISTANT EDITOR
ALLISON STOCK

ASSOCIATE EDITOR
DEVIN LEWIS

EDITOR
NICK LOWE

COLLECTION EDITOR
JENNIFER GRÜNWALD
ASSOCIATE MANAGING EDITOR
KATERI WOODY
ASSOCIATE EDITOR
SARAH BRUNSTAD
EDITOR, SPECIAL PROJECTS
MARK D. BEAZLEY
VP PRODUCTION & SPECIAL PROJECTS
JEFF YOUNGQUIST
SVP PRINT, SALES & MARKETING
DAVID GABRIEL

BOOK DESIGNER
JAY BOWEN

EDITOR IN CHIEF
AXEL ALONSO
CHIEF CREATIVE OFFICER
JOE QUESADA
PUBLISHER
DAN BUCKLEY
EXECUTIVE PRODUCER
ALAN FINE

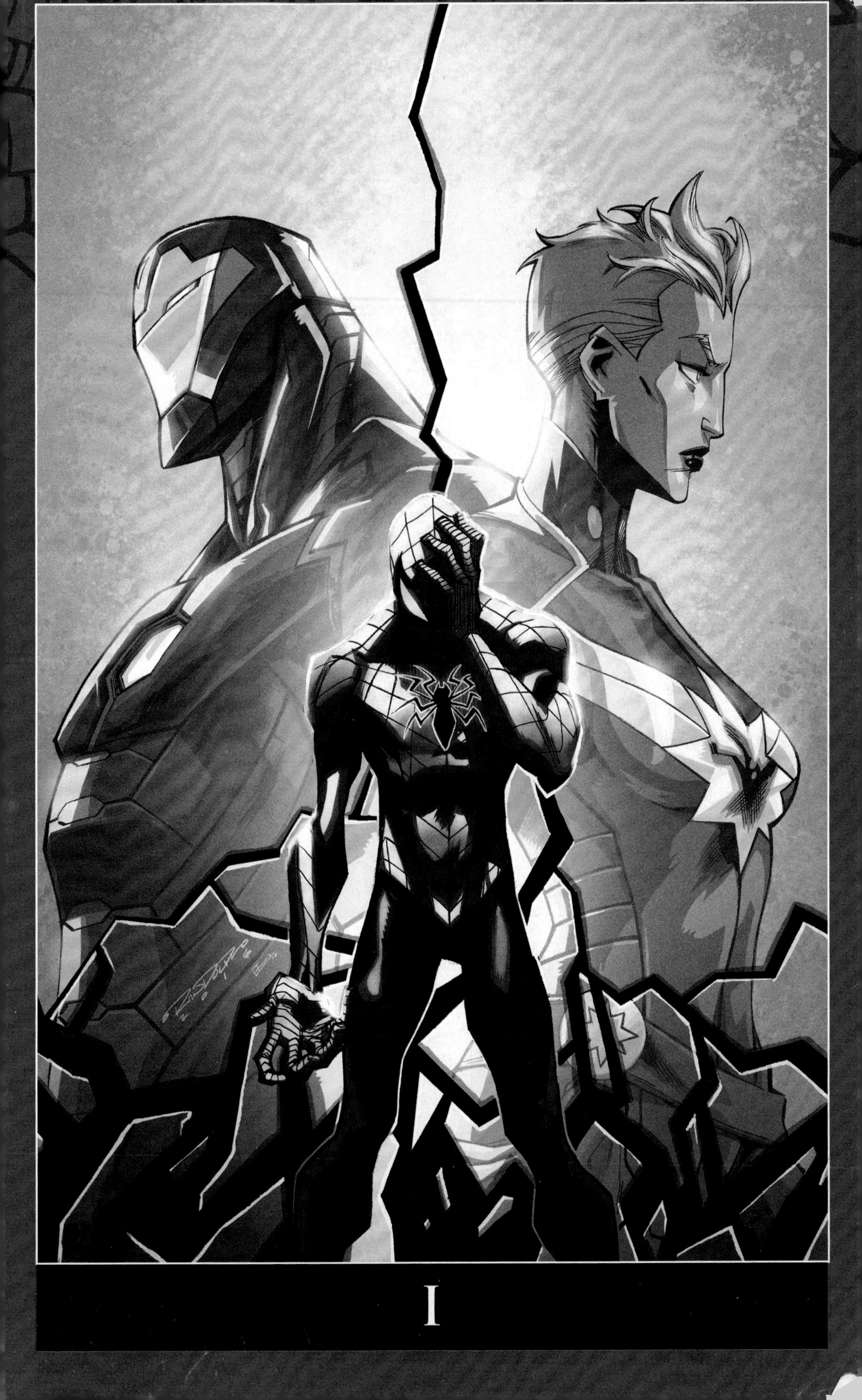

I

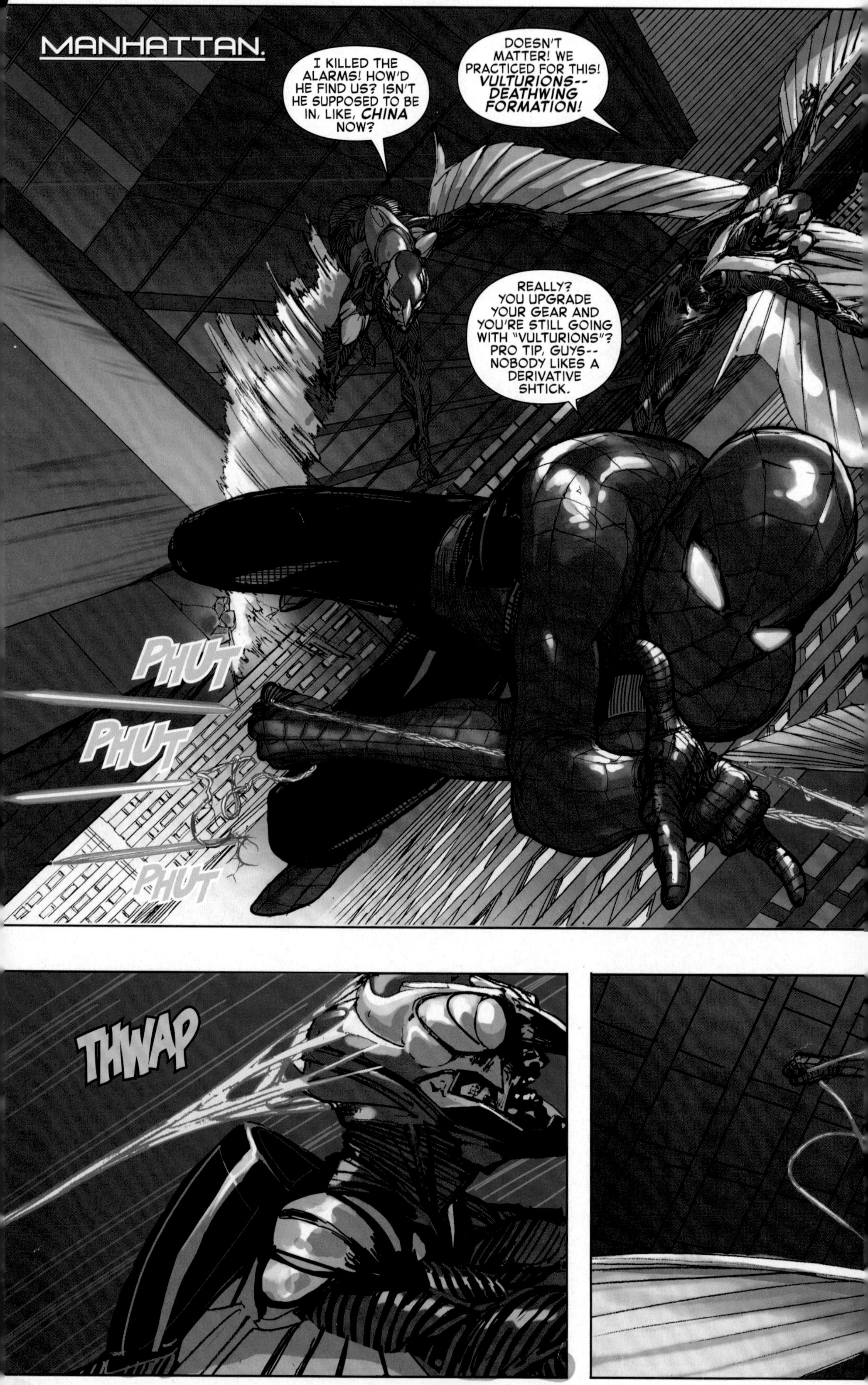

MANHATTAN.
I KILLED THE ALARMS! HOW'D HE FIND US? ISN'T HE SUPPOSED TO BE IN, LIKE, *CHINA* NOW?
DOESN'T MATTER! WE PRACTICED FOR THIS! *VULTURIONS--DEATHWING FORMATION!*
REALLY? YOU UPGRADE YOUR GEAR AND YOU'RE STILL GOING WITH "VULTURIONS"? PRO TIP, GUYS--NOBODY LIKES A DERIVATIVE SHTICK.
PHUT
PHUT
PHUT
THWAP

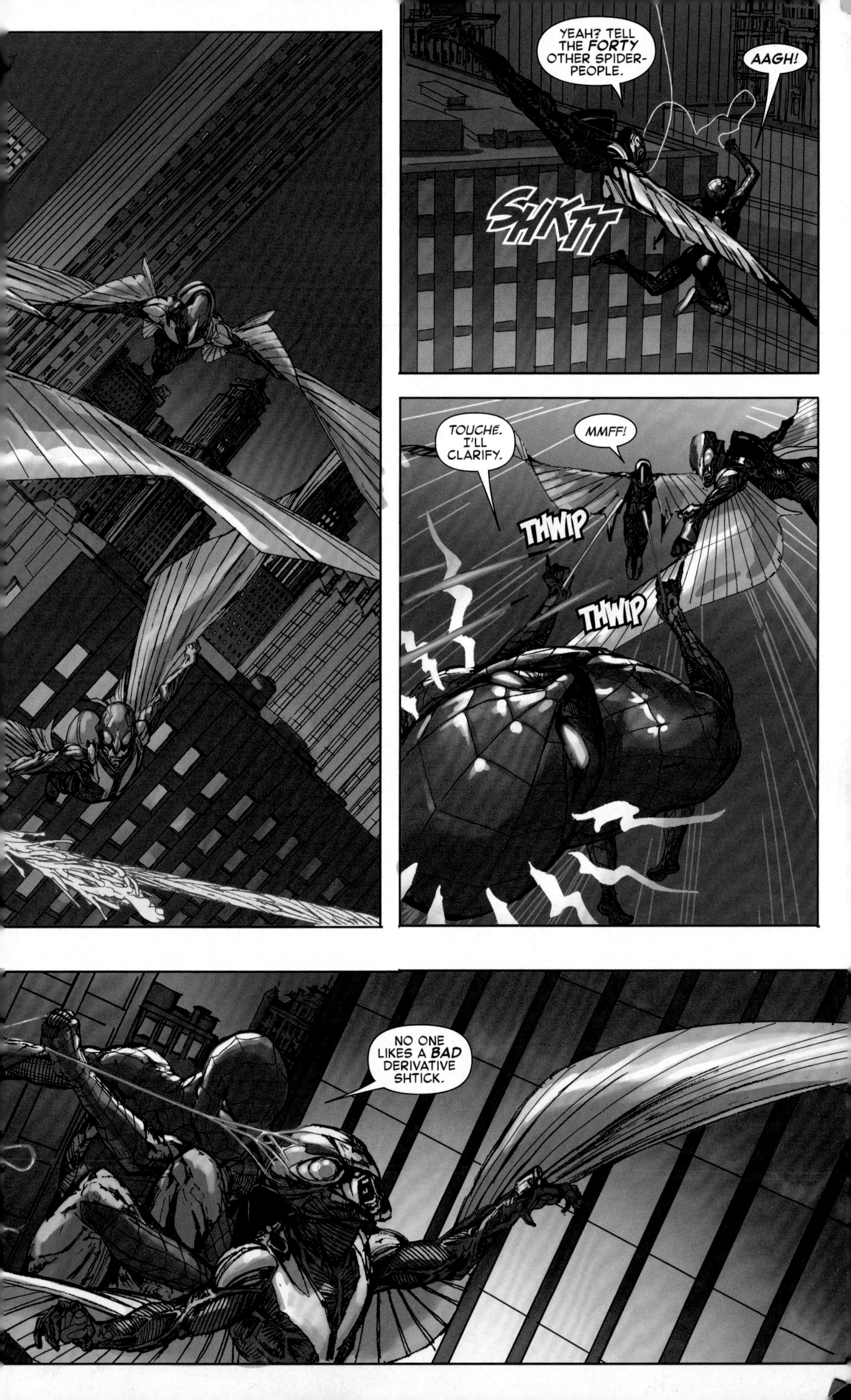
YEAH? TELL THE FORTY OTHER SPIDER-PEOPLE.
AAGH!
SHKTT
TOUCHÉ. I'LL CLARIFY.
MMFF!
THWIP
THWIP
NO ONE LIKES A BAD DERIVATIVE SHTICK.

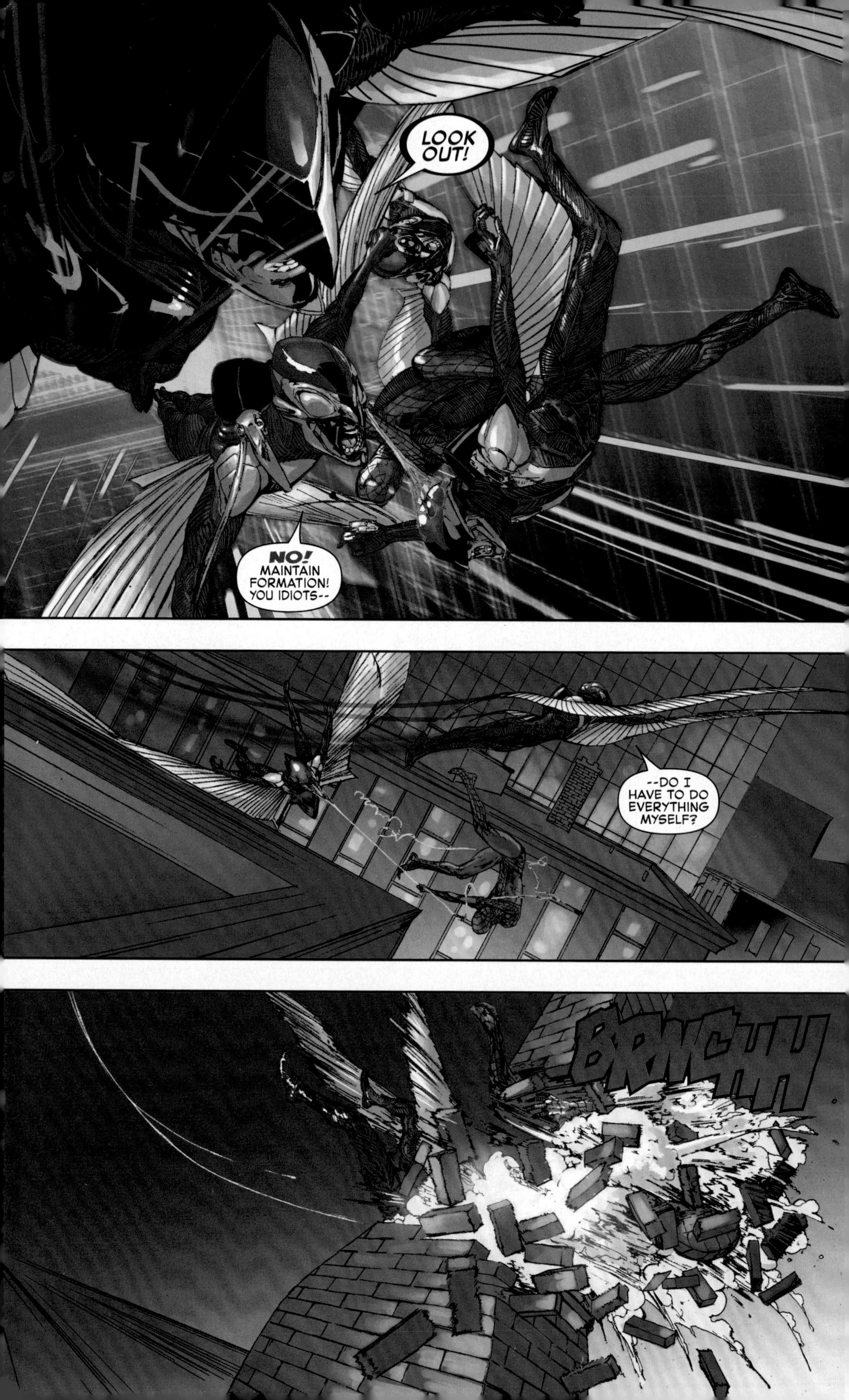
LOOK OUT!
NO! MAINTAIN FORMATION! YOU IDIOTS--
--DO I HAVE TO DO EVERYTHING MYSELF?
BRAKCHH

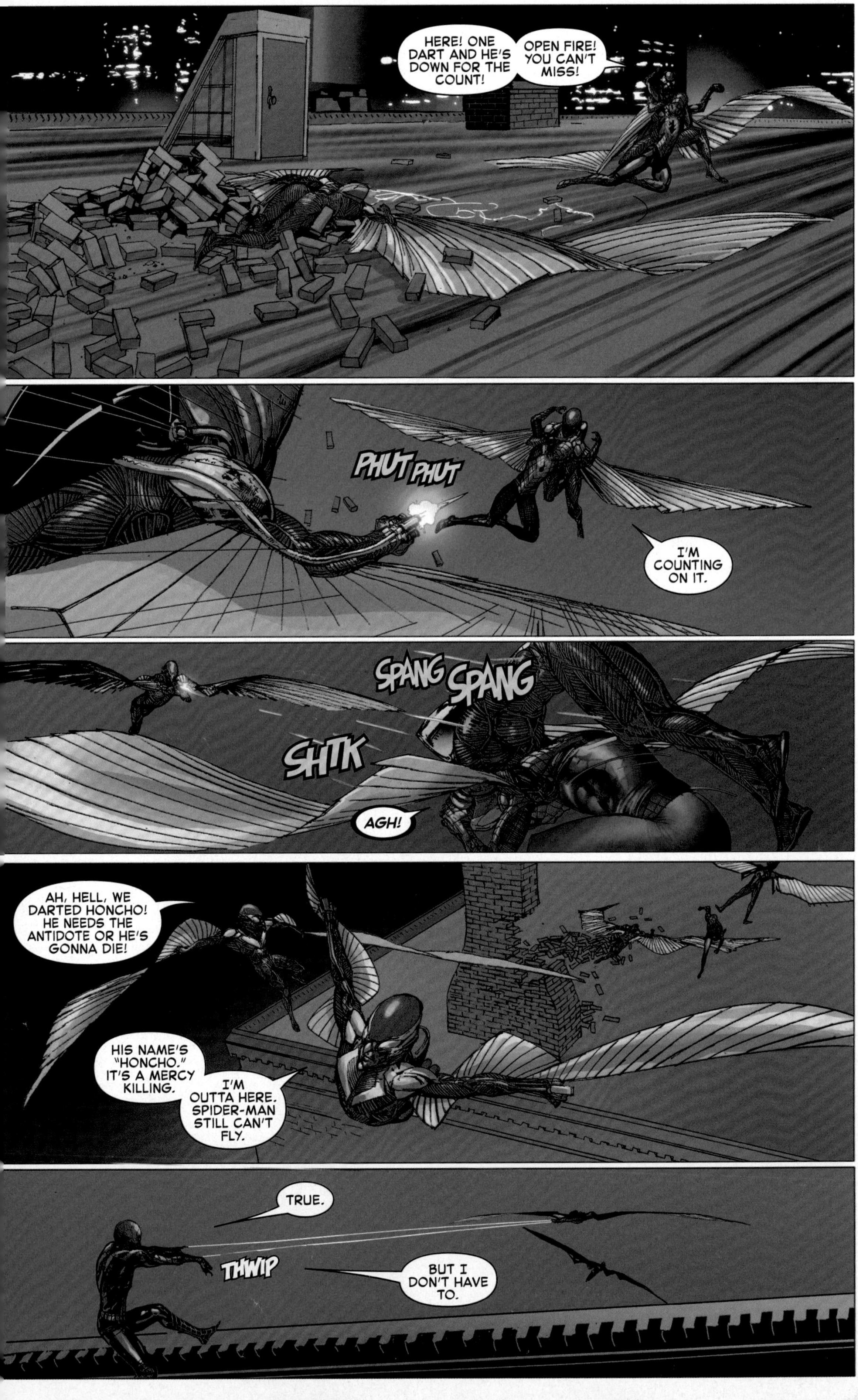
HERE! ONE DART AND HE'S DOWN FOR THE COUNT!
OPEN FIRE! YOU CAN'T MISS!
PHUT PHUT
I'M COUNTING ON IT.
SPANG SPANG
SHTK
AGH!
AH, HELL, WE DARTED HONCHO! HE NEEDS THE ANTIDOTE OR HE'S GONNA DIE!
HIS NAME'S "HONCHO." IT'S A MERCY KILLING.
I'M OUTTA HERE. SPIDER-MAN STILL CAN'T FLY.
TRUE.
THWIP
BUT I DON'T HAVE TO.

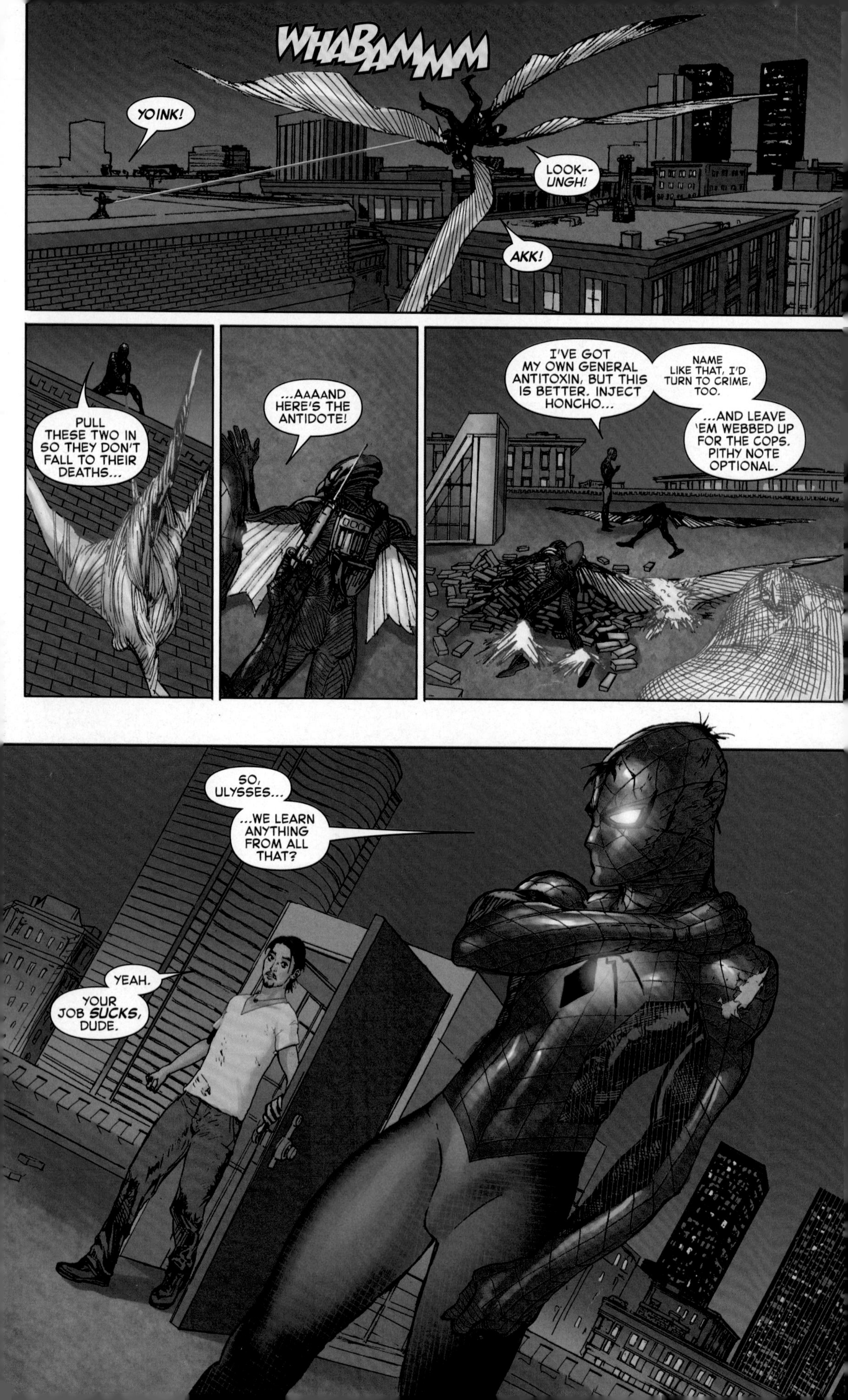
WHABAMMMM
YOINK!
LOOK-- UNGH!
AKK!
PULL THESE TWO IN SO THEY DON'T FALL TO THEIR DEATHS...
...AAAAND HERE'S THE ANTIDOTE!
I'VE GOT MY OWN GENERAL ANTITOXIN, BUT THIS IS BETTER. INJECT HONCHO...
NAME LIKE THAT, I'D TURN TO CRIME, TOO.
...AND LEAVE 'EM WEBBED UP FOR THE COPS. PITHY NOTE OPTIONAL.
SO, ULYSSES...
...WE LEARN ANYTHING FROM ALL THAT?
YEAH.
YOUR JOB SUCKS, DUDE.

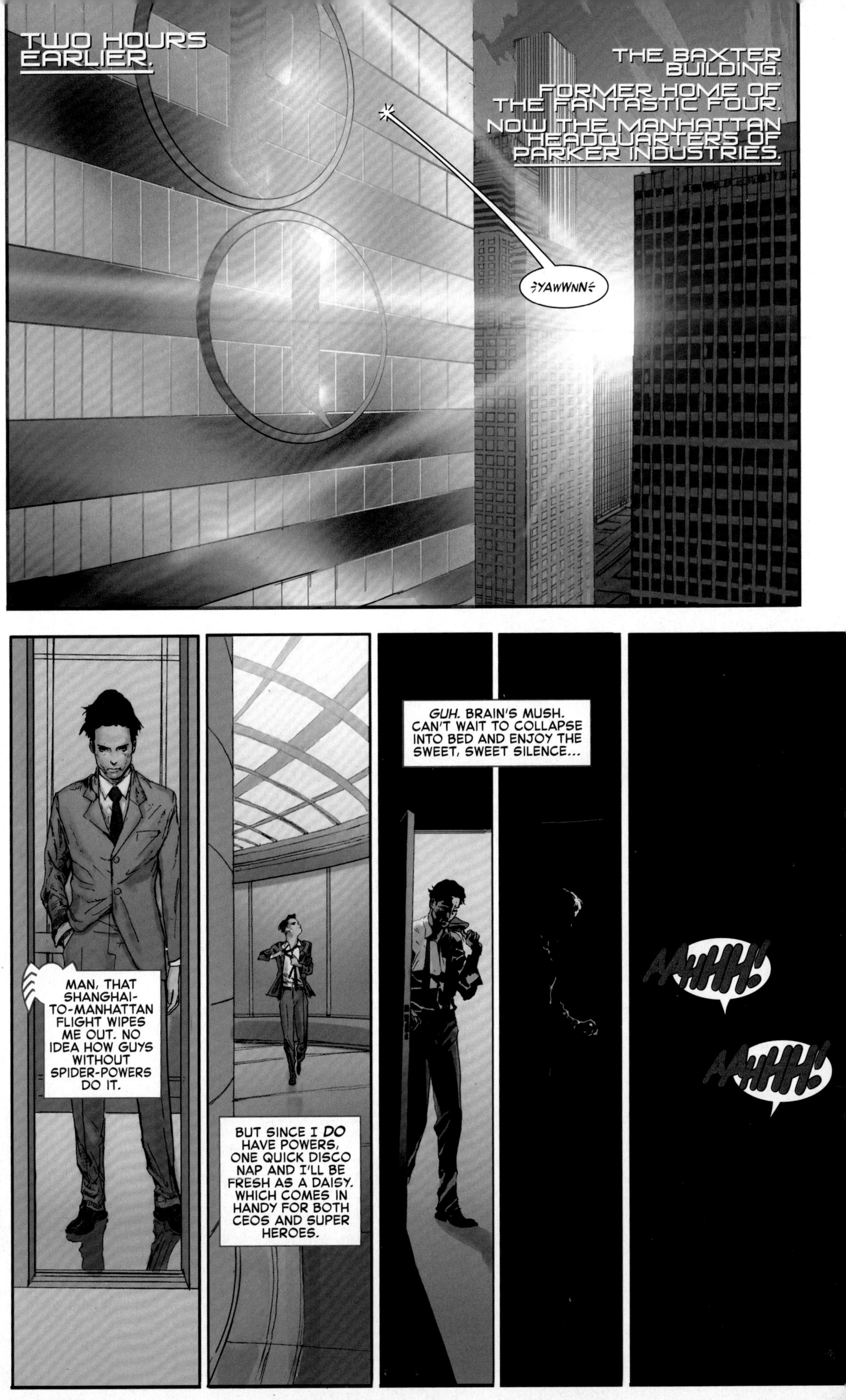
TWO HOURS EARLIER.
THE BAXTER BUILDING.
FORMER HOME OF THE FANTASTIC FOUR.
NOW THE MANHATTAN HEADQUARTERS OF PARKER INDUSTRIES.
YAWWNN
MAN, THAT SHANGHAI-TO-MANHATTAN FLIGHT WIPES ME OUT. NO IDEA HOW GUYS WITHOUT SPIDER-POWERS DO IT.
BUT SINCE I DO HAVE POWERS, ONE QUICK DISCO NAP AND I'LL BE FRESH AS A DAISY. WHICH COMES IN HANDY FOR BOTH CEOS AND SUPER HEROES.
GUH. BRAIN'S MUSH. CAN'T WAIT TO COLLAPSE INTO BED AND ENJOY THE SWEET, SWEET SILENCE...
AAHHH!
AAHHH!

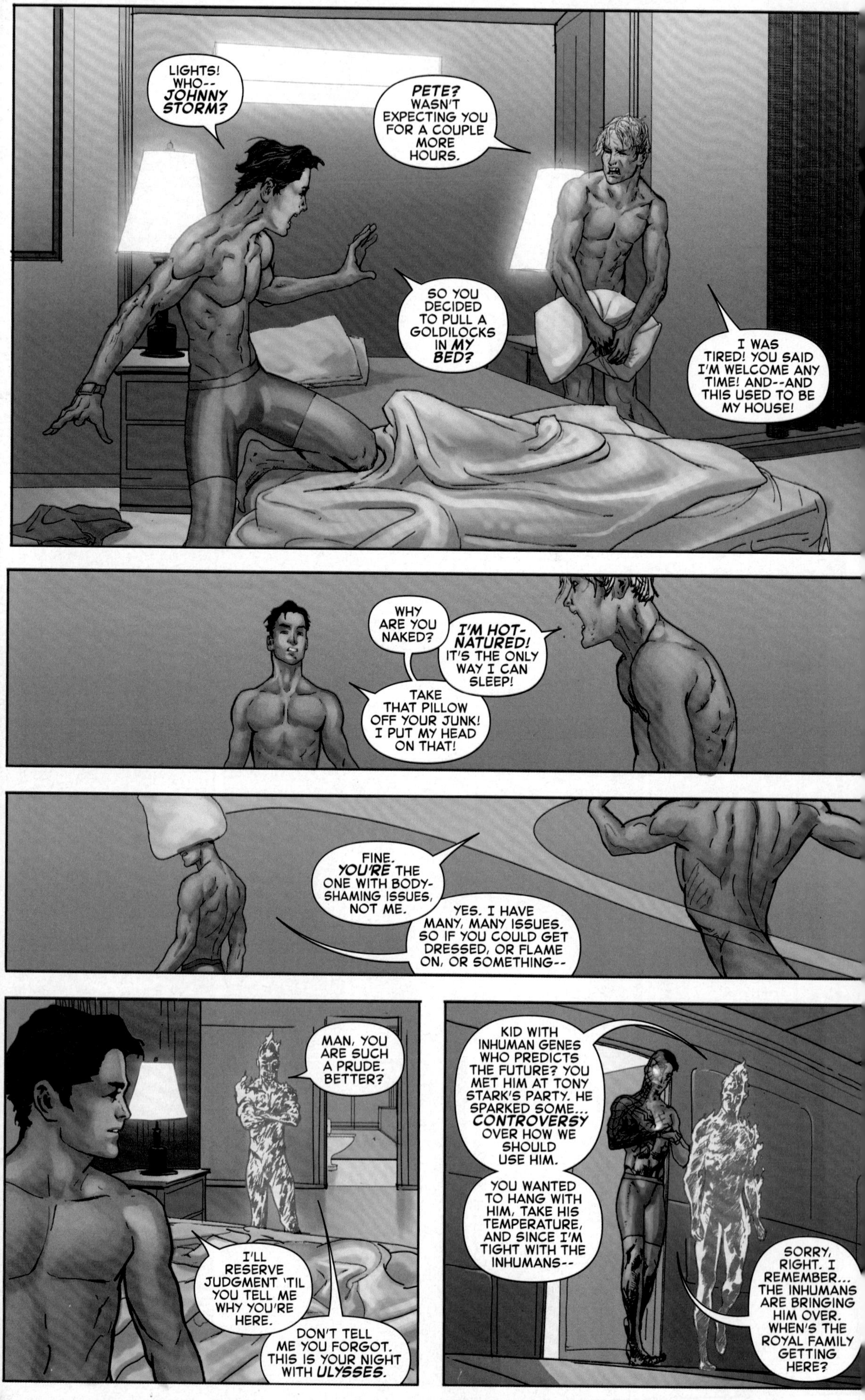
LIGHTS! WHO-- JOHNNY STORM?
PETE? WASN'T EXPECTING YOU FOR A COUPLE MORE HOURS.
SO YOU DECIDED TO PULL A GOLDILOCKS IN MY BED?
I WAS TIRED! YOU SAID I'M WELCOME ANY TIME! AND--AND THIS USED TO BE MY HOUSE!
WHY ARE YOU NAKED?
I'M HOT-NATURED! IT'S THE ONLY WAY I CAN SLEEP!
TAKE THAT PILLOW OFF YOUR JUNK! I PUT MY HEAD ON THAT!
FINE. YOU'RE THE ONE WITH BODY-SHAMING ISSUES, NOT ME.
YES. I HAVE MANY, MANY ISSUES. SO IF YOU COULD GET DRESSED, OR FLAME ON, OR SOMETHING--
MAN, YOU ARE SUCH A PRUDE. BETTER?
I'LL RESERVE JUDGMENT 'TIL YOU TELL ME WHY YOU'RE HERE.
DON'T TELL ME YOU FORGOT. THIS IS YOUR NIGHT WITH ULYSSES.
KID WITH INHUMAN GENES WHO PREDICTS THE FUTURE? YOU MET HIM AT TONY STARK'S PARTY. HE SPARKED SOME... CONTROVERSY OVER HOW WE SHOULD USE HIM.
YOU WANTED TO HANG WITH HIM, TAKE HIS TEMPERATURE, AND SINCE I'M TIGHT WITH THE INHUMANS--
SORRY, RIGHT. I REMEMBER... THE INHUMANS ARE BRINGING HIM OVER. WHEN'S THE ROYAL FAMILY GETTING HERE?

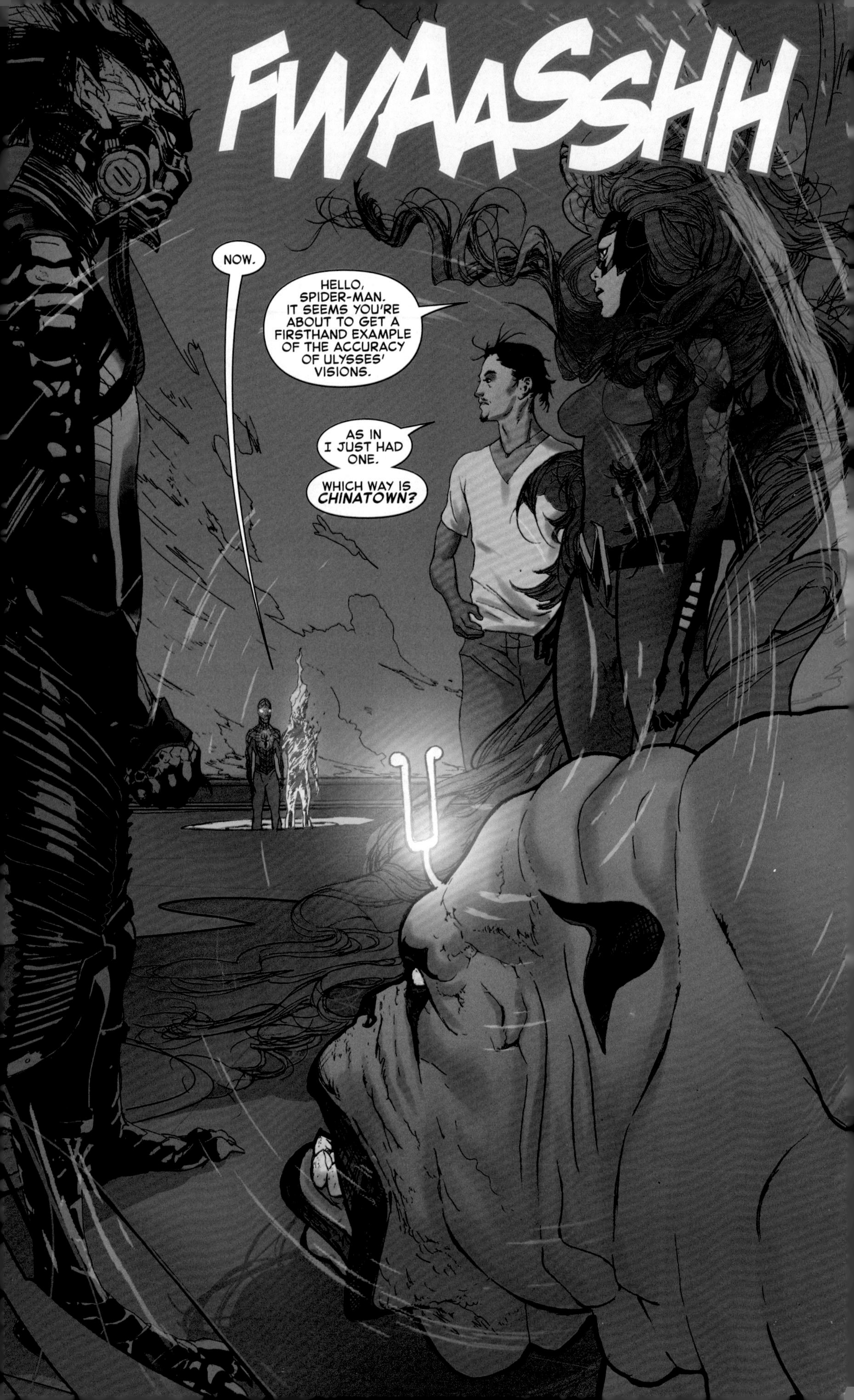
FWAASSHH
NOW.
HELLO, SPIDER-MAN. IT SEEMS YOU'RE ABOUT TO GET A FIRSTHAND EXAMPLE OF THE ACCURACY OF ULYSSES' VISIONS.
AS IN I JUST HAD ONE.
WHICH WAY IS CHINATOWN?

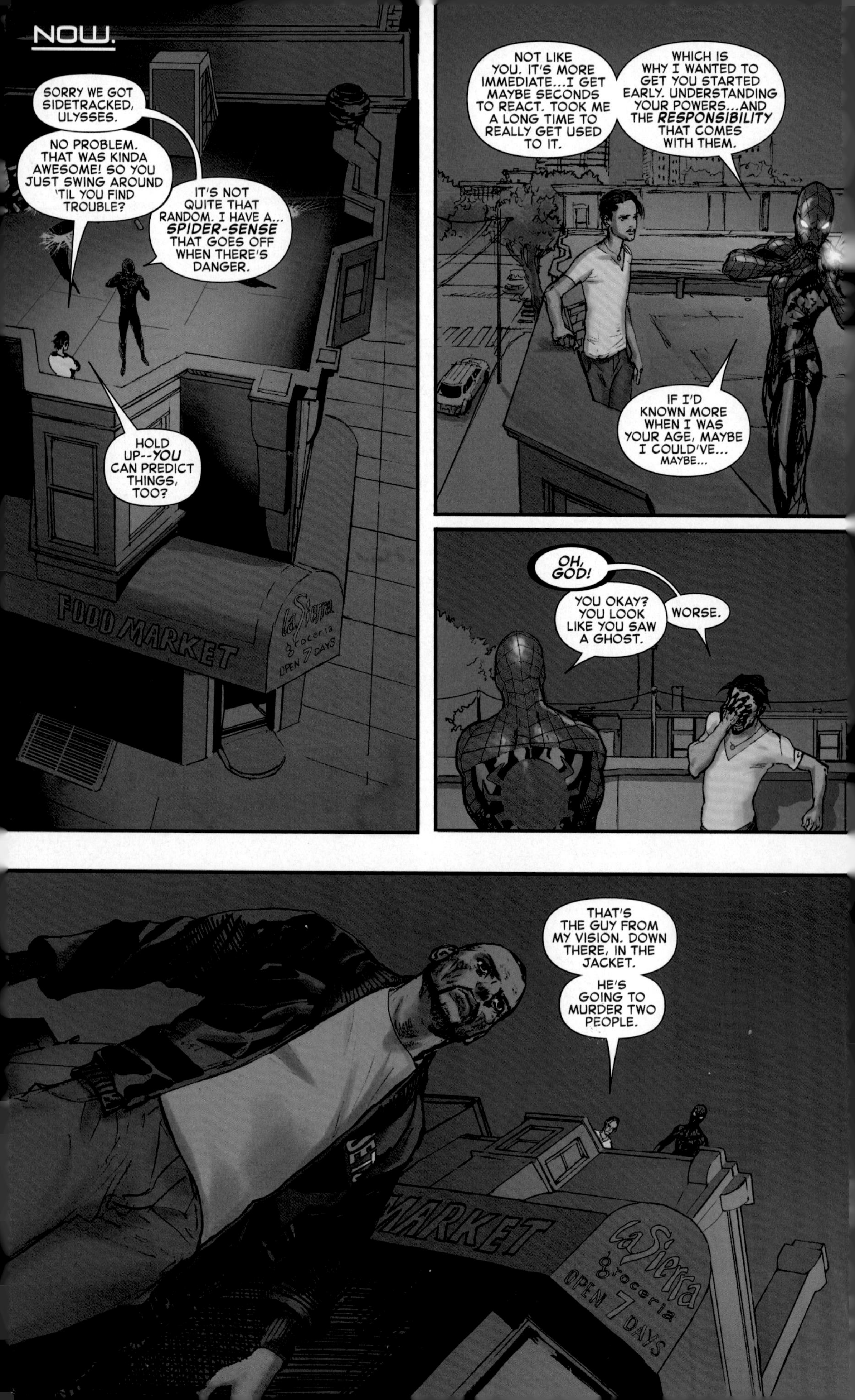
NOW.
SORRY WE GOT SIDETRACKED, ULYSSES.
NO PROBLEM. THAT WAS KINDA AWESOME! SO YOU JUST SWING AROUND 'TIL YOU FIND TROUBLE?
IT'S NOT QUITE THAT RANDOM. I HAVE A... SPIDER-SENSE THAT GOES OFF WHEN THERE'S DANGER.
HOLD UP--YOU CAN PREDICT THINGS, TOO?
FOOD MARKET
La Sierra groceria OPEN 7 DAYS
NOT LIKE YOU. IT'S MORE IMMEDIATE...I GET MAYBE SECONDS TO REACT. TOOK ME A LONG TIME TO REALLY GET USED TO IT.
WHICH IS WHY I WANTED TO GET YOU STARTED EARLY. UNDERSTANDING YOUR POWERS...AND THE RESPONSIBILITY THAT COMES WITH THEM.
IF I'D KNOWN MORE WHEN I WAS YOUR AGE, MAYBE I COULD'VE... MAYBE...
OH, GOD!
YOU OKAY? YOU LOOK LIKE YOU SAW A GHOST.
WORSE.
THAT'S THE GUY FROM MY VISION. DOWN THERE, IN THE JACKET.
HE'S GOING TO MURDER TWO PEOPLE.
MARKET
La Sierra groceria OPEN 7 DAYS

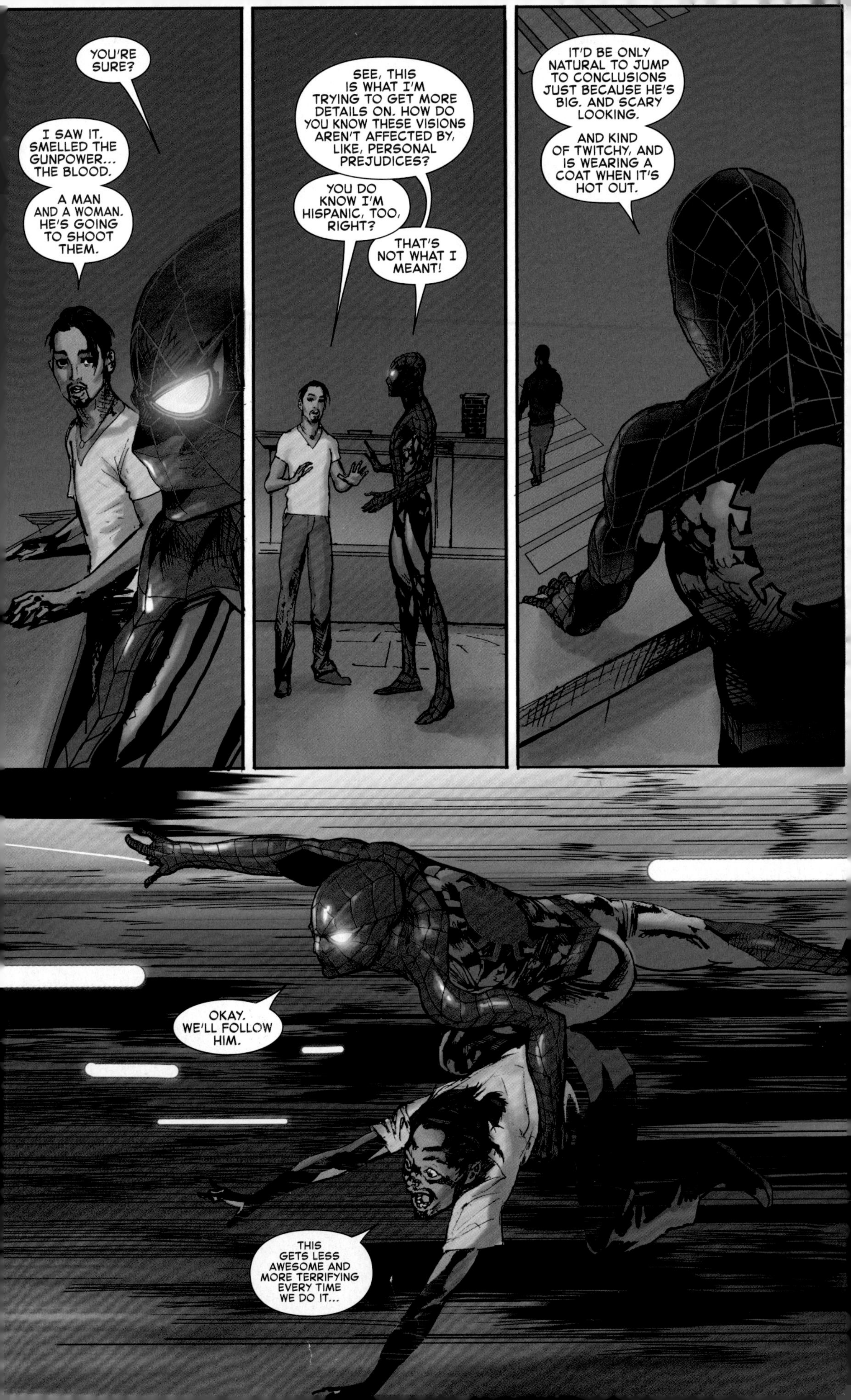
YOU'RE SURE?
I SAW IT. SMELLED THE GUNPOWER... THE BLOOD.
A MAN AND A WOMAN. HE'S GOING TO SHOOT THEM.
SEE, THIS IS WHAT I'M TRYING TO GET MORE DETAILS ON. HOW DO YOU KNOW THESE VISIONS AREN'T AFFECTED BY, LIKE, PERSONAL PREJUDICES?
YOU DO KNOW I'M HISPANIC, TOO, RIGHT?
THAT'S NOT WHAT I MEANT!
IT'D BE ONLY NATURAL TO JUMP TO CONCLUSIONS JUST BECAUSE HE'S BIG. AND SCARY LOOKING.
AND KIND OF TWITCHY, AND IS WEARING A COAT WHEN IT'S HOT OUT.
OKAY. WE'LL FOLLOW HIM.
THIS GETS LESS AWESOME AND MORE TERRIFYING EVERY TIME WE DO IT...

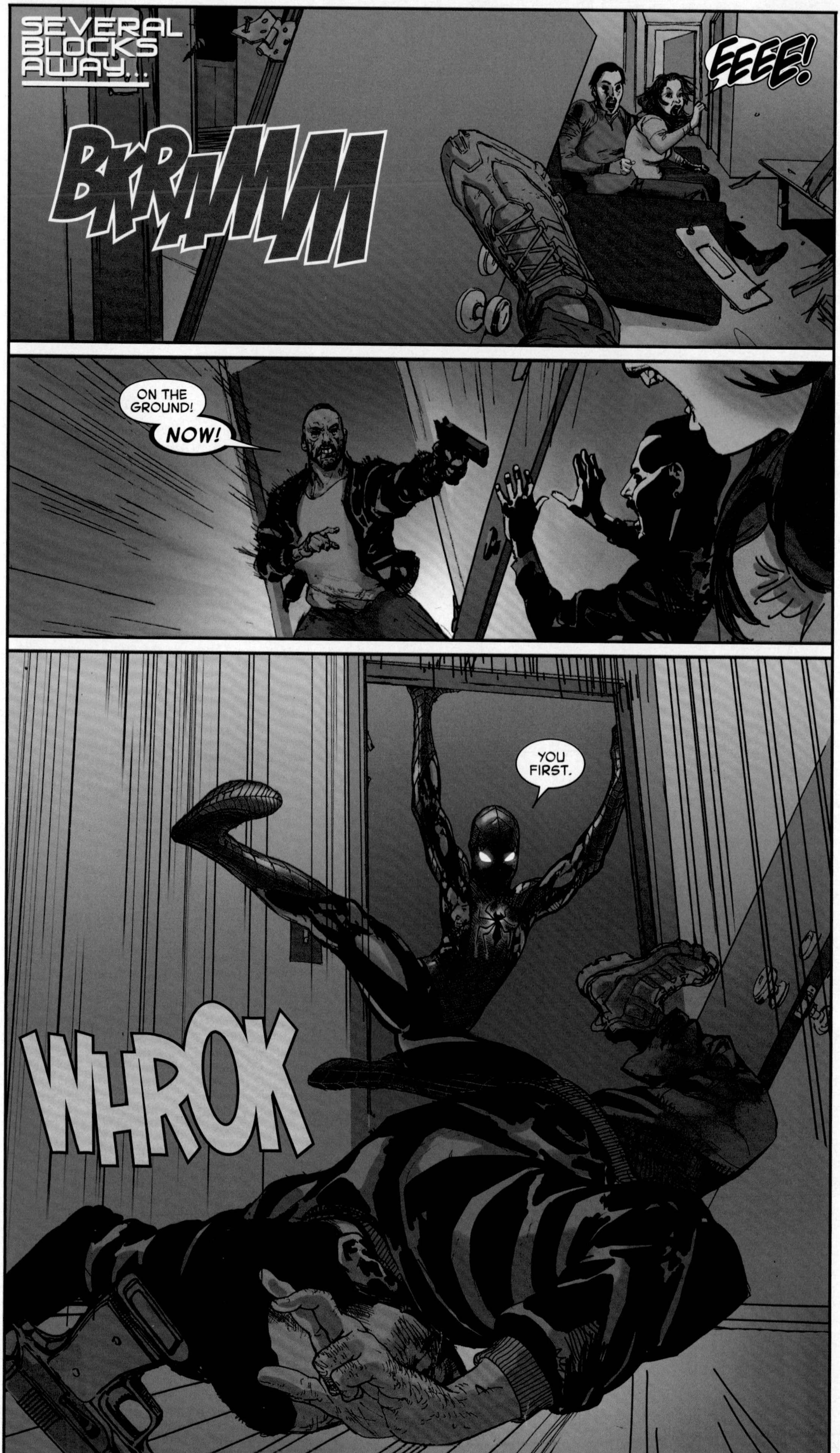
SEVERAL BLOCKS AWAY...
BKRAMM
EEEE!
ON THE GROUND! NOW!
YOU FIRST.
WHROK

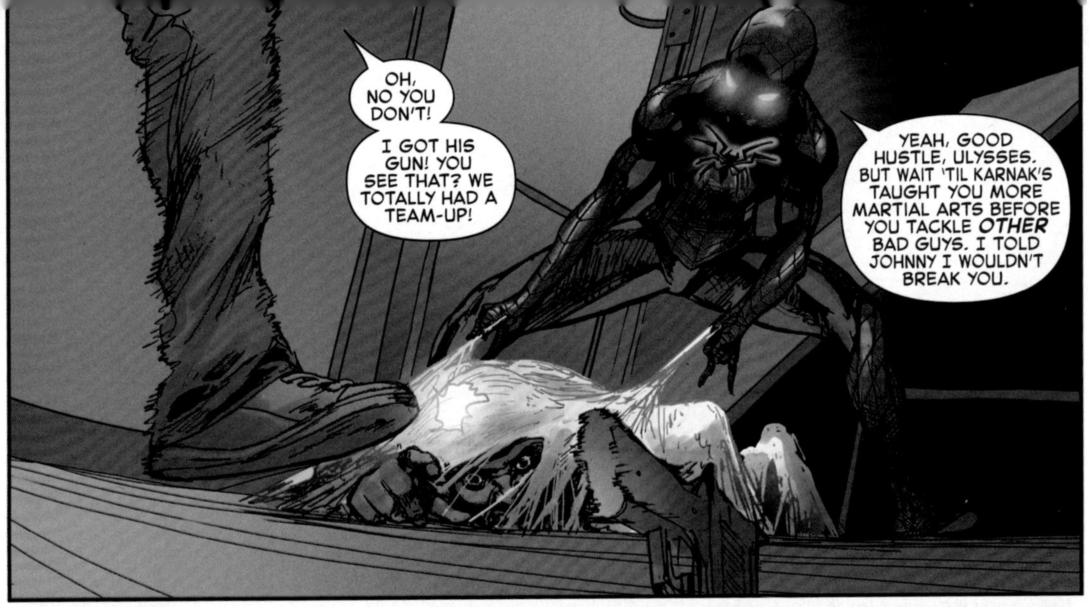
OH, NO YOU DON'T!
I GOT HIS GUN! YOU SEE THAT? WE TOTALLY HAD A TEAM-UP!
YEAH, GOOD HUSTLE, ULYSSES. BUT WAIT 'TIL KARNAK'S TAUGHT YOU MORE MARTIAL ARTS BEFORE YOU TACKLE OTHER BAD GUYS. I TOLD JOHNNY I WOULDN'T BREAK YOU.

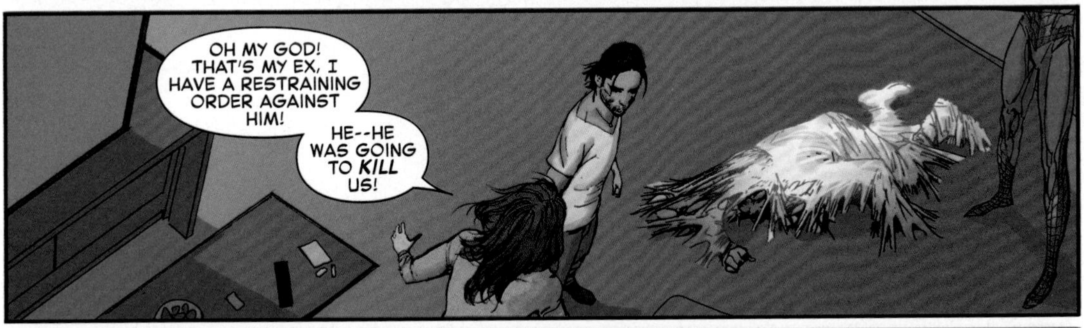
OH MY GOD! THAT'S MY EX, I HAVE A RESTRAINING ORDER AGAINST HIM!
HE--HE WAS GOING TO KILL US!

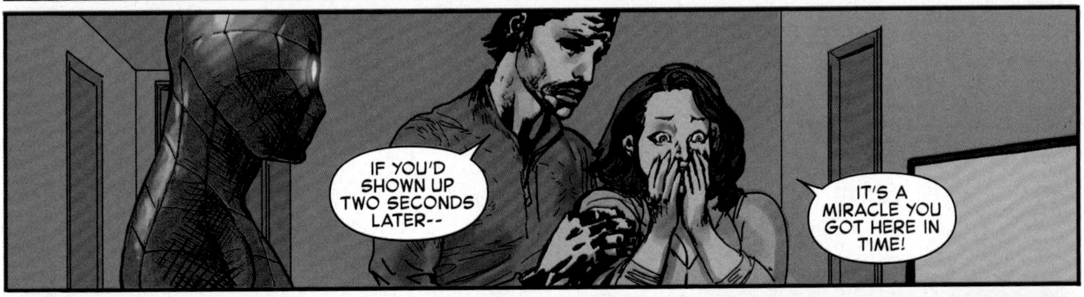
IF YOU'D SHOWN UP TWO SECONDS LATER--
IT'S A MIRACLE YOU GOT HERE IN TIME!

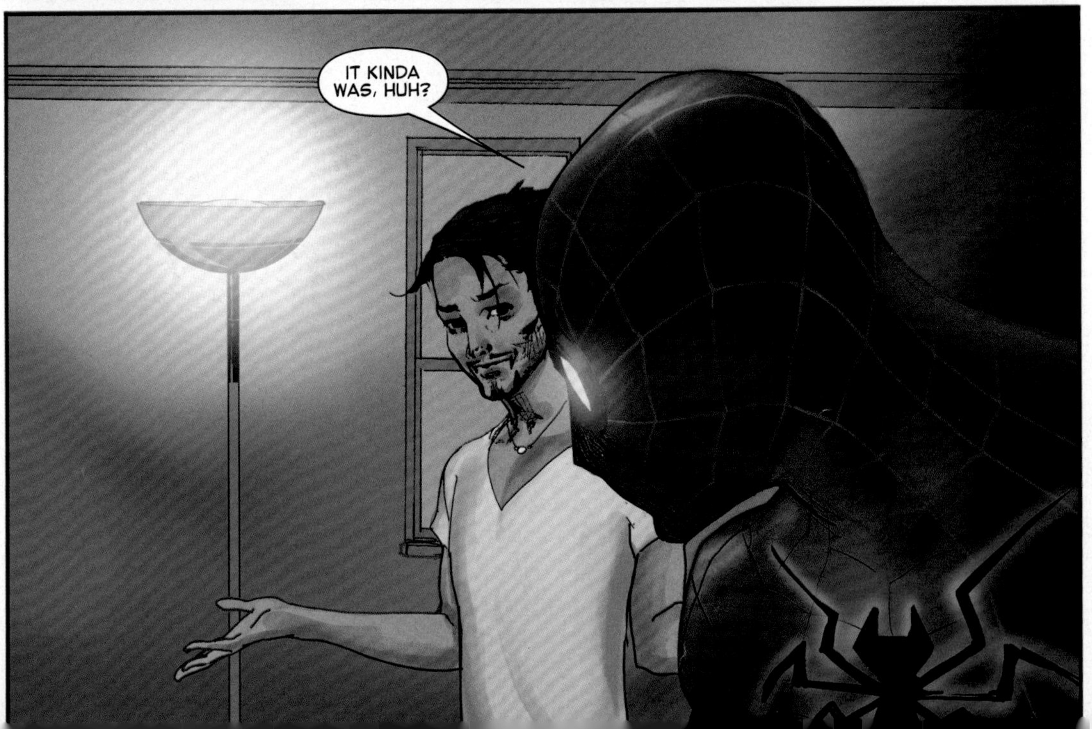
IT KINDA WAS, HUH?

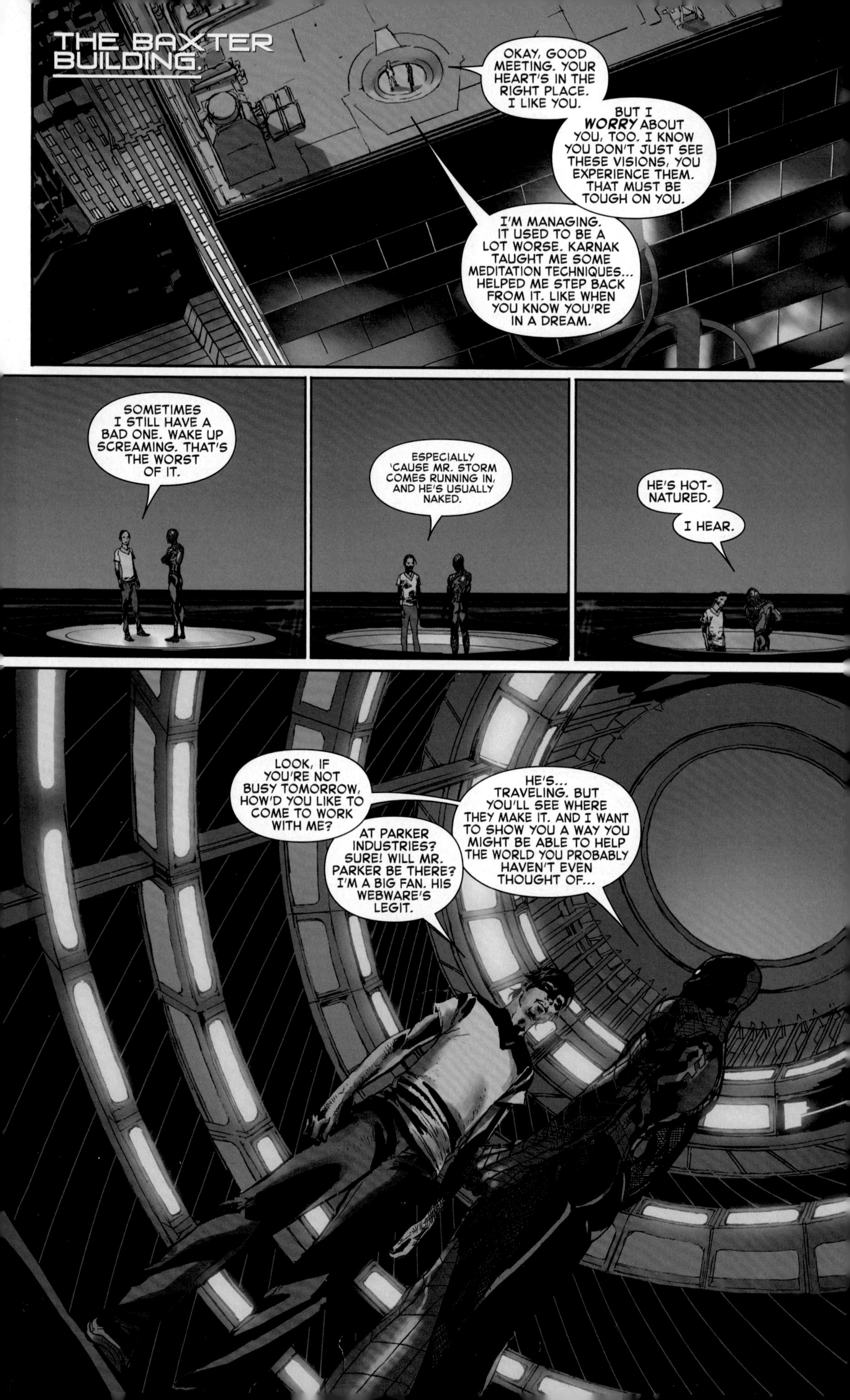
THE BAXTER BUILDING.
OKAY, GOOD MEETING. YOUR HEART'S IN THE RIGHT PLACE. I LIKE YOU.
BUT I WORRY ABOUT YOU, TOO. I KNOW YOU DON'T JUST SEE THESE VISIONS, YOU EXPERIENCE THEM. THAT MUST BE TOUGH ON YOU.
I'M MANAGING. IT USED TO BE A LOT WORSE. KARNAK TAUGHT ME SOME MEDITATION TECHNIQUES... HELPED ME STEP BACK FROM IT. LIKE WHEN YOU KNOW YOU'RE IN A DREAM.
SOMETIMES I STILL HAVE A BAD ONE. WAKE UP SCREAMING. THAT'S THE WORST OF IT.
ESPECIALLY 'CAUSE MR. STORM COMES RUNNING IN, AND HE'S USUALLY NAKED.
HE'S HOT-NATURED.
I HEAR.
LOOK, IF YOU'RE NOT BUSY TOMORROW, HOW'D YOU LIKE TO COME TO WORK WITH ME?
AT PARKER INDUSTRIES? SURE! WILL MR. PARKER BE THERE? I'M A BIG FAN. HIS WEBWARE'S LEGIT.
HE'S... TRAVELING. BUT YOU'LL SEE WHERE THEY MAKE IT. AND I WANT TO SHOW YOU A WAY YOU MIGHT BE ABLE TO HELP THE WORLD YOU PROBABLY HAVEN'T EVEN THOUGHT OF...

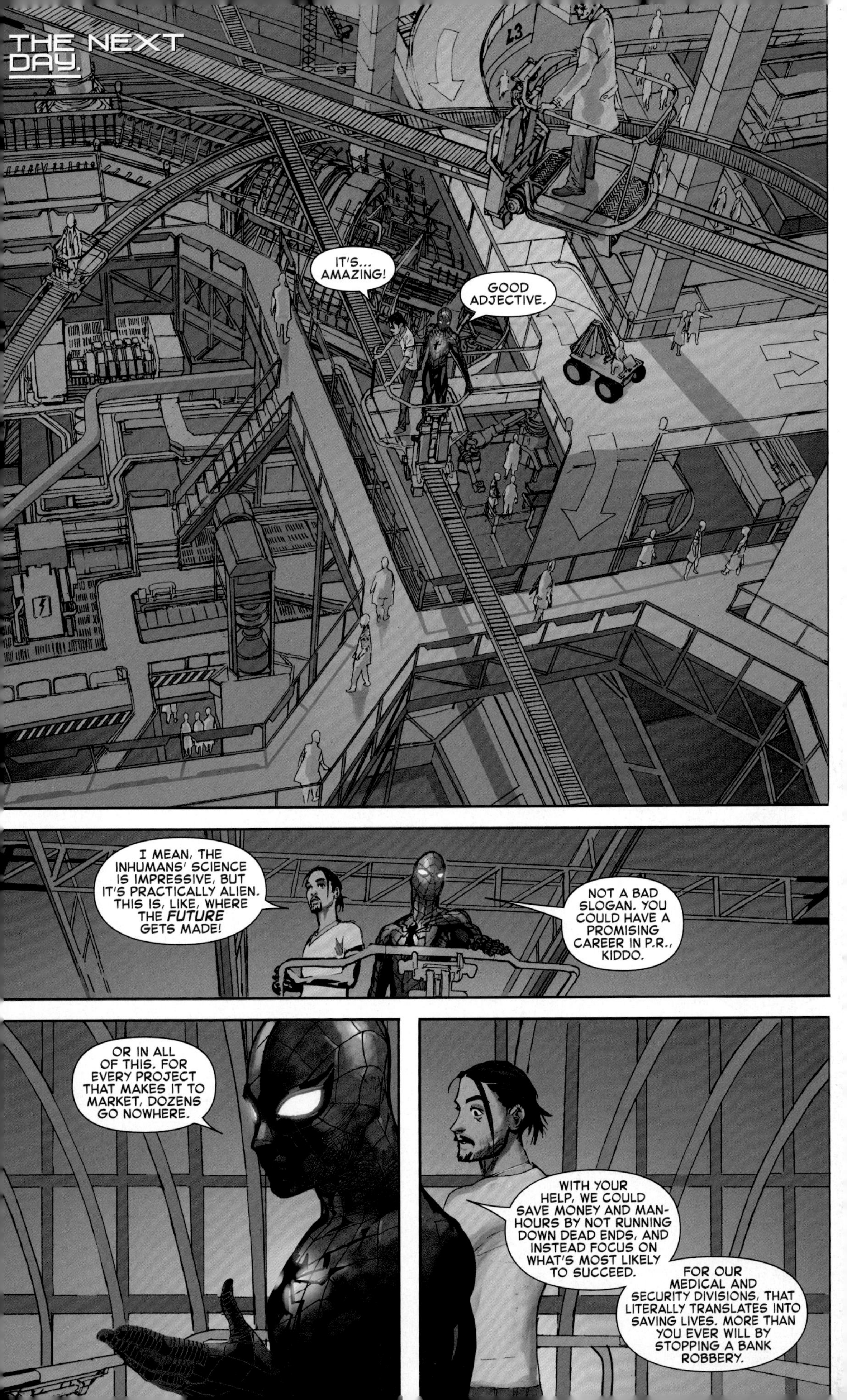
THE NEXT DAY.
IT'S... AMAZING!
GOOD ADJECTIVE.
I MEAN, THE INHUMANS' SCIENCE IS IMPRESSIVE, BUT IT'S PRACTICALLY ALIEN. THIS IS, LIKE, WHERE THE *FUTURE* GETS MADE!
NOT A BAD SLOGAN. YOU COULD HAVE A PROMISING CAREER IN P.R., KIDDO.
OR IN ALL OF THIS. FOR EVERY PROJECT THAT MAKES IT TO MARKET, DOZENS GO NOWHERE.
WITH YOUR HELP, WE COULD SAVE MONEY AND MAN-HOURS BY NOT RUNNING DOWN DEAD ENDS, AND INSTEAD FOCUS ON WHAT'S MOST LIKELY TO SUCCEED.
FOR OUR MEDICAL AND SECURITY DIVISIONS, THAT LITERALLY TRANSLATES INTO SAVING LIVES. MORE THAN YOU EVER WILL BY STOPPING A BANK ROBBERY.

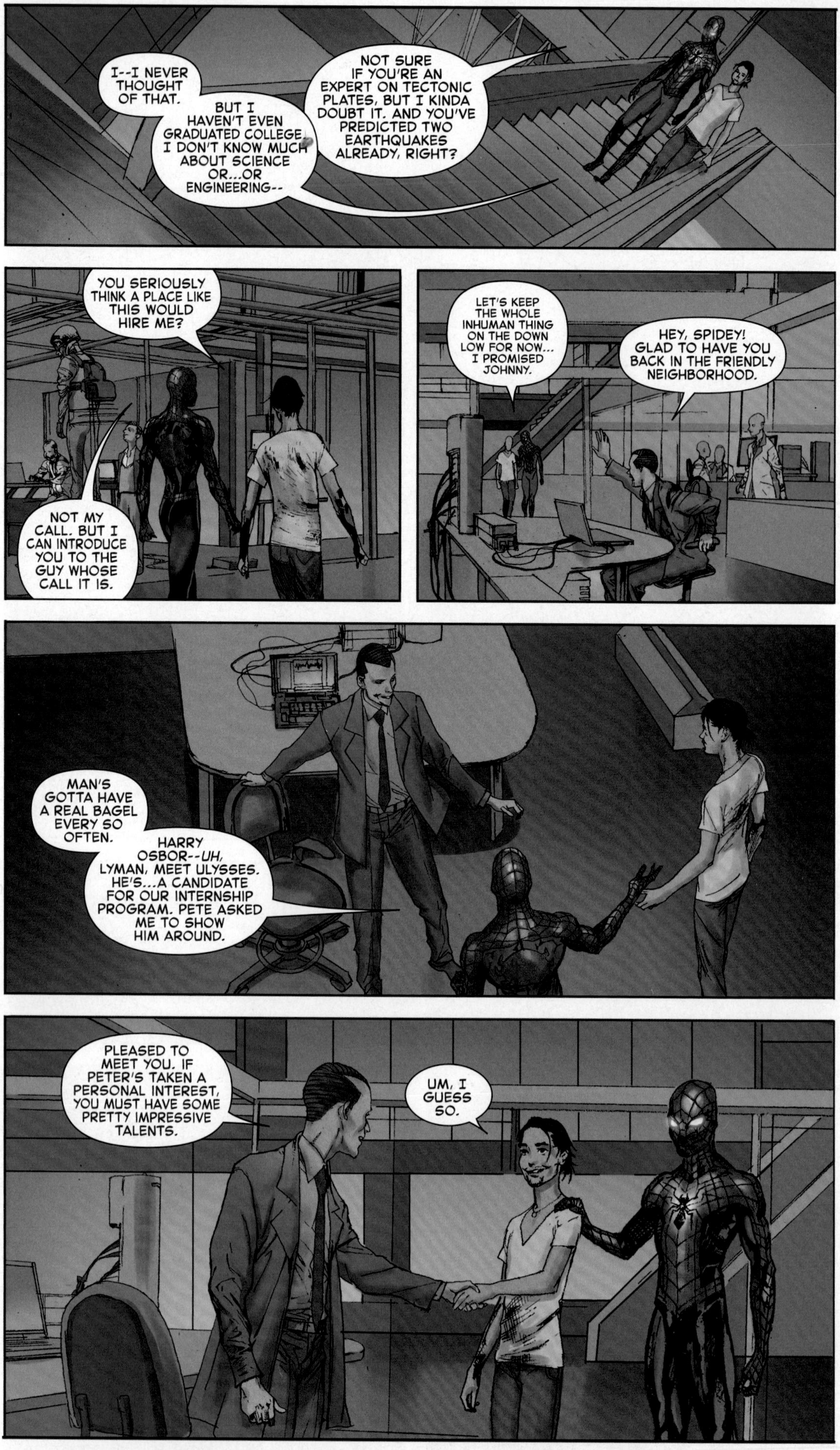

I--I NEVER THOUGHT OF THAT.
BUT I HAVEN'T EVEN GRADUATED COLLEGE. I DON'T KNOW MUCH ABOUT SCIENCE OR...OR ENGINEERING--
NOT SURE IF YOU'RE AN EXPERT ON TECTONIC PLATES, BUT I KINDA DOUBT IT. AND YOU'VE PREDICTED TWO EARTHQUAKES ALREADY, RIGHT?
YOU SERIOUSLY THINK A PLACE LIKE THIS WOULD HIRE ME?
NOT MY CALL. BUT I CAN INTRODUCE YOU TO THE GUY WHOSE CALL IT IS.
LET'S KEEP THE WHOLE INHUMAN THING ON THE DOWN LOW FOR NOW... I PROMISED JOHNNY.
HEY, SPIDEY! GLAD TO HAVE YOU BACK IN THE FRIENDLY NEIGHBORHOOD.
MAN'S GOTTA HAVE A REAL BAGEL EVERY SO OFTEN.
HARRY OSBOR--*UH*, LYMAN, MEET ULYSSES. HE'S...A CANDIDATE FOR OUR INTERNSHIP PROGRAM. PETE ASKED ME TO SHOW HIM AROUND.
PLEASED TO MEET YOU. IF PETER'S TAKEN A PERSONAL INTEREST, YOU MUST HAVE SOME PRETTY IMPRESSIVE TALENTS.
UM, I GUESS SO.

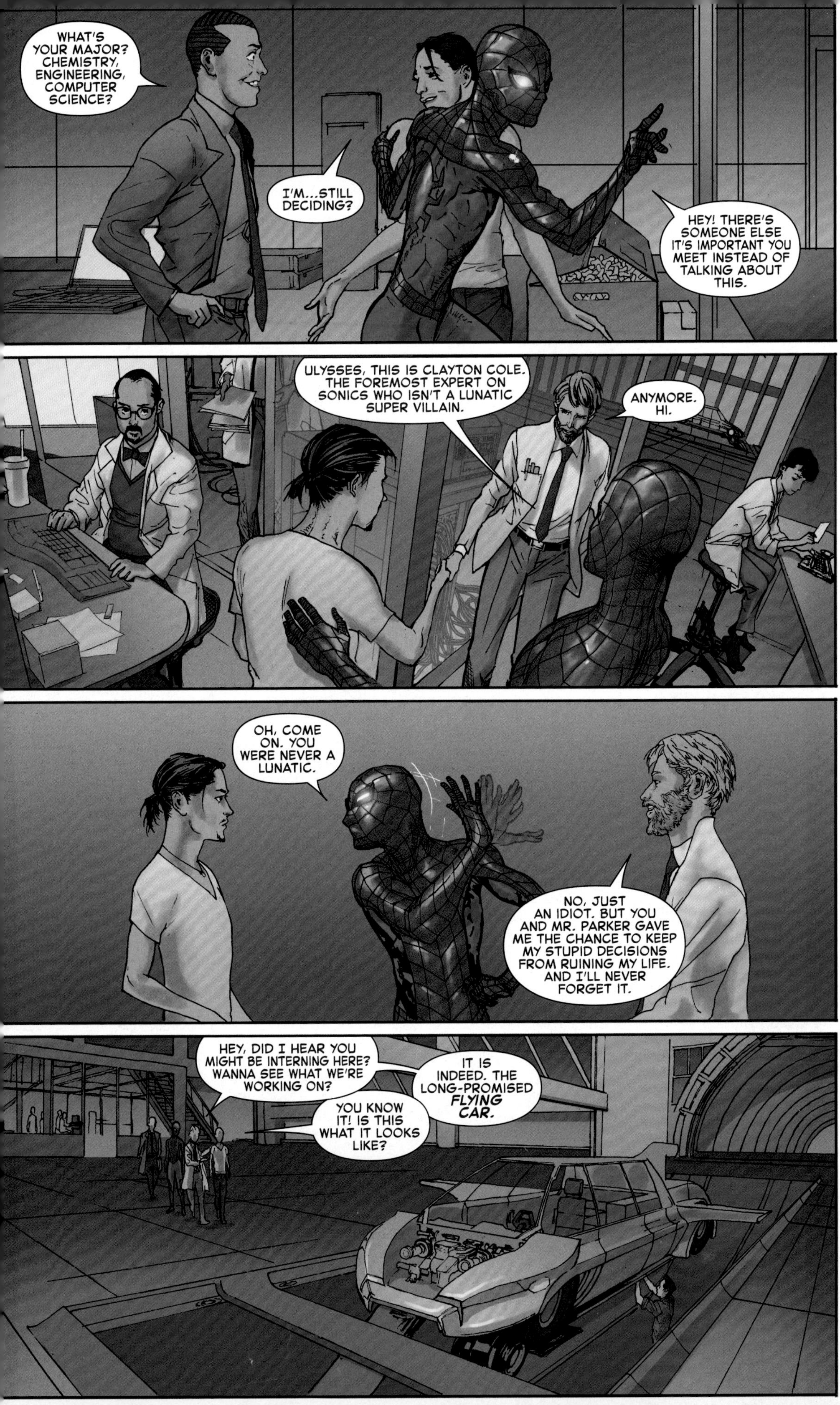
WHAT'S YOUR MAJOR? CHEMISTRY, ENGINEERING, COMPUTER SCIENCE?
I'M...STILL DECIDING?
HEY! THERE'S SOMEONE ELSE IT'S IMPORTANT YOU MEET INSTEAD OF TALKING ABOUT THIS.
ULYSSES, THIS IS CLAYTON COLE. THE FOREMOST EXPERT ON SONICS WHO ISN'T A LUNATIC SUPER VILLAIN.
ANYMORE. HI.
OH, COME ON. YOU WERE NEVER A LUNATIC.
NO, JUST AN IDIOT. BUT YOU AND MR. PARKER GAVE ME THE CHANCE TO KEEP MY STUPID DECISIONS FROM RUINING MY LIFE. AND I'LL NEVER FORGET IT.
HEY, DID I HEAR YOU MIGHT BE INTERNING HERE? WANNA SEE WHAT WE'RE WORKING ON?
YOU KNOW IT! IS THIS WHAT IT LOOKS LIKE?
IT IS INDEED. THE LONG-PROMISED *FLYING CAR.*

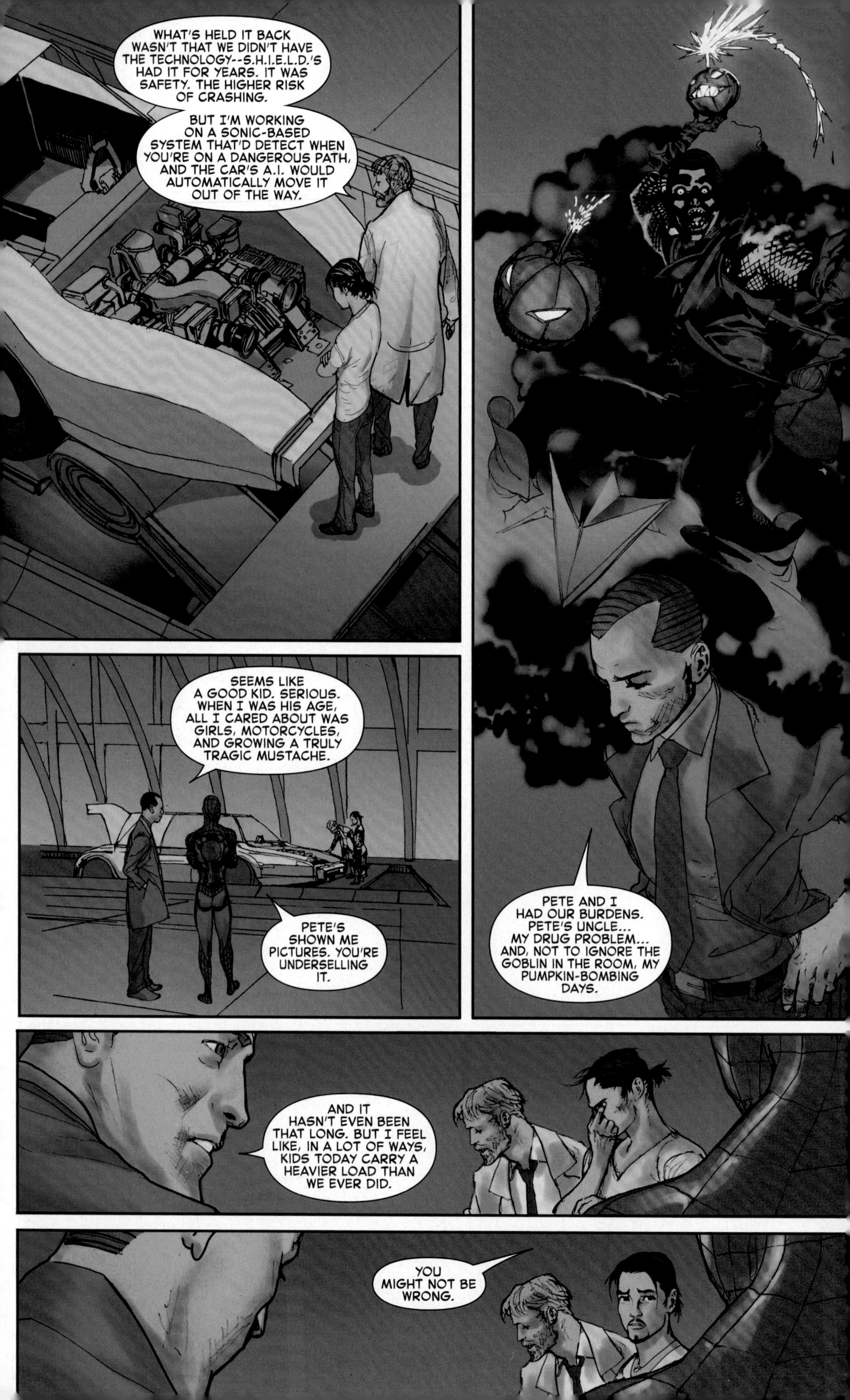
WHAT'S HELD IT BACK WASN'T THAT WE DIDN'T HAVE THE TECHNOLOGY--S.H.I.E.L.D.'S HAD IT FOR YEARS. IT WAS SAFETY. THE HIGHER RISK OF CRASHING.
BUT I'M WORKING ON A SONIC-BASED SYSTEM THAT'D DETECT WHEN YOU'RE ON A DANGEROUS PATH, AND THE CAR'S A.I. WOULD AUTOMATICALLY MOVE IT OUT OF THE WAY.
SEEMS LIKE A GOOD KID. SERIOUS. WHEN I WAS HIS AGE, ALL I CARED ABOUT WAS GIRLS, MOTORCYCLES, AND GROWING A TRULY TRAGIC MUSTACHE.
PETE'S SHOWN ME PICTURES. YOU'RE UNDERSELLING IT.
PETE AND I HAD OUR BURDENS. PETE'S UNCLE... MY DRUG PROBLEM... AND, NOT TO IGNORE THE GOBLIN IN THE ROOM, MY PUMPKIN-BOMBING DAYS.
AND IT HASN'T EVEN BEEN THAT LONG. BUT I FEEL LIKE, IN A LOT OF WAYS, KIDS TODAY CARRY A HEAVIER LOAD THAN WE EVER DID.
YOU MIGHT NOT BE WRONG.

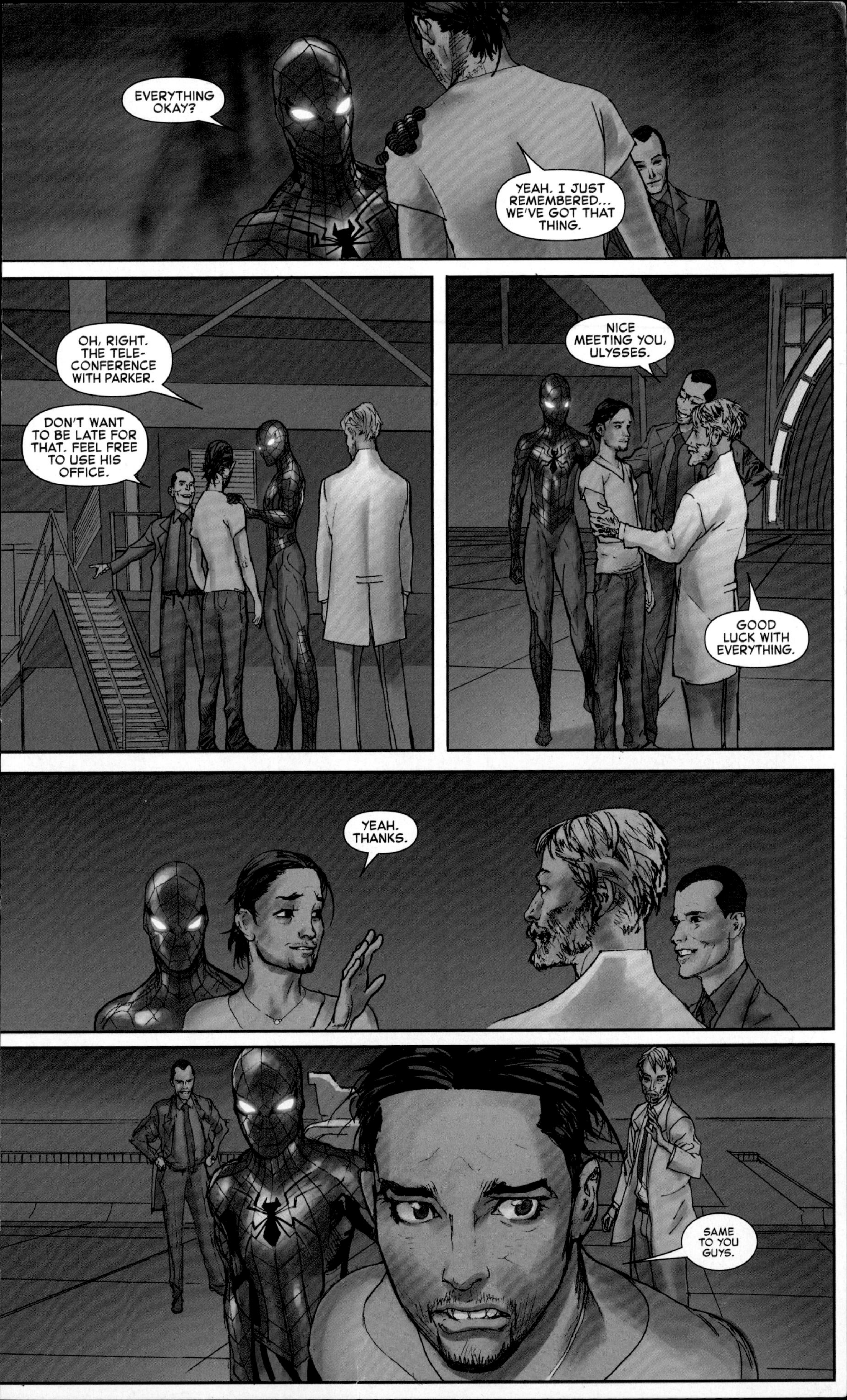
EVERYTHING OKAY?
YEAH. I JUST REMEMBERED... WE'VE GOT THAT THING.
OH, RIGHT. THE TELE-CONFERENCE WITH PARKER.
DON'T WANT TO BE LATE FOR THAT. FEEL FREE TO USE HIS OFFICE.
NICE MEETING YOU, ULYSSES.
GOOD LUCK WITH EVERYTHING.
YEAH. THANKS.
SAME TO YOU GUYS.

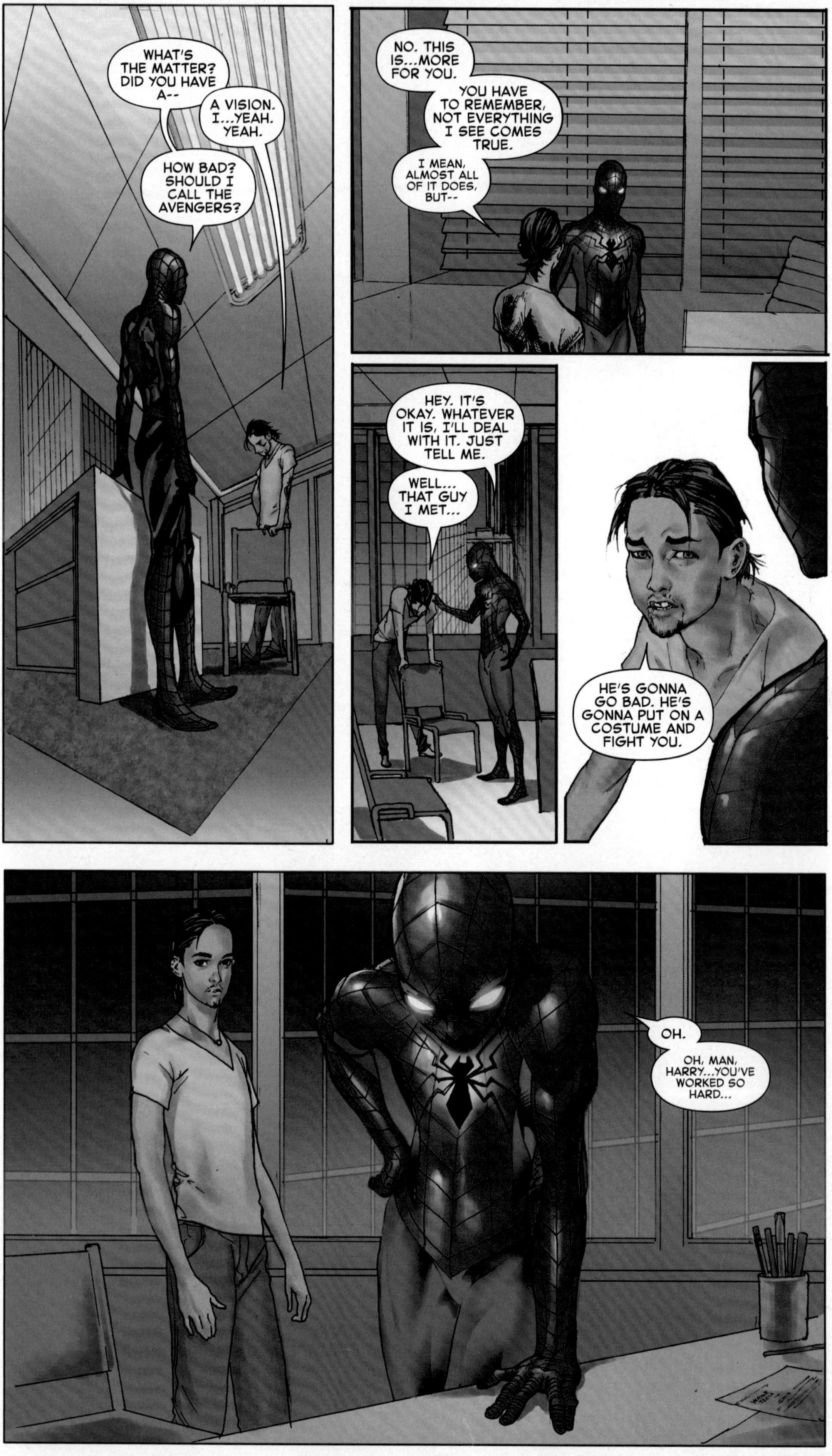
WHAT'S THE MATTER? DID YOU HAVE A--
A VISION. I...YEAH. YEAH.
HOW BAD? SHOULD I CALL THE AVENGERS?
NO. THIS IS...MORE FOR YOU.
YOU HAVE TO REMEMBER, NOT EVERYTHING I SEE COMES TRUE.
I MEAN, ALMOST ALL OF IT DOES, BUT--
HEY. IT'S OKAY. WHATEVER IT IS, I'LL DEAL WITH IT. JUST TELL ME.
WELL... THAT GUY I MET...
HE'S GONNA GO BAD. HE'S GONNA PUT ON A COSTUME AND FIGHT YOU.
OH.
OH, MAN, HARRY...YOU'VE WORKED SO HARD...

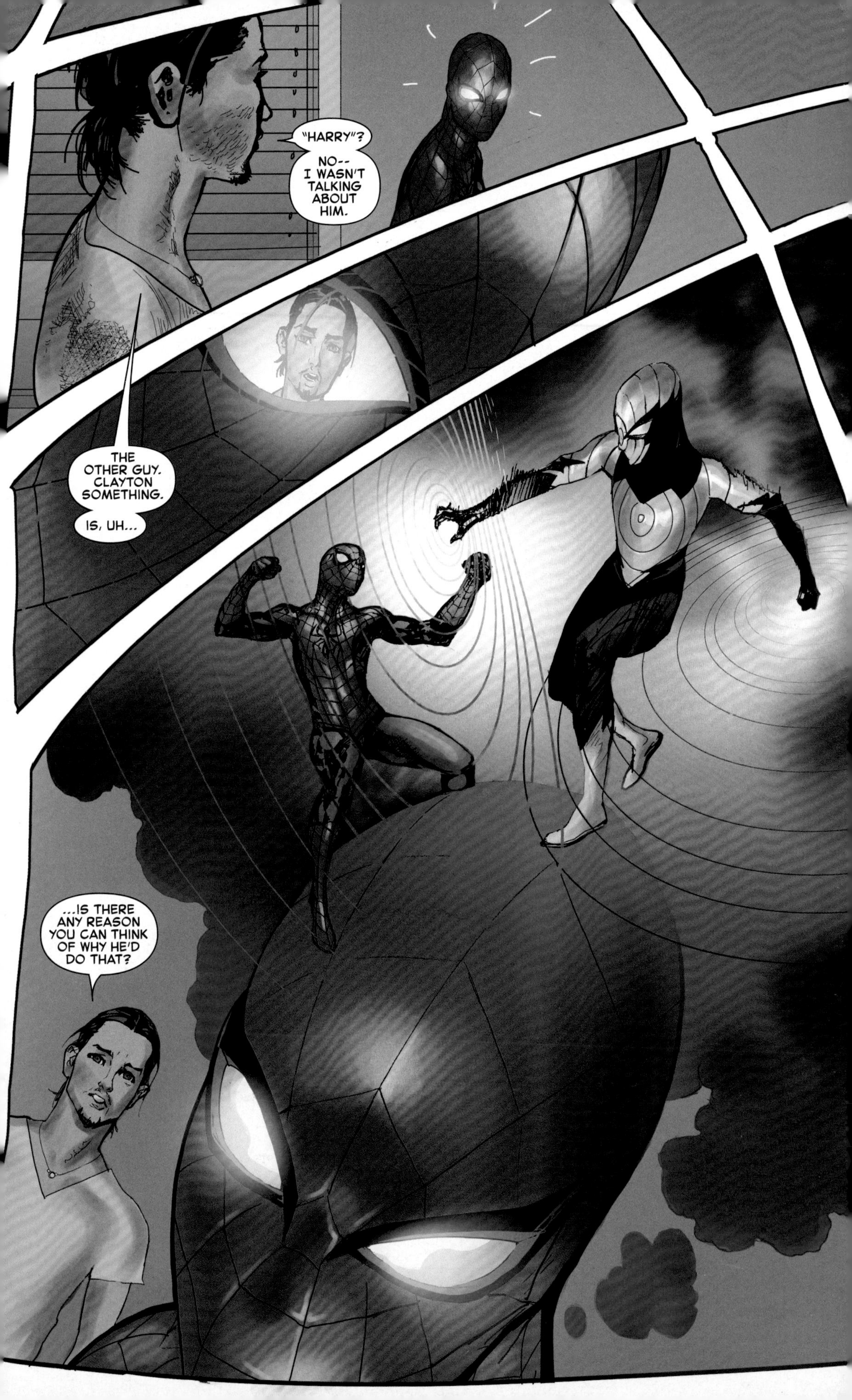
"HARRY"?
NO-- I WASN'T TALKING ABOUT HIM.
THE OTHER GUY. CLAYTON SOMETHING.
IS, UH...
...IS THERE ANY REASON YOU CAN THINK OF WHY HE'D DO THAT?

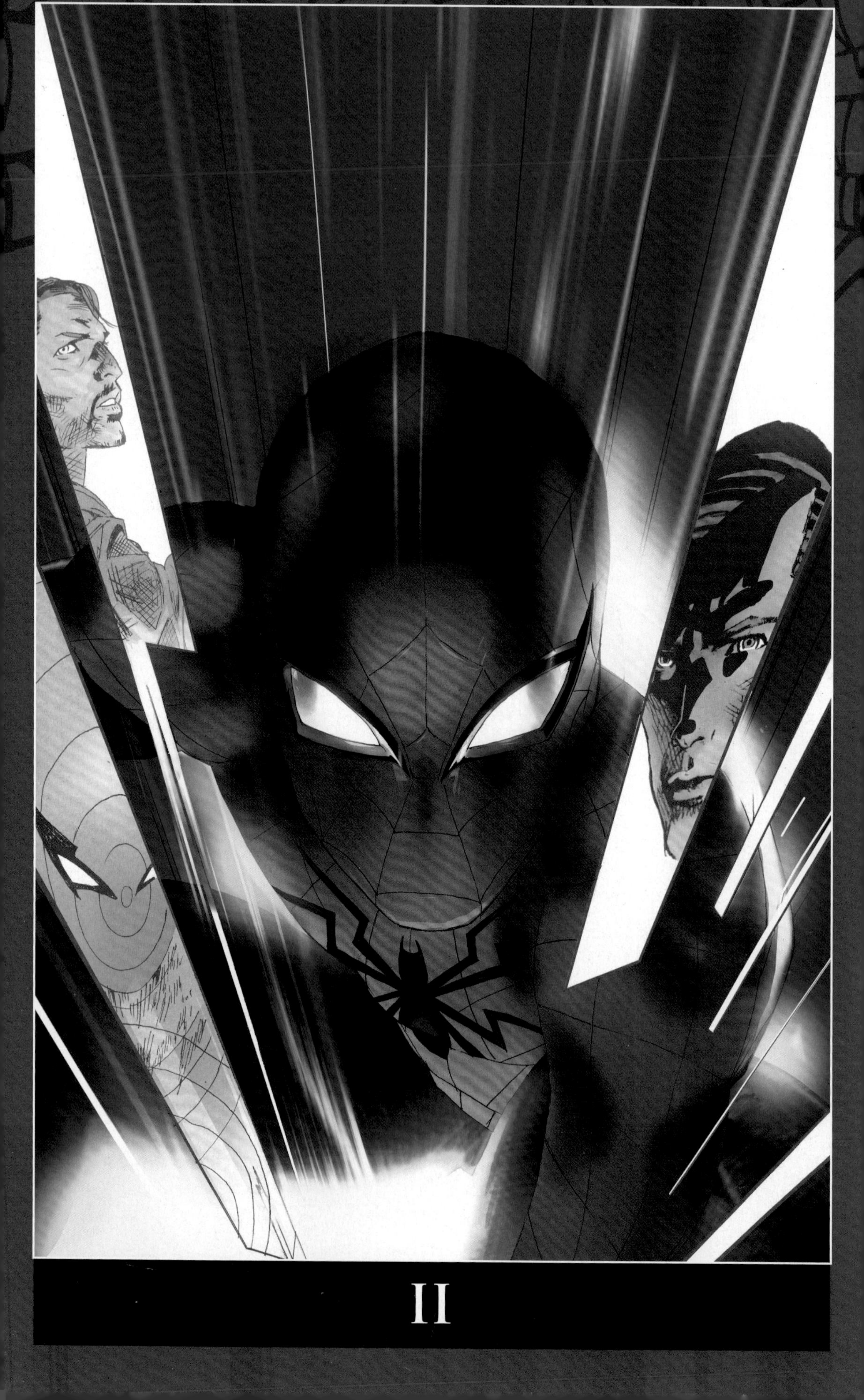

II

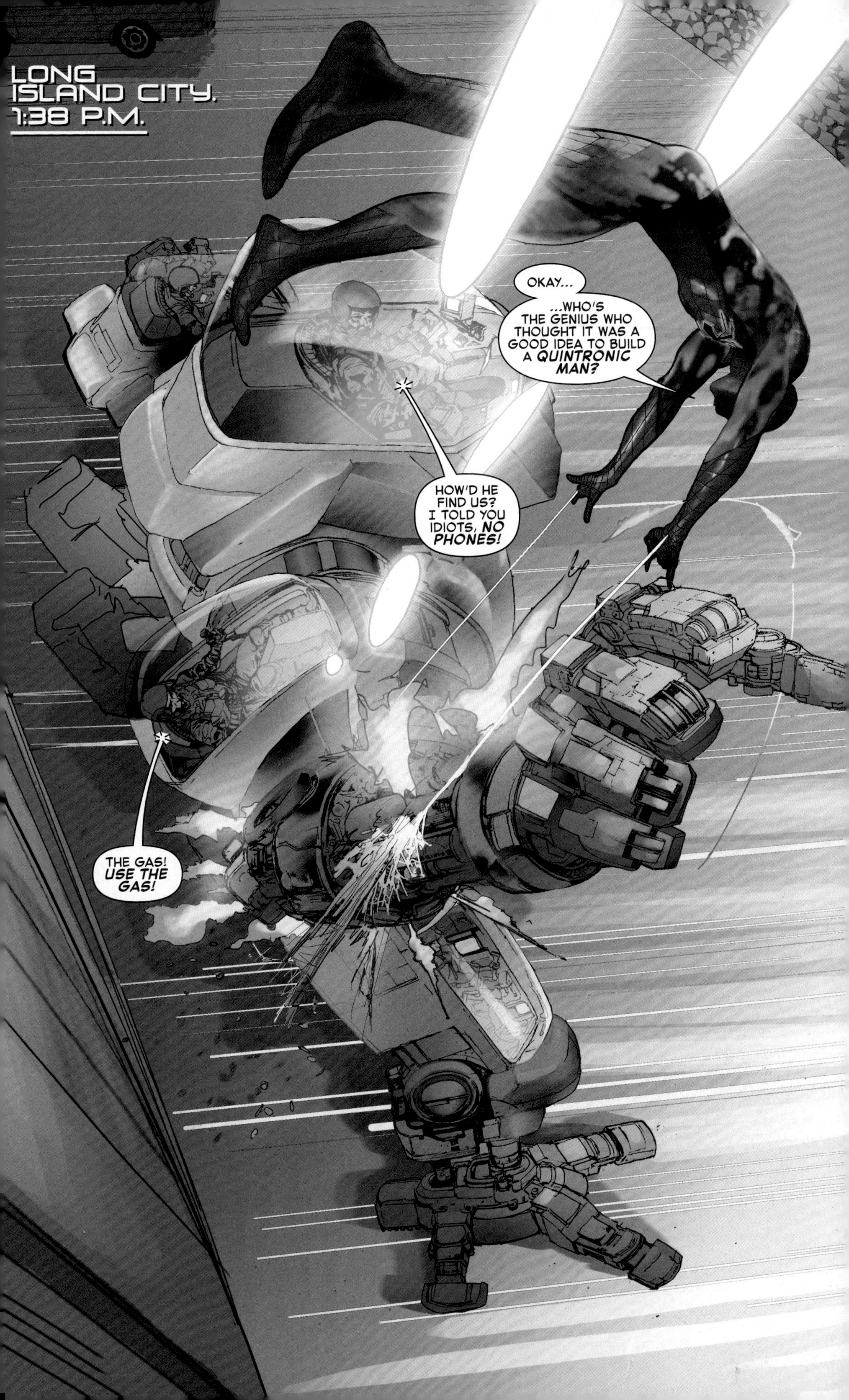
LONG ISLAND CITY. 1:38 P.M.
OKAY...
...WHO'S THE GENIUS WHO THOUGHT IT WAS A GOOD IDEA TO BUILD A QUINTRONIC MAN?
HOW'D HE FIND US? I TOLD YOU IDIOTS, NO PHONES!
THE GAS! USE THE GAS!

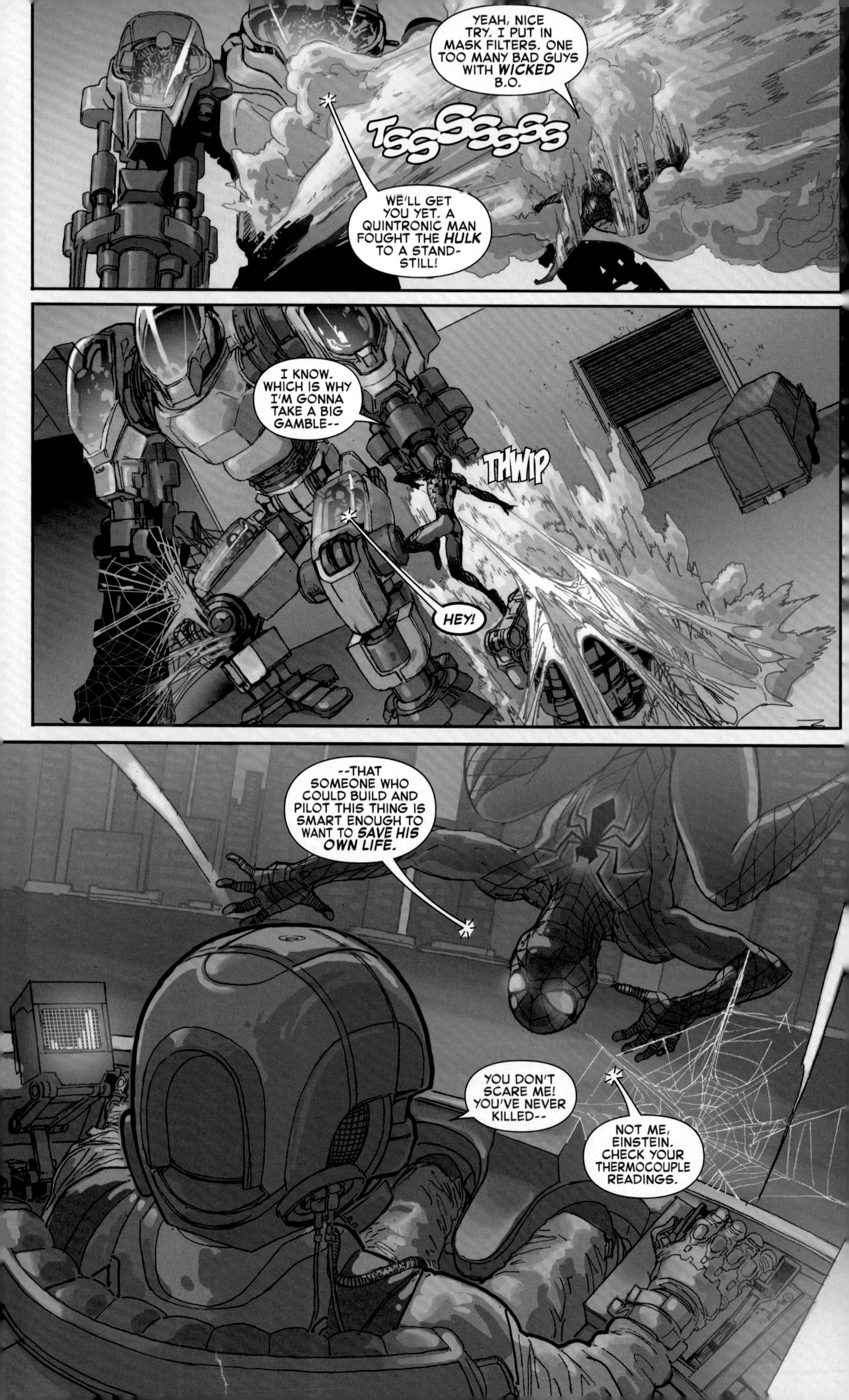

YEAH, NICE TRY. I PUT IN MASK FILTERS. ONE TOO MANY BAD GUYS WITH WICKED B.O.
TSSSSSSSS
WE'LL GET YOU YET. A QUINTRONIC MAN FOUGHT THE HULK TO A STAND-STILL!
I KNOW. WHICH IS WHY I'M GONNA TAKE A BIG GAMBLE--
THWIP
HEY!
--THAT SOMEONE WHO COULD BUILD AND PILOT THIS THING IS SMART ENOUGH TO WANT TO SAVE HIS OWN LIFE.
YOU DON'T SCARE ME! YOU'VE NEVER KILLED--
NOT ME, EINSTEIN. CHECK YOUR THERMOCOUPLE READINGS.

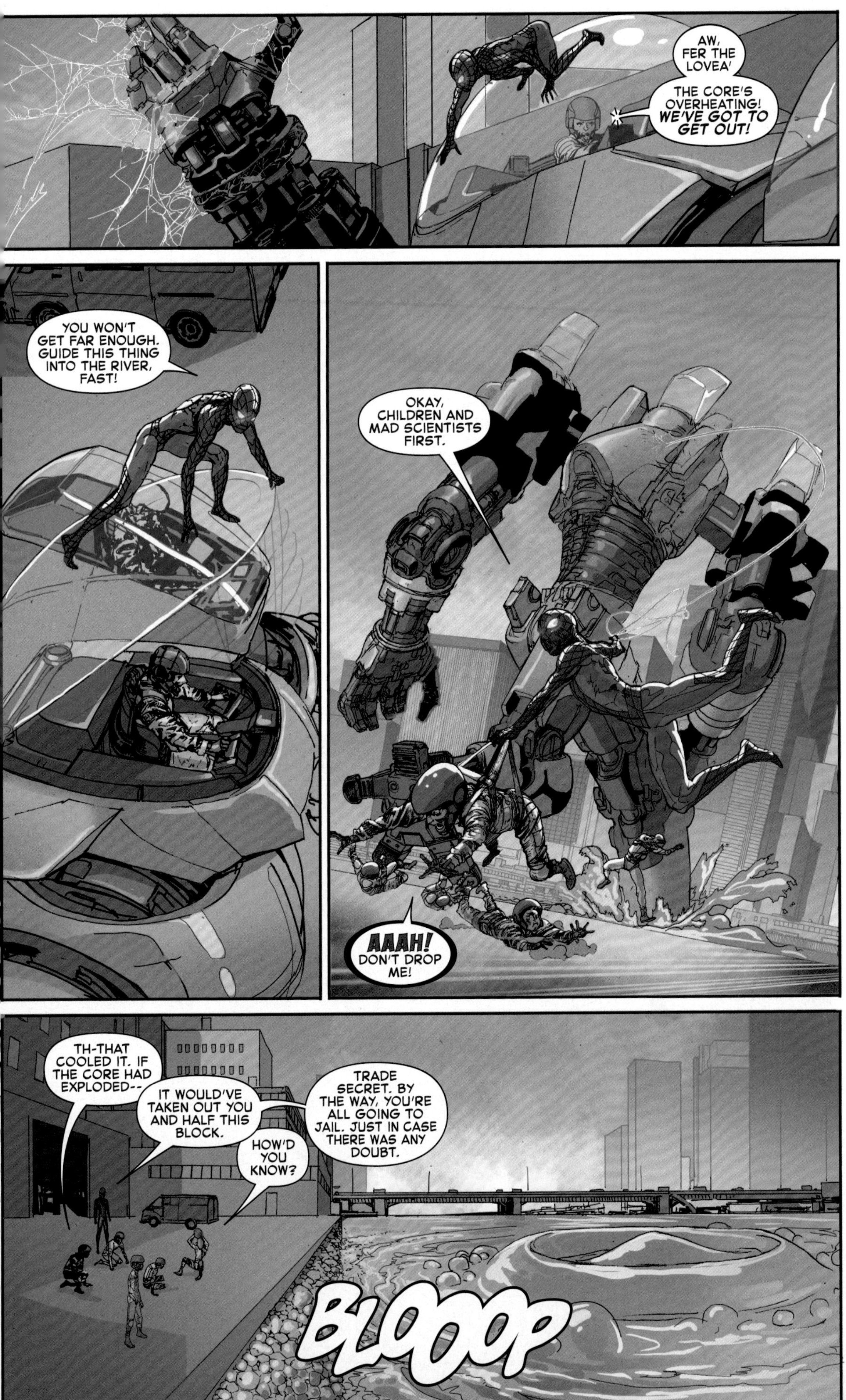
AW, FER THE LOVEA'
THE CORE'S OVERHEATING! WE'VE GOT TO GET OUT!
YOU WON'T GET FAR ENOUGH. GUIDE THIS THING INTO THE RIVER, FAST!
OKAY, CHILDREN AND MAD SCIENTISTS FIRST.
AAAH! DON'T DROP ME!
TH-THAT COOLED IT. IF THE CORE HAD EXPLODED--
IT WOULD'VE TAKEN OUT YOU AND HALF THIS BLOCK.
HOW'D YOU KNOW?
TRADE SECRET. BY THE WAY, YOU'RE ALL GOING TO JAIL. JUST IN CASE THERE WAS ANY DOUBT.
BLOOOP

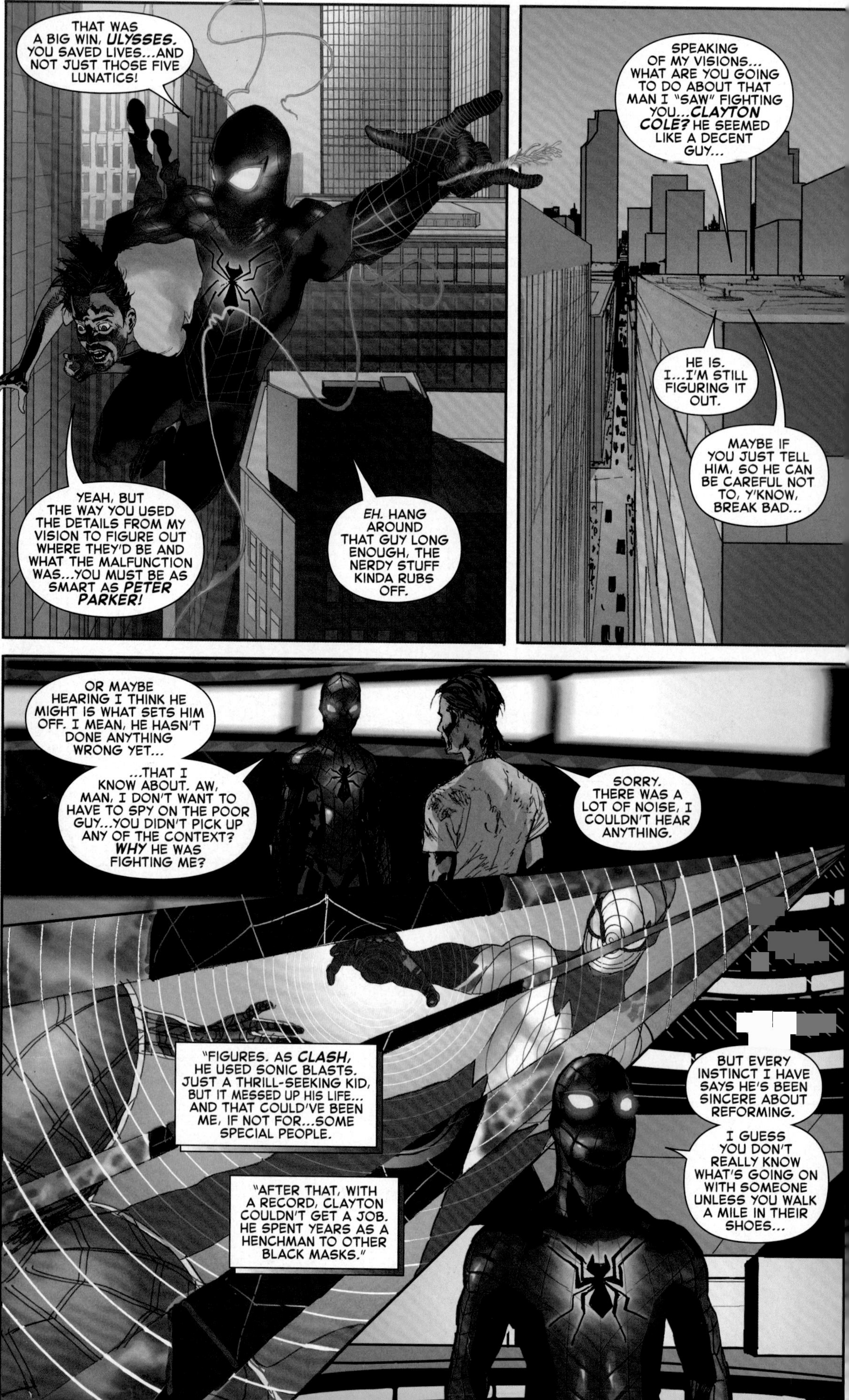
THAT WAS A BIG WIN, ULYSSES. YOU SAVED LIVES...AND NOT JUST THOSE FIVE LUNATICS!
YEAH, BUT THE WAY YOU USED THE DETAILS FROM MY VISION TO FIGURE OUT WHERE THEY'D BE AND WHAT THE MALFUNCTION WAS...YOU MUST BE AS SMART AS PETER PARKER!
EH. HANG AROUND THAT GUY LONG ENOUGH, THE NERDY STUFF KINDA RUBS OFF.
SPEAKING OF MY VISIONS... WHAT ARE YOU GOING TO DO ABOUT THAT MAN I "SAW" FIGHTING YOU...CLAYTON COLE? HE SEEMED LIKE A DECENT GUY...
HE IS. I...I'M STILL FIGURING IT OUT.
MAYBE IF YOU JUST TELL HIM, SO HE CAN BE CAREFUL NOT TO, Y'KNOW, BREAK BAD...
OR MAYBE HEARING I THINK HE MIGHT IS WHAT SETS HIM OFF. I MEAN, HE HASN'T DONE ANYTHING WRONG YET...
...THAT I KNOW ABOUT. AW, MAN, I DON'T WANT TO HAVE TO SPY ON THE POOR GUY...YOU DIDN'T PICK UP ANY OF THE CONTEXT? WHY HE WAS FIGHTING ME?
SORRY. THERE WAS A LOT OF NOISE, I COULDN'T HEAR ANYTHING.
"FIGURES. AS CLASH, HE USED SONIC BLASTS. JUST A THRILL-SEEKING KID, BUT IT MESSED UP HIS LIFE... AND THAT COULD'VE BEEN ME, IF NOT FOR...SOME SPECIAL PEOPLE.
"AFTER THAT, WITH A RECORD, CLAYTON COULDN'T GET A JOB. HE SPENT YEARS AS A HENCHMAN TO OTHER BLACK MASKS."
BUT EVERY INSTINCT I HAVE SAYS HE'S BEEN SINCERE ABOUT REFORMING.
I GUESS YOU DON'T REALLY KNOW WHAT'S GOING ON WITH SOMEONE UNLESS YOU WALK A MILE IN THEIR SHOES...

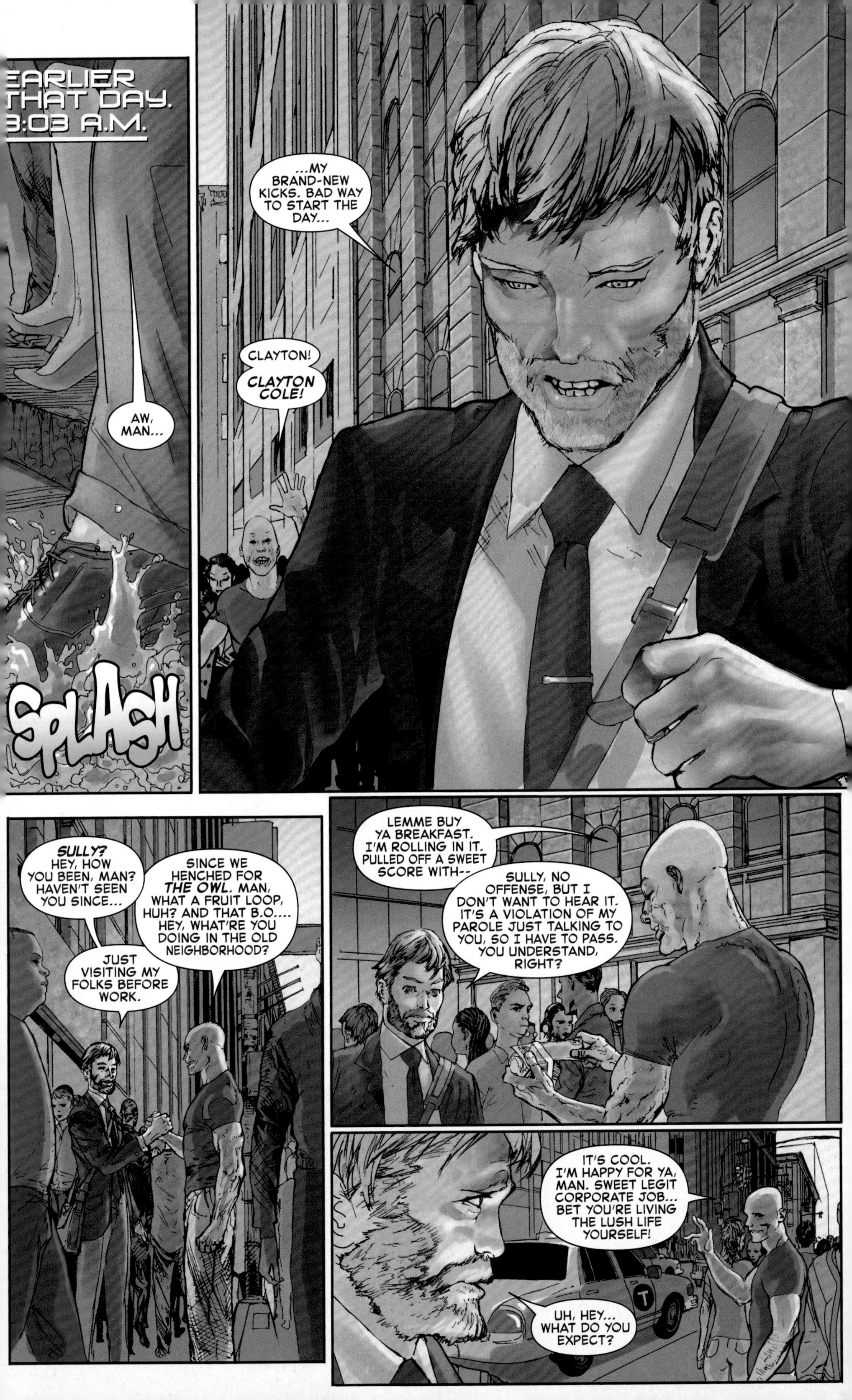
EARLIER THAT DAY. 8:03 A.M.
AW, MAN...
SPLASH
...MY BRAND-NEW KICKS. BAD WAY TO START THE DAY...
CLAYTON! CLAYTON COLE!
SULLY? HEY, HOW YOU BEEN, MAN? HAVEN'T SEEN YOU SINCE...
SINCE WE HENCHED FOR THE OWL. MAN, WHAT A FRUIT LOOP, HUH? AND THAT B.O.... HEY, WHAT'RE YOU DOING IN THE OLD NEIGHBORHOOD?
JUST VISITING MY FOLKS BEFORE WORK.
LEMME BUY YA BREAKFAST. I'M ROLLING IN IT. PULLED OFF A SWEET SCORE WITH--
SULLY, NO OFFENSE, BUT I DON'T WANT TO HEAR IT. IT'S A VIOLATION OF MY PAROLE JUST TALKING TO YOU, SO I HAVE TO PASS. YOU UNDERSTAND, RIGHT?
IT'S COOL. I'M HAPPY FOR YA, MAN. SWEET LEGIT CORPORATE JOB... BET YOU'RE LIVING THE LUSH LIFE YOURSELF!
UH, HEY... WHAT DO YOU EXPECT?

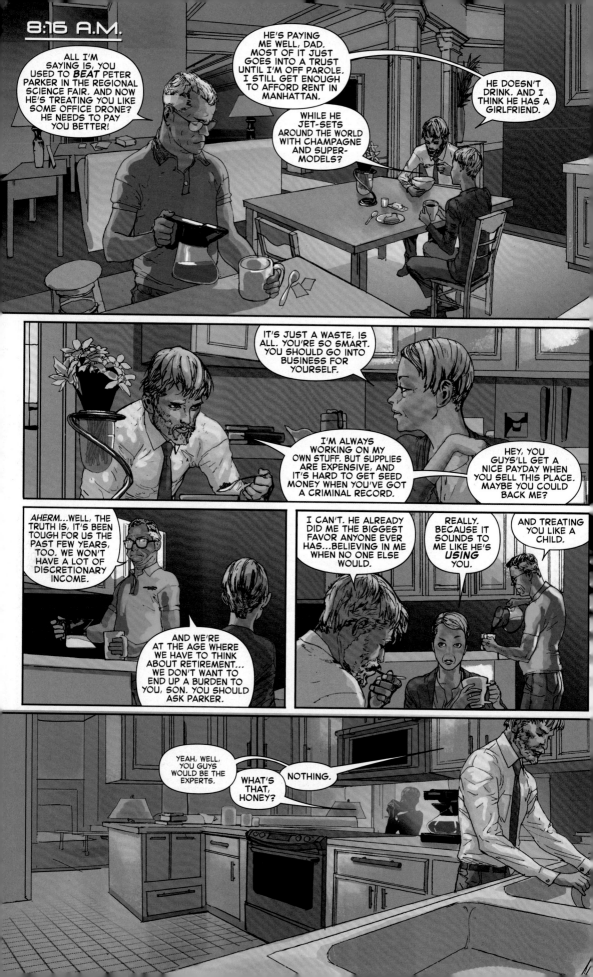

8:16 A.M.

ALL I'M SAYING IS, YOU USED TO **BEAT** PETER PARKER IN THE REGIONAL SCIENCE FAIR. AND NOW HE'S TREATING YOU LIKE SOME OFFICE DRONE? HE NEEDS TO PAY YOU BETTER!

HE'S PAYING ME WELL, DAD. MOST OF IT JUST GOES INTO A TRUST UNTIL I'M OFF PAROLE. I STILL GET ENOUGH TO AFFORD RENT IN MANHATTAN.

HE DOESN'T DRINK. AND I THINK HE HAS A GIRLFRIEND.

WHILE HE JET-SETS AROUND THE WORLD WITH CHAMPAGNE AND SUPER-MODELS?

IT'S JUST A WASTE, IS ALL. YOU'RE SO SMART. YOU SHOULD GO INTO BUSINESS FOR YOURSELF.

I'M ALWAYS WORKING ON MY OWN STUFF. BUT SUPPLIES ARE EXPENSIVE, AND IT'S HARD TO GET SEED MONEY WHEN YOU'VE GOT A CRIMINAL RECORD.

HEY, YOU GUYS'LL GET A NICE PAYDAY WHEN YOU SELL THIS PLACE. MAYBE YOU COULD BACK ME?

AHERM...WELL, THE TRUTH IS, IT'S BEEN TOUGH FOR US THE PAST FEW YEARS, TOO. WE WON'T HAVE A LOT OF DISCRETIONARY INCOME.

AND WE'RE AT THE AGE WHERE WE HAVE TO THINK ABOUT RETIREMENT... WE DON'T WANT TO END UP A BURDEN TO YOU, SON. YOU SHOULD ASK PARKER.

I CAN'T. HE ALREADY DID ME THE BIGGEST FAVOR ANYONE EVER HAS...BELIEVING IN ME WHEN NO ONE ELSE WOULD.

REALLY. BECAUSE IT SOUNDS TO ME LIKE HE'S **USING** YOU.

AND TREATING YOU LIKE A CHILD.

YEAH, WELL, YOU GUYS WOULD BE THE EXPERTS.

WHAT'S THAT, HONEY?

NOTHING.

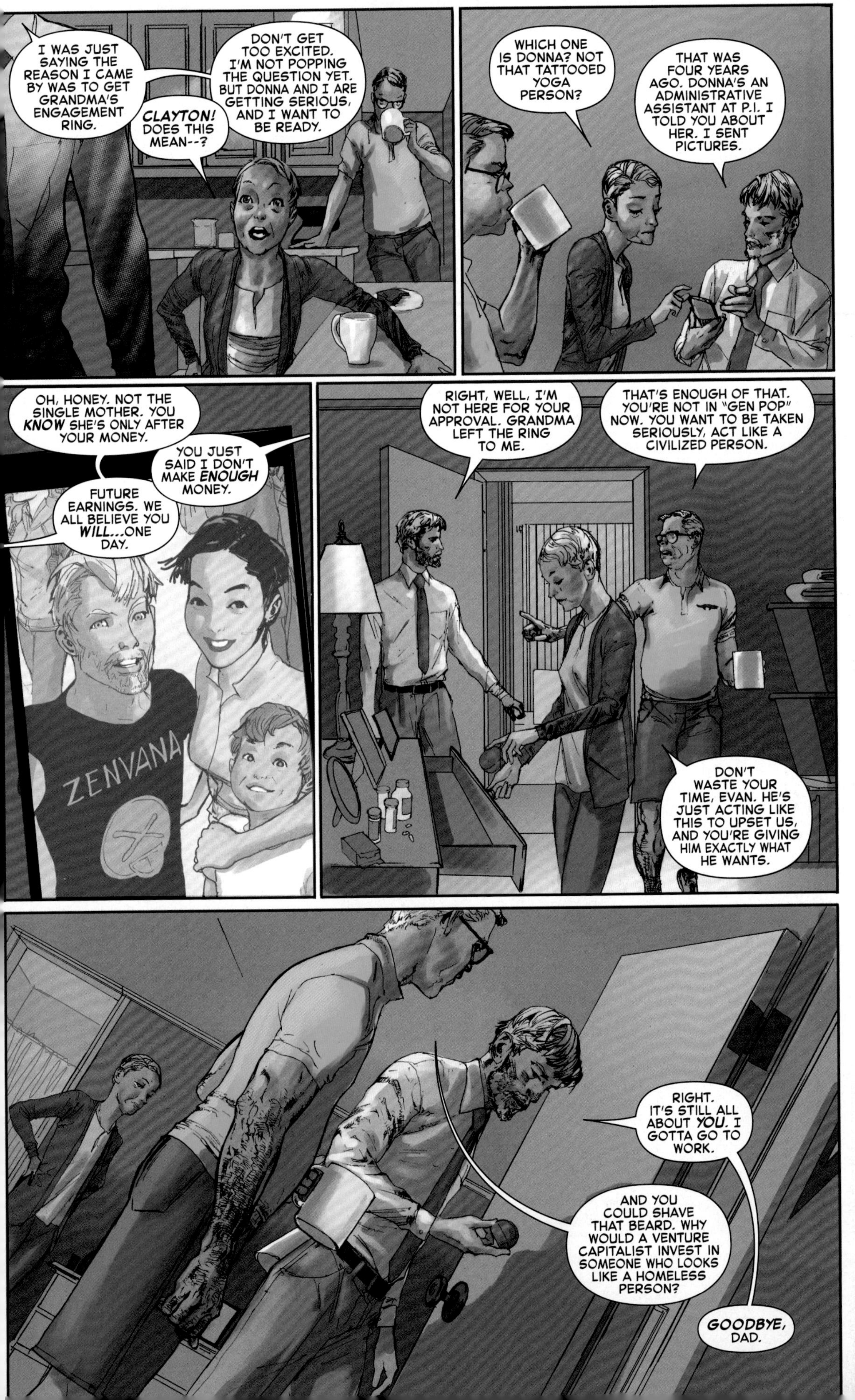
I WAS JUST SAYING THE REASON I CAME BY WAS TO GET GRANDMA'S ENGAGEMENT RING.
CLAYTON! DOES THIS MEAN--?
DON'T GET TOO EXCITED. I'M NOT POPPING THE QUESTION YET. BUT DONNA AND I ARE GETTING SERIOUS, AND I WANT TO BE READY.
WHICH ONE IS DONNA? NOT THAT TATTOOED YOGA PERSON?
THAT WAS FOUR YEARS AGO. DONNA'S AN ADMINISTRATIVE ASSISTANT AT P.I. I TOLD YOU ABOUT HER. I SENT PICTURES.
OH, HONEY. NOT THE SINGLE MOTHER. YOU KNOW SHE'S ONLY AFTER YOUR MONEY.
YOU JUST SAID I DON'T MAKE ENOUGH MONEY.
FUTURE EARNINGS. WE ALL BELIEVE YOU WILL...ONE DAY.
ZENVANA
RIGHT, WELL, I'M NOT HERE FOR YOUR APPROVAL. GRANDMA LEFT THE RING TO ME.
THAT'S ENOUGH OF THAT. YOU'RE NOT IN "GEN POP" NOW. YOU WANT TO BE TAKEN SERIOUSLY, ACT LIKE A CIVILIZED PERSON.
DON'T WASTE YOUR TIME, EVAN. HE'S JUST ACTING LIKE THIS TO UPSET US, AND YOU'RE GIVING HIM EXACTLY WHAT HE WANTS.
RIGHT. IT'S STILL ALL ABOUT YOU. I GOTTA GO TO WORK.
AND YOU COULD SHAVE THAT BEARD. WHY WOULD A VENTURE CAPITALIST INVEST IN SOMEONE WHO LOOKS LIKE A HOMELESS PERSON?
GOODBYE, DAD.

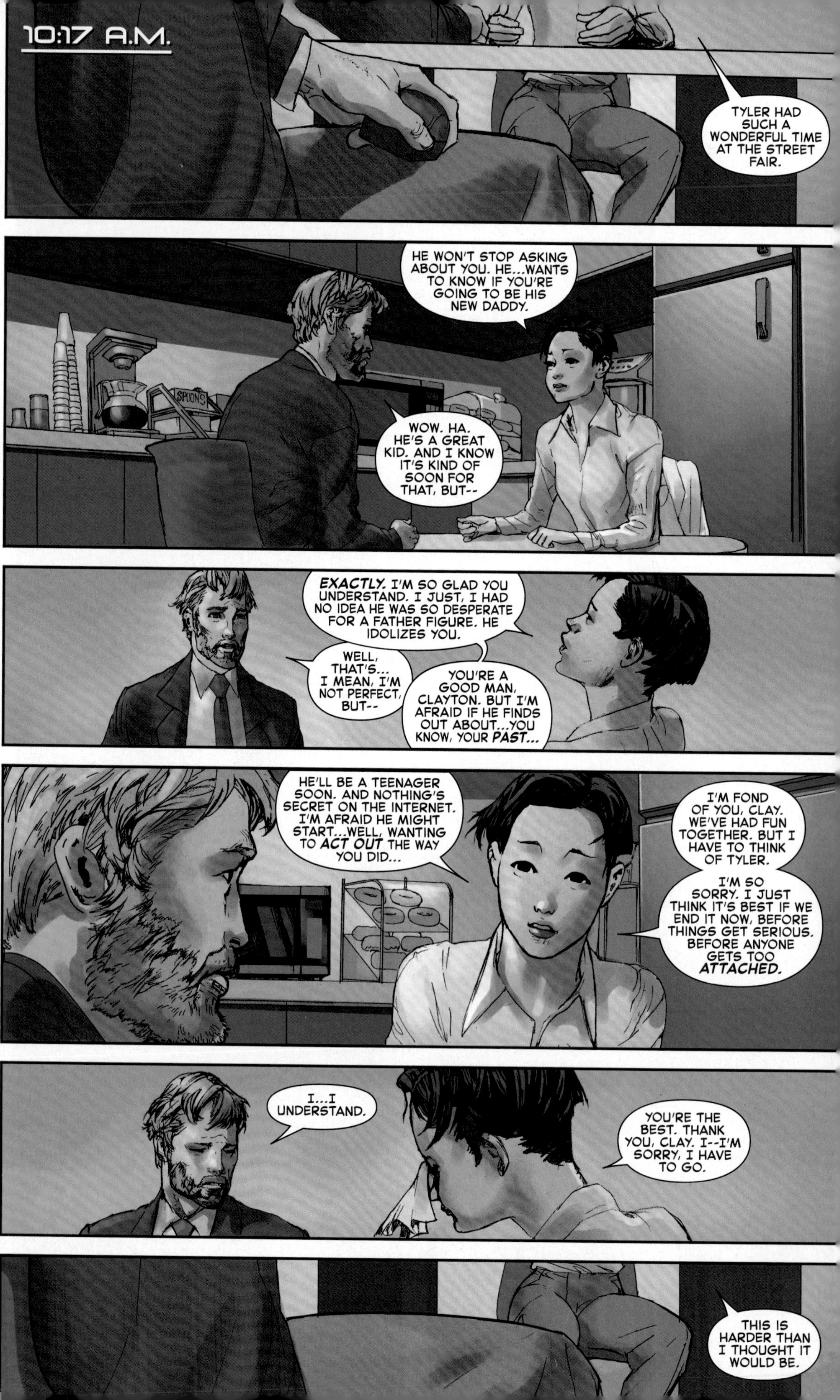
10:17 A.M.
TYLER HAD SUCH A WONDERFUL TIME AT THE STREET FAIR.
HE WON'T STOP ASKING ABOUT YOU. HE...WANTS TO KNOW IF YOU'RE GOING TO BE HIS NEW DADDY.
SPOONS
WOW. HA. HE'S A GREAT KID. AND I KNOW IT'S KIND OF SOON FOR THAT, BUT--
EXACTLY. I'M SO GLAD YOU UNDERSTAND. I JUST, I HAD NO IDEA HE WAS SO DESPERATE FOR A FATHER FIGURE. HE IDOLIZES YOU.
WELL, THAT'S... I MEAN, I'M NOT PERFECT, BUT--
YOU'RE A GOOD MAN, CLAYTON. BUT I'M AFRAID IF HE FINDS OUT ABOUT...YOU KNOW, YOUR *PAST...*
HE'LL BE A TEENAGER SOON. AND NOTHING'S SECRET ON THE INTERNET. I'M AFRAID HE MIGHT START...WELL, WANTING TO *ACT OUT* THE WAY YOU DID...
I'M FOND OF YOU, CLAY. WE'VE HAD FUN TOGETHER. BUT I HAVE TO THINK OF TYLER.
I'M SO SORRY. I JUST THINK IT'S BEST IF WE END IT NOW, BEFORE THINGS GET SERIOUS. BEFORE ANYONE GETS TOO *ATTACHED.*
I...I UNDERSTAND.
YOU'RE THE BEST. THANK YOU, CLAY. I--I'M SORRY, I HAVE TO GO.
THIS IS HARDER THAN I THOUGHT IT WOULD BE.

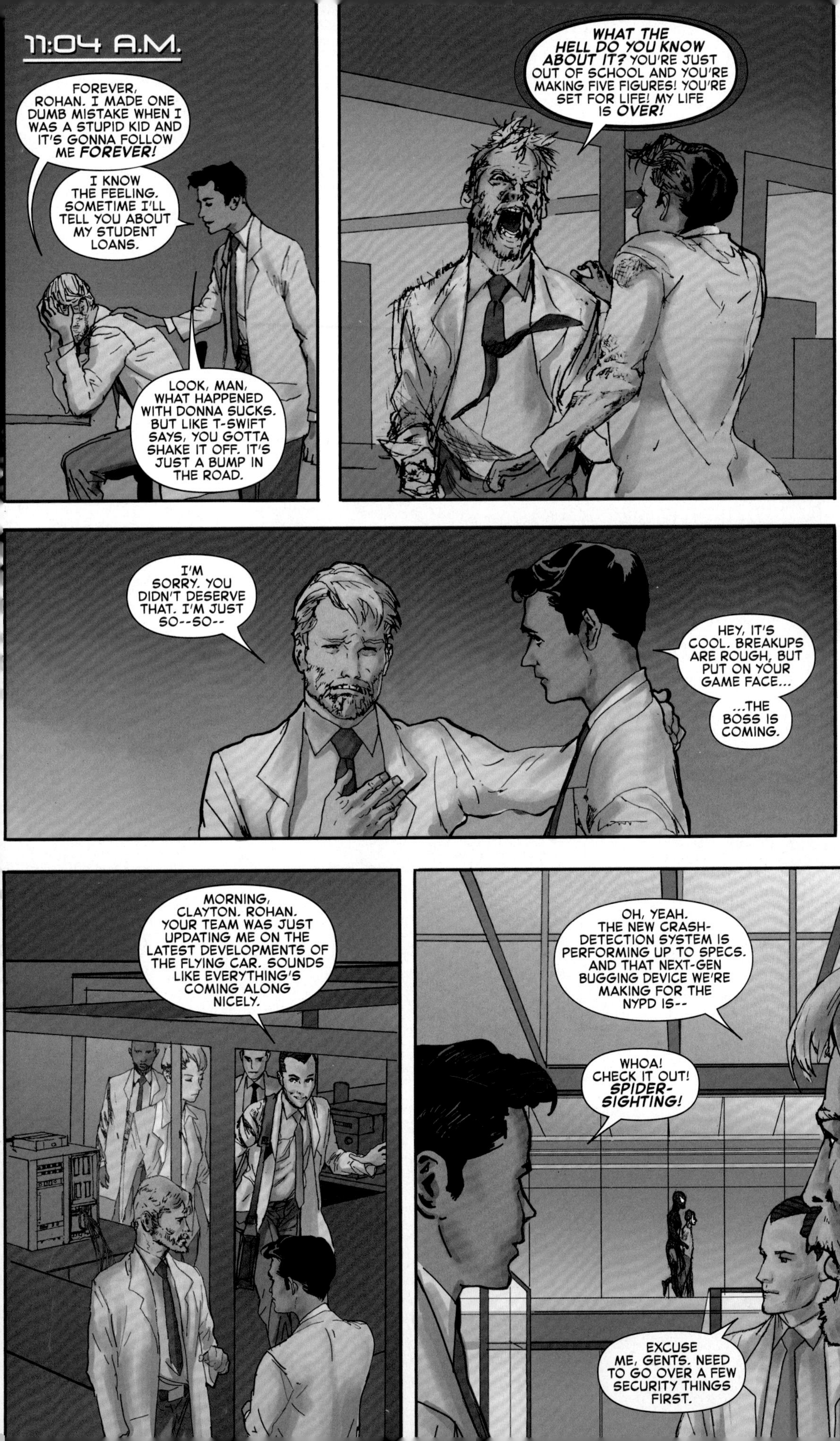
11:04 A.M.
FOREVER, ROHAN. I MADE ONE DUMB MISTAKE WHEN I WAS A STUPID KID AND IT'S GONNA FOLLOW ME FOREVER!
I KNOW THE FEELING. SOMETIME I'LL TELL YOU ABOUT MY STUDENT LOANS.
LOOK, MAN, WHAT HAPPENED WITH DONNA SUCKS. BUT LIKE T-SWIFT SAYS, YOU GOTTA SHAKE IT OFF. IT'S JUST A BUMP IN THE ROAD.
WHAT THE HELL DO YOU KNOW ABOUT IT? YOU'RE JUST OUT OF SCHOOL AND YOU'RE MAKING FIVE FIGURES! YOU'RE SET FOR LIFE! MY LIFE IS OVER!
I'M SORRY. YOU DIDN'T DESERVE THAT. I'M JUST SO--SO--
HEY, IT'S COOL. BREAKUPS ARE ROUGH, BUT PUT ON YOUR GAME FACE...
...THE BOSS IS COMING.
MORNING, CLAYTON. ROHAN. YOUR TEAM WAS JUST UPDATING ME ON THE LATEST DEVELOPMENTS OF THE FLYING CAR. SOUNDS LIKE EVERYTHING'S COMING ALONG NICELY.
OH, YEAH. THE NEW CRASH-DETECTION SYSTEM IS PERFORMING UP TO SPECS. AND THAT NEXT-GEN BUGGING DEVICE WE'RE MAKING FOR THE NYPD IS--
WHOA! CHECK IT OUT! SPIDER-SIGHTING!
EXCUSE ME, GENTS. NEED TO GO OVER A FEW SECURITY THINGS FIRST.

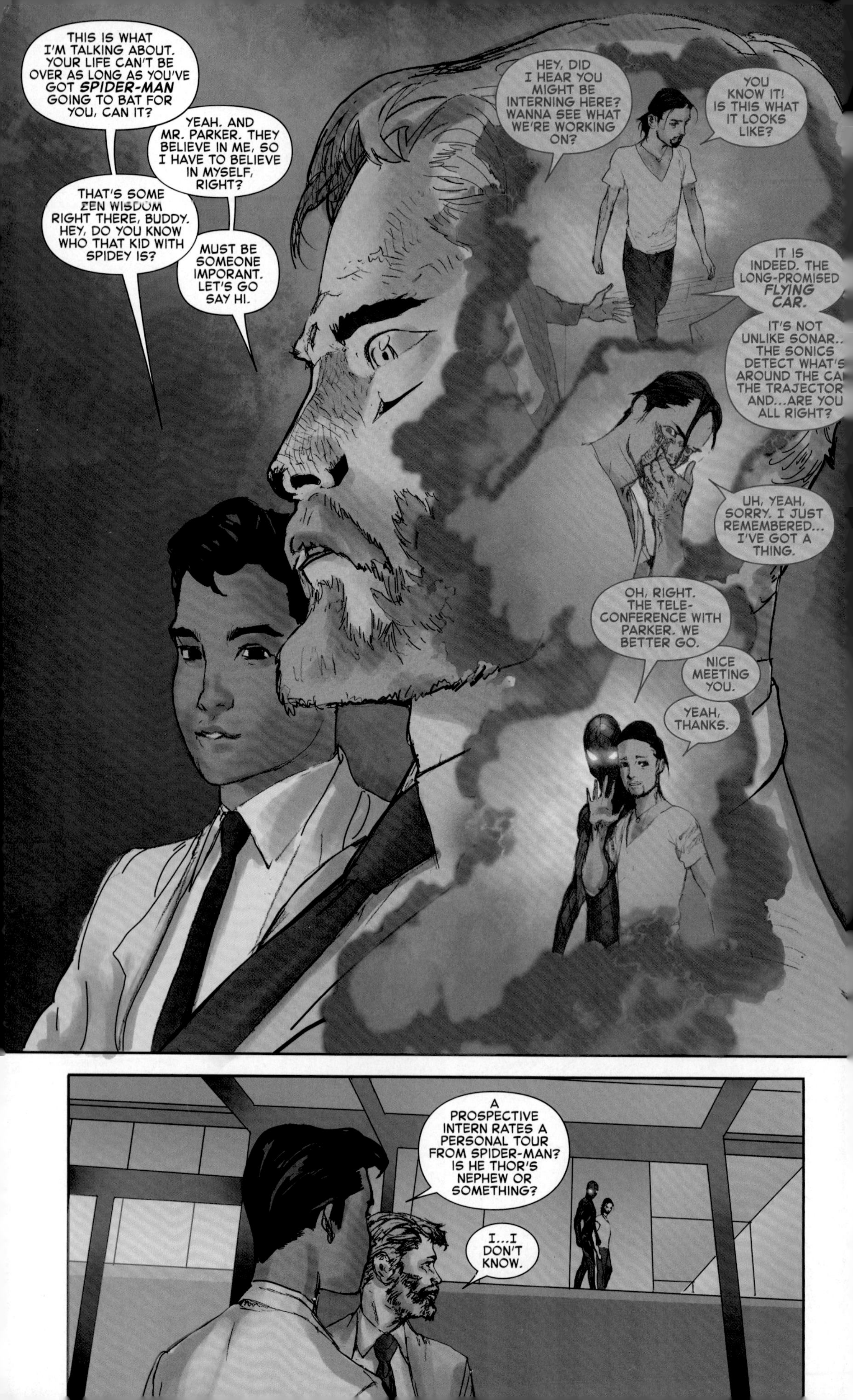
THIS IS WHAT I'M TALKING ABOUT. YOUR LIFE CAN'T BE OVER AS LONG AS YOU'VE GOT SPIDER-MAN GOING TO BAT FOR YOU, CAN IT?
YEAH. AND MR. PARKER. THEY BELIEVE IN ME, SO I HAVE TO BELIEVE IN MYSELF, RIGHT?
THAT'S SOME ZEN WISDOM RIGHT THERE, BUDDY. HEY, DO YOU KNOW WHO THAT KID WITH SPIDEY IS?
MUST BE SOMEONE IMPORANT. LET'S GO SAY HI.
HEY, DID I HEAR YOU MIGHT BE INTERNING HERE? WANNA SEE WHAT WE'RE WORKING ON?
YOU KNOW IT! IS THIS WHAT IT LOOKS LIKE?
IT IS INDEED. THE LONG-PROMISED FLYING CAR.
IT'S NOT UNLIKE SONAR.. THE SONICS DETECT WHAT'S AROUND THE CA THE TRAJECTOR AND...ARE YOU ALL RIGHT?
UH, YEAH, SORRY. I JUST REMEMBERED... I'VE GOT A THING.
OH, RIGHT. THE TELE-CONFERENCE WITH PARKER. WE BETTER GO.
NICE MEETING YOU.
YEAH, THANKS.
A PROSPECTIVE INTERN RATES A PERSONAL TOUR FROM SPIDER-MAN? IS HE THOR'S NEPHEW OR SOMETHING?
I...I DON'T KNOW.

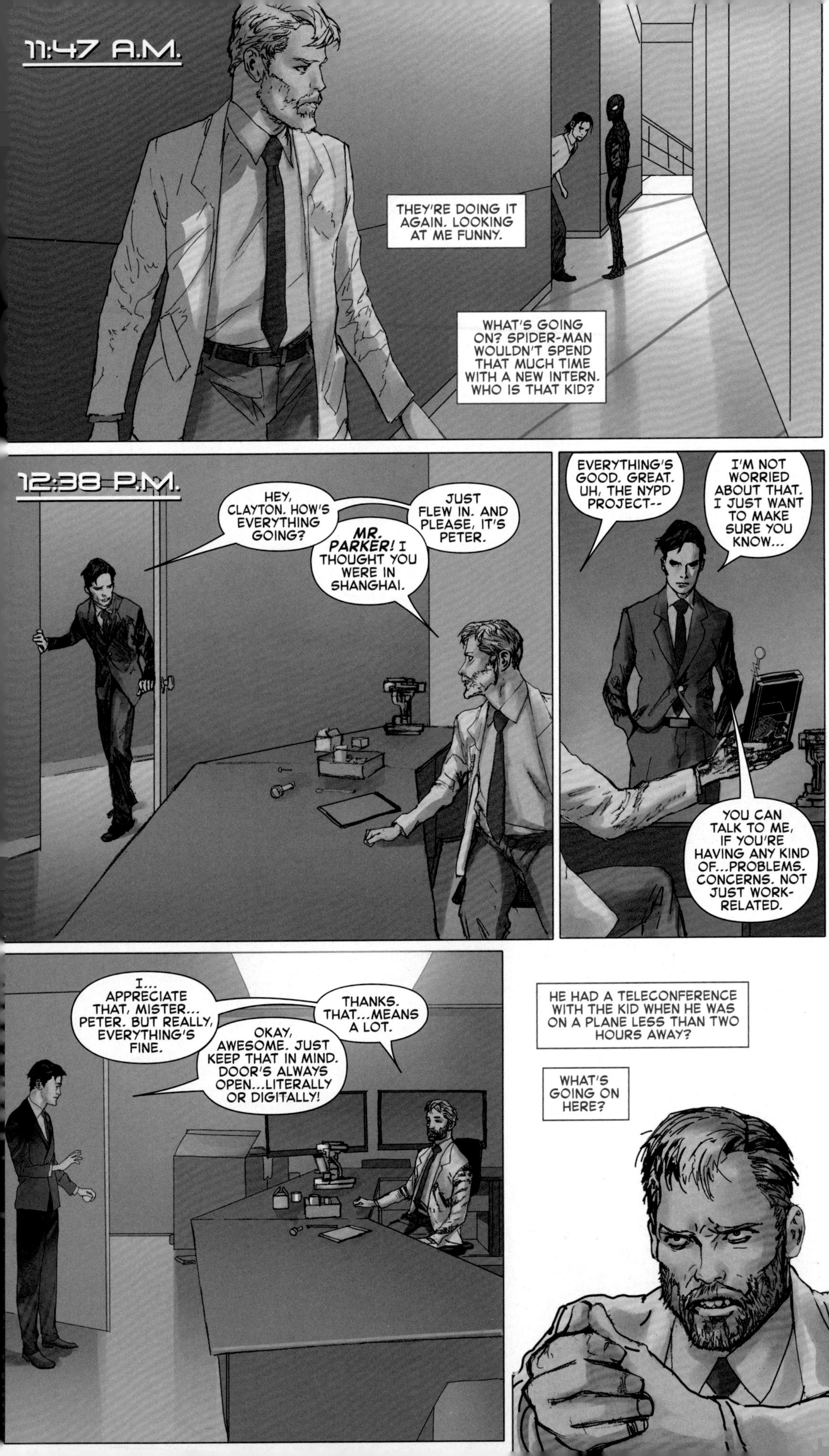
11:47 A.M.
THEY'RE DOING IT AGAIN. LOOKING AT ME FUNNY.
WHAT'S GOING ON? SPIDER-MAN WOULDN'T SPEND THAT MUCH TIME WITH A NEW INTERN. WHO IS THAT KID?
12:38 P.M.
HEY, CLAYTON. HOW'S EVERYTHING GOING?
MR. PARKER! I THOUGHT YOU WERE IN SHANGHAI.
JUST FLEW IN. AND PLEASE, IT'S PETER.
EVERYTHING'S GOOD. GREAT. UH, THE NYPD PROJECT--
I'M NOT WORRIED ABOUT THAT. I JUST WANT TO MAKE SURE YOU KNOW...
YOU CAN TALK TO ME, IF YOU'RE HAVING ANY KIND OF...PROBLEMS. CONCERNS. NOT JUST WORK-RELATED.
I... APPRECIATE THAT, MISTER... PETER. BUT REALLY, EVERYTHING'S FINE.
OKAY, AWESOME. JUST KEEP THAT IN MIND. DOOR'S ALWAYS OPEN...LITERALLY OR DIGITALLY!
THANKS. THAT...MEANS A LOT.
HE HAD A TELECONFERENCE WITH THE KID WHEN HE WAS ON A PLANE LESS THAN TWO HOURS AWAY?
WHAT'S GOING ON HERE?

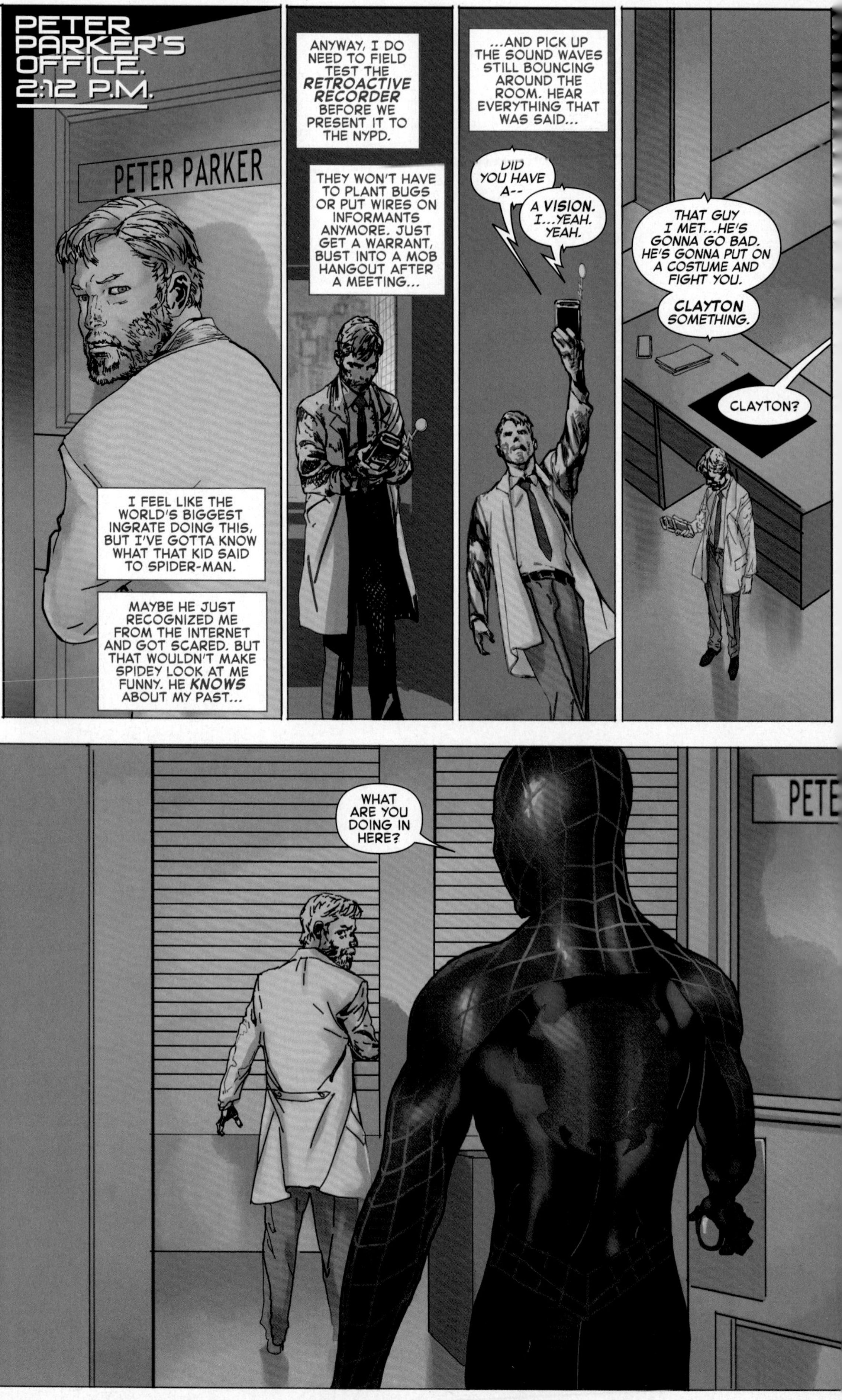
PETER PARKER'S OFFICE. 2:12 P.M.
PETER PARKER
I FEEL LIKE THE WORLD'S BIGGEST INGRATE DOING THIS, BUT I'VE GOTTA KNOW WHAT THAT KID SAID TO SPIDER-MAN.
MAYBE HE JUST RECOGNIZED ME FROM THE INTERNET AND GOT SCARED. BUT THAT WOULDN'T MAKE SPIDEY LOOK AT ME FUNNY. HE KNOWS ABOUT MY PAST...
ANYWAY, I DO NEED TO FIELD TEST THE RETROACTIVE RECORDER BEFORE WE PRESENT IT TO THE NYPD.
THEY WON'T HAVE TO PLANT BUGS OR PUT WIRES ON INFORMANTS ANYMORE. JUST GET A WARRANT, BUST INTO A MOB HANGOUT AFTER A MEETING...
...AND PICK UP THE SOUND WAVES STILL BOUNCING AROUND THE ROOM. HEAR EVERYTHING THAT WAS SAID...
DID YOU HAVE A--
A VISION. I...YEAH. YEAH.
THAT GUY I MET...HE'S GONNA GO BAD. HE'S GONNA PUT ON A COSTUME AND FIGHT YOU.
CLAYTON SOMETHING.
CLAYTON?
WHAT ARE YOU DOING IN HERE?
PETE

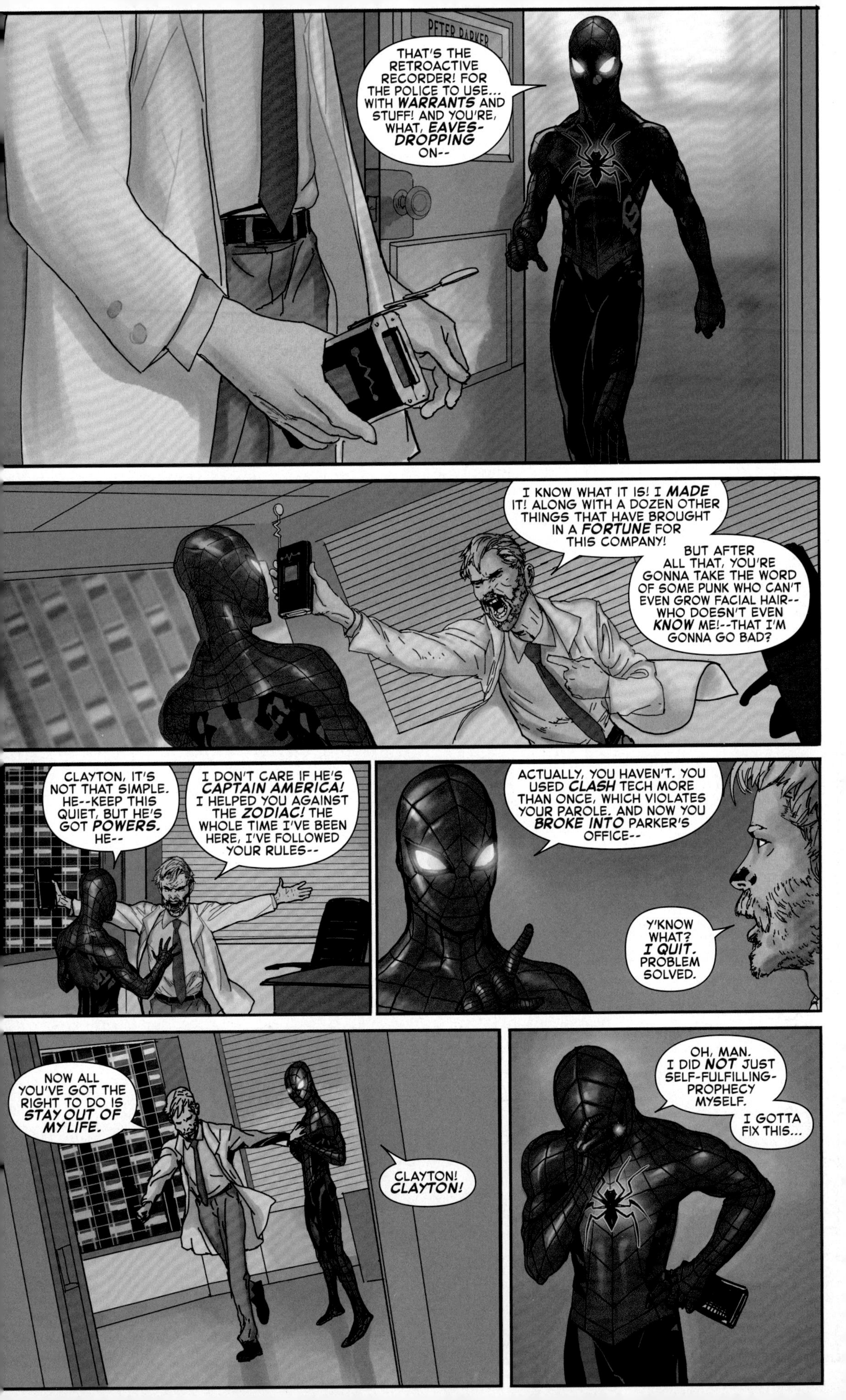
PETER PARKER
THAT'S THE RETROACTIVE RECORDER! FOR THE POLICE TO USE... WITH WARRANTS AND STUFF! AND YOU'RE, WHAT, EAVES-DROPPING ON--
I KNOW WHAT IT IS! I MADE IT! ALONG WITH A DOZEN OTHER THINGS THAT HAVE BROUGHT IN A FORTUNE FOR THIS COMPANY!
BUT AFTER ALL THAT, YOU'RE GONNA TAKE THE WORD OF SOME PUNK WHO CAN'T EVEN GROW FACIAL HAIR-- WHO DOESN'T EVEN KNOW ME!--THAT I'M GONNA GO BAD?
CLAYTON, IT'S NOT THAT SIMPLE. HE--KEEP THIS QUIET, BUT HE'S GOT POWERS. HE--
I DON'T CARE IF HE'S CAPTAIN AMERICA! I HELPED YOU AGAINST THE ZODIAC! THE WHOLE TIME I'VE BEEN HERE, I'VE FOLLOWED YOUR RULES--
ACTUALLY, YOU HAVEN'T. YOU USED CLASH TECH MORE THAN ONCE, WHICH VIOLATES YOUR PAROLE. AND NOW YOU BROKE INTO PARKER'S OFFICE--
Y'KNOW WHAT? I QUIT. PROBLEM SOLVED.
NOW ALL YOU'VE GOT THE RIGHT TO DO IS STAY OUT OF MY LIFE.
CLAYTON! CLAYTON!
OH, MAN. I DID NOT JUST SELF-FULFILLING-PROPHECY MYSELF.
I GOTTA FIX THIS...

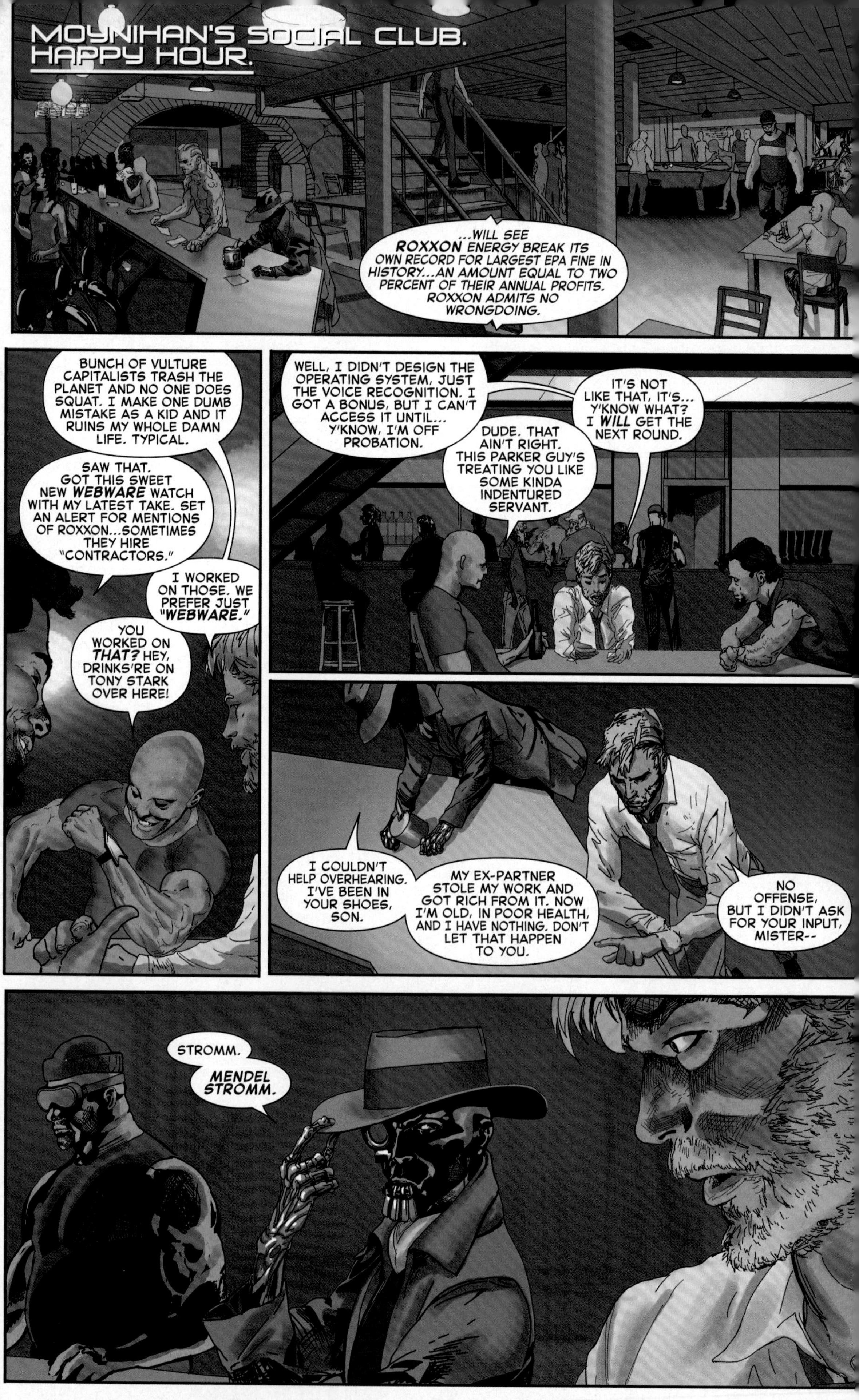
MOYNIHAN'S SOCIAL CLUB. HAPPY HOUR.
...WILL SEE ROXXON ENERGY BREAK ITS OWN RECORD FOR LARGEST EPA FINE IN HISTORY...AN AMOUNT EQUAL TO TWO PERCENT OF THEIR ANNUAL PROFITS. ROXXON ADMITS NO WRONGDOING.
BUNCH OF VULTURE CAPITALISTS TRASH THE PLANET AND NO ONE DOES SQUAT. I MAKE ONE DUMB MISTAKE AS A KID AND IT RUINS MY WHOLE DAMN LIFE. TYPICAL.
SAW THAT. GOT THIS SWEET NEW WEBWARE WATCH WITH MY LATEST TAKE. SET AN ALERT FOR MENTIONS OF ROXXON...SOMETIMES THEY HIRE "CONTRACTORS."
I WORKED ON THOSE. WE PREFER JUST "WEBWARE."
YOU WORKED ON THAT? HEY, DRINKS'RE ON TONY STARK OVER HERE!
WELL, I DIDN'T DESIGN THE OPERATING SYSTEM, JUST THE VOICE RECOGNITION. I GOT A BONUS, BUT I CAN'T ACCESS IT UNTIL... Y'KNOW, I'M OFF PROBATION.
DUDE. THAT AIN'T RIGHT. THIS PARKER GUY'S TREATING YOU LIKE SOME KINDA INDENTURED SERVANT.
IT'S NOT LIKE THAT, IT'S... Y'KNOW WHAT? I WILL GET THE NEXT ROUND.
I COULDN'T HELP OVERHEARING. I'VE BEEN IN YOUR SHOES, SON.
MY EX-PARTNER STOLE MY WORK AND GOT RICH FROM IT. NOW I'M OLD, IN POOR HEALTH, AND I HAVE NOTHING. DON'T LET THAT HAPPEN TO YOU.
NO OFFENSE, BUT I DIDN'T ASK FOR YOUR INPUT, MISTER--
STROMM.
MENDEL STROMM.

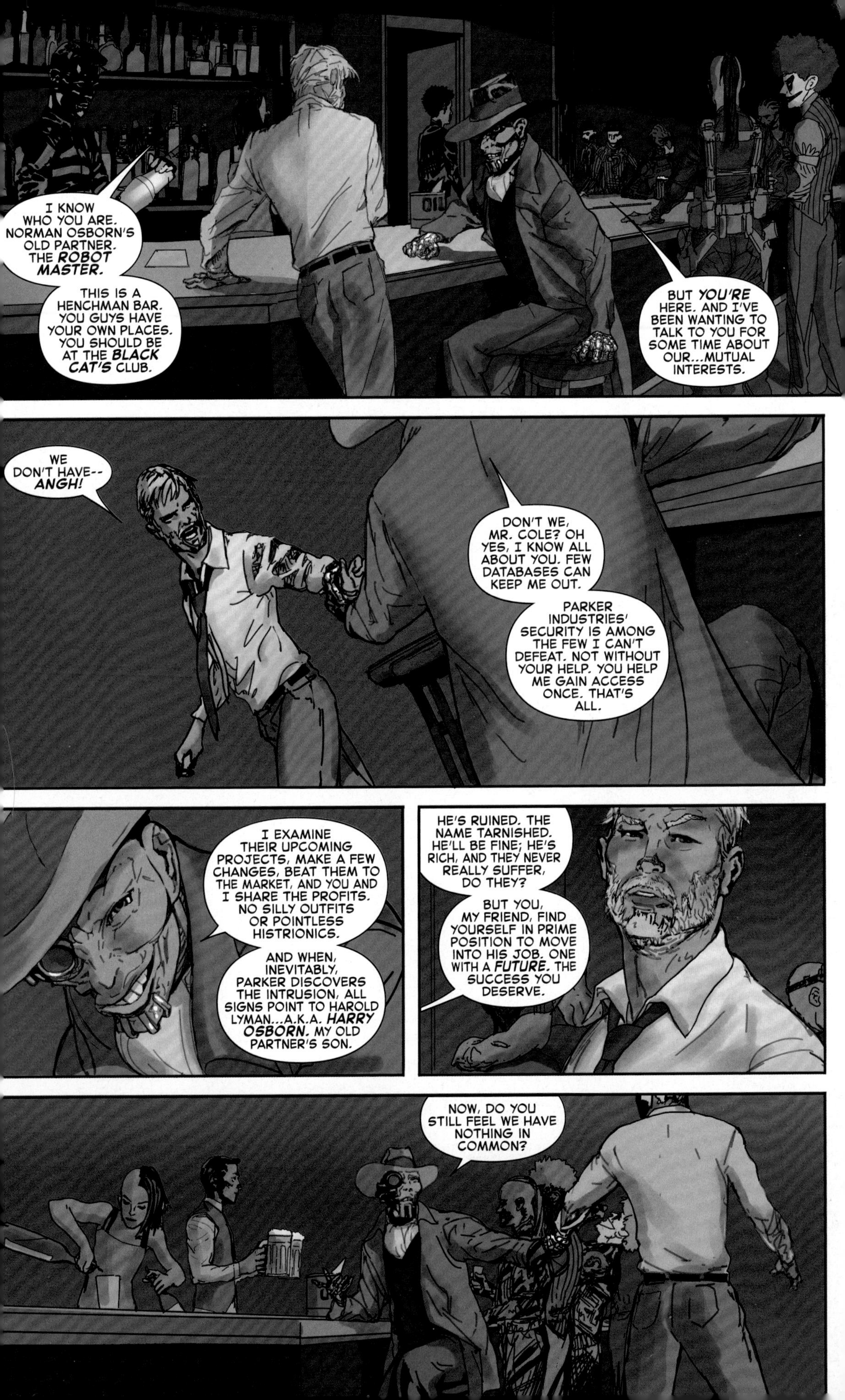
I KNOW WHO YOU ARE. NORMAN OSBORN'S OLD PARTNER. THE ROBOT MASTER.
THIS IS A HENCHMAN BAR. YOU GUYS HAVE YOUR OWN PLACES. YOU SHOULD BE AT THE BLACK CAT'S CLUB.
BUT YOU'RE HERE. AND I'VE BEEN WANTING TO TALK TO YOU FOR SOME TIME ABOUT OUR...MUTUAL INTERESTS.
WE DON'T HAVE-- ANGH!
DON'T WE, MR. COLE? OH YES, I KNOW ALL ABOUT YOU. FEW DATABASES CAN KEEP ME OUT.
PARKER INDUSTRIES' SECURITY IS AMONG THE FEW I CAN'T DEFEAT. NOT WITHOUT YOUR HELP. YOU HELP ME GAIN ACCESS ONCE. THAT'S ALL.
I EXAMINE THEIR UPCOMING PROJECTS, MAKE A FEW CHANGES, BEAT THEM TO THE MARKET, AND YOU AND I SHARE THE PROFITS. NO SILLY OUTFITS OR POINTLESS HISTRIONICS.
AND WHEN, INEVITABLY, PARKER DISCOVERS THE INTRUSION, ALL SIGNS POINT TO HAROLD LYMAN...A.K.A. HARRY OSBORN. MY OLD PARTNER'S SON.
HE'S RUINED. THE NAME TARNISHED. HE'LL BE FINE; HE'S RICH, AND THEY NEVER REALLY SUFFER, DO THEY?
BUT YOU, MY FRIEND, FIND YOURSELF IN PRIME POSITION TO MOVE INTO HIS JOB. ONE WITH A FUTURE. THE SUCCESS YOU DESERVE.
NOW, DO YOU STILL FEEL WE HAVE NOTHING IN COMMON?

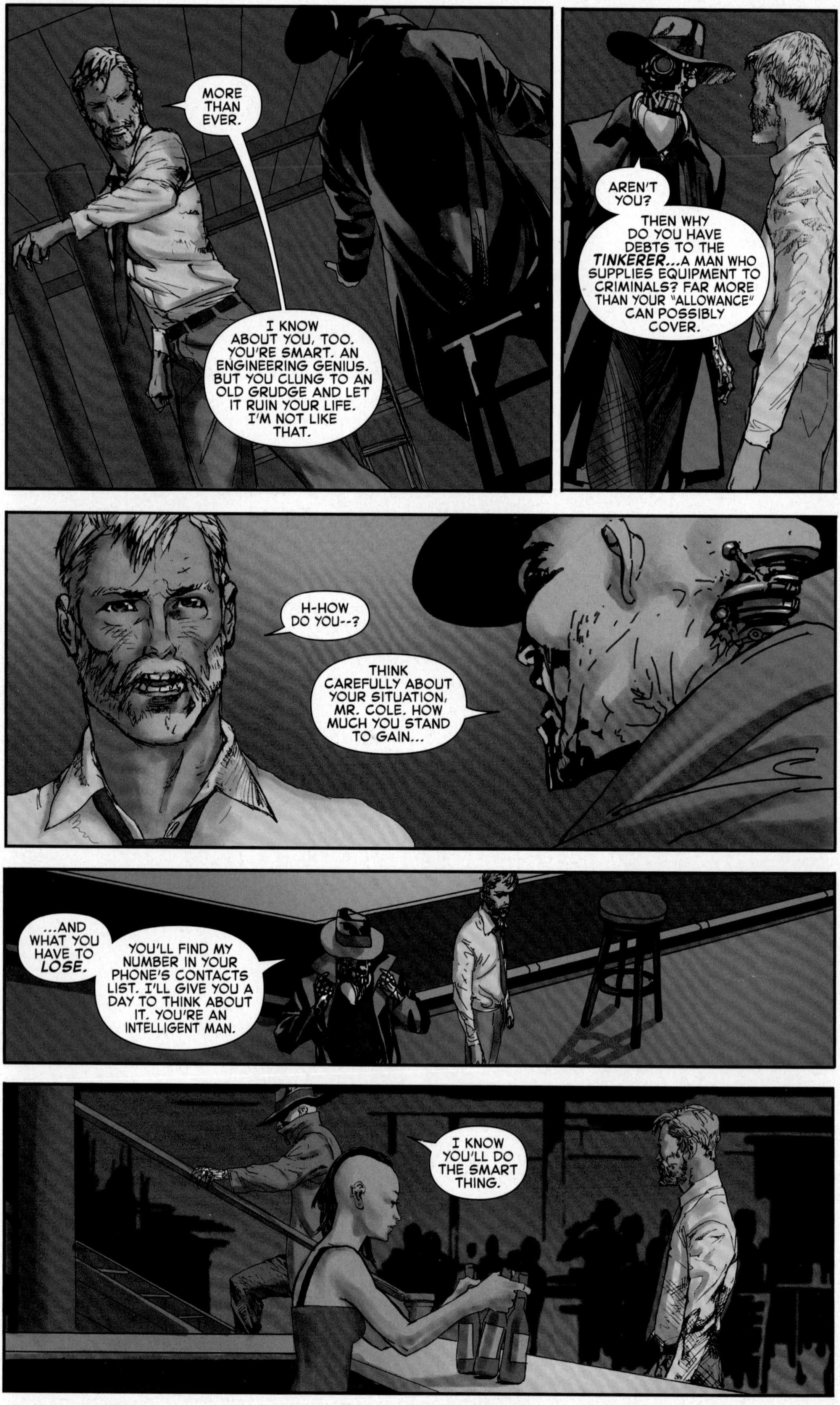
MORE THAN EVER.
I KNOW ABOUT YOU, TOO. YOU'RE SMART. AN ENGINEERING GENIUS. BUT YOU CLUNG TO AN OLD GRUDGE AND LET IT RUIN YOUR LIFE. I'M NOT LIKE THAT.
AREN'T YOU?
THEN WHY DO YOU HAVE DEBTS TO THE TINKERER...A MAN WHO SUPPLIES EQUIPMENT TO CRIMINALS? FAR MORE THAN YOUR "ALLOWANCE" CAN POSSIBLY COVER.
H-HOW DO YOU--?
THINK CAREFULLY ABOUT YOUR SITUATION, MR. COLE. HOW MUCH YOU STAND TO GAIN...
...AND WHAT YOU HAVE TO LOSE.
YOU'LL FIND MY NUMBER IN YOUR PHONE'S CONTACTS LIST. I'LL GIVE YOU A DAY TO THINK ABOUT IT. YOU'RE AN INTELLIGENT MAN.
I KNOW YOU'LL DO THE SMART THING.

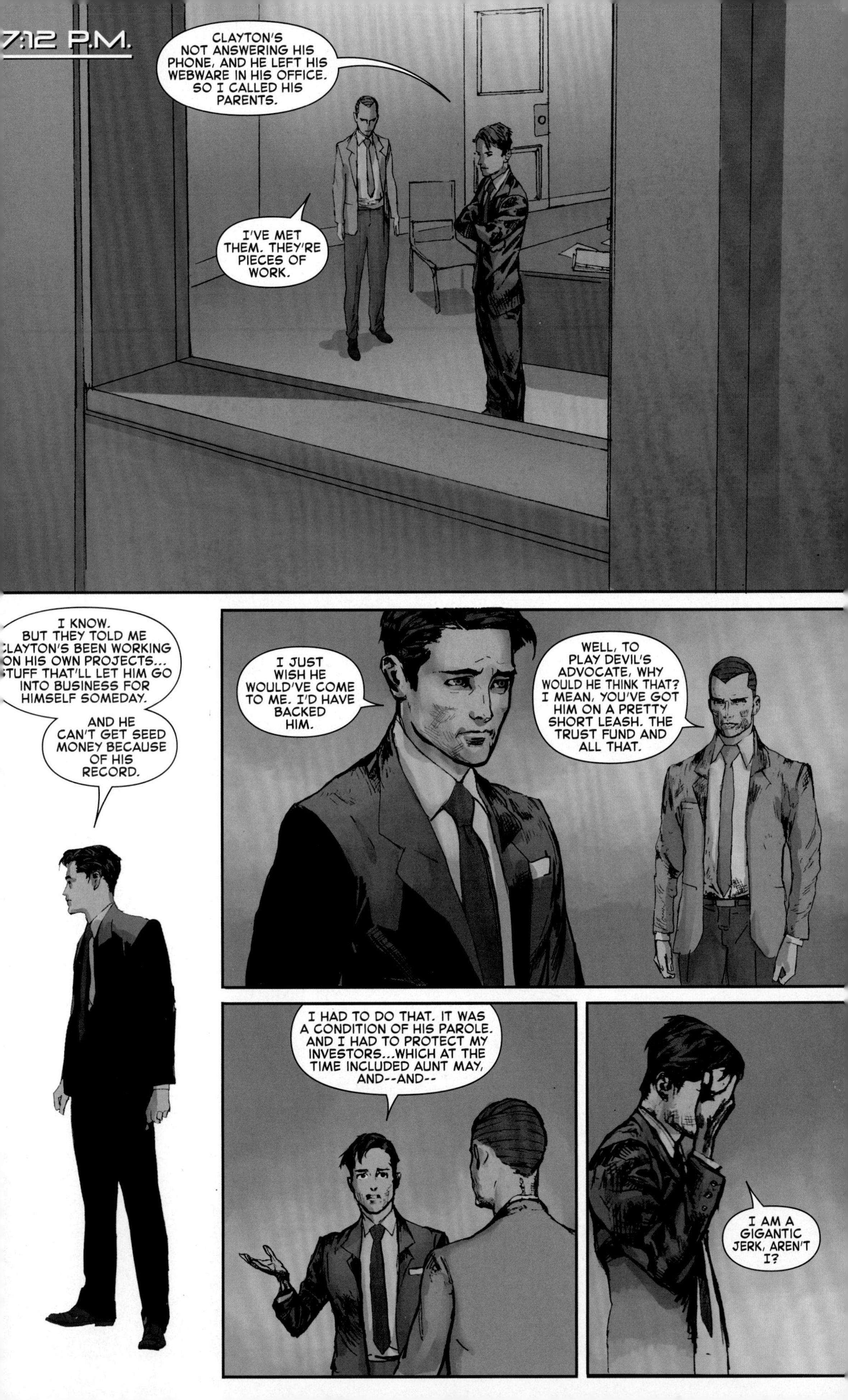
7:12 P.M.
CLAYTON'S NOT ANSWERING HIS PHONE, AND HE LEFT HIS WEBWARE IN HIS OFFICE. SO I CALLED HIS PARENTS.
I'VE MET THEM. THEY'RE PIECES OF WORK.
I KNOW. BUT THEY TOLD ME CLAYTON'S BEEN WORKING ON HIS OWN PROJECTS... STUFF THAT'LL LET HIM GO INTO BUSINESS FOR HIMSELF SOMEDAY.
AND HE CAN'T GET SEED MONEY BECAUSE OF HIS RECORD.
I JUST WISH HE WOULD'VE COME TO ME. I'D HAVE BACKED HIM.
WELL, TO PLAY DEVIL'S ADVOCATE, WHY WOULD HE THINK THAT? I MEAN, YOU'VE GOT HIM ON A PRETTY SHORT LEASH. THE TRUST FUND AND ALL THAT.
I HAD TO DO THAT. IT WAS A CONDITION OF HIS PAROLE. AND I HAD TO PROTECT MY INVESTORS...WHICH AT THE TIME INCLUDED AUNT MAY, AND--AND--
I AM A GIGANTIC JERK, AREN'T I?

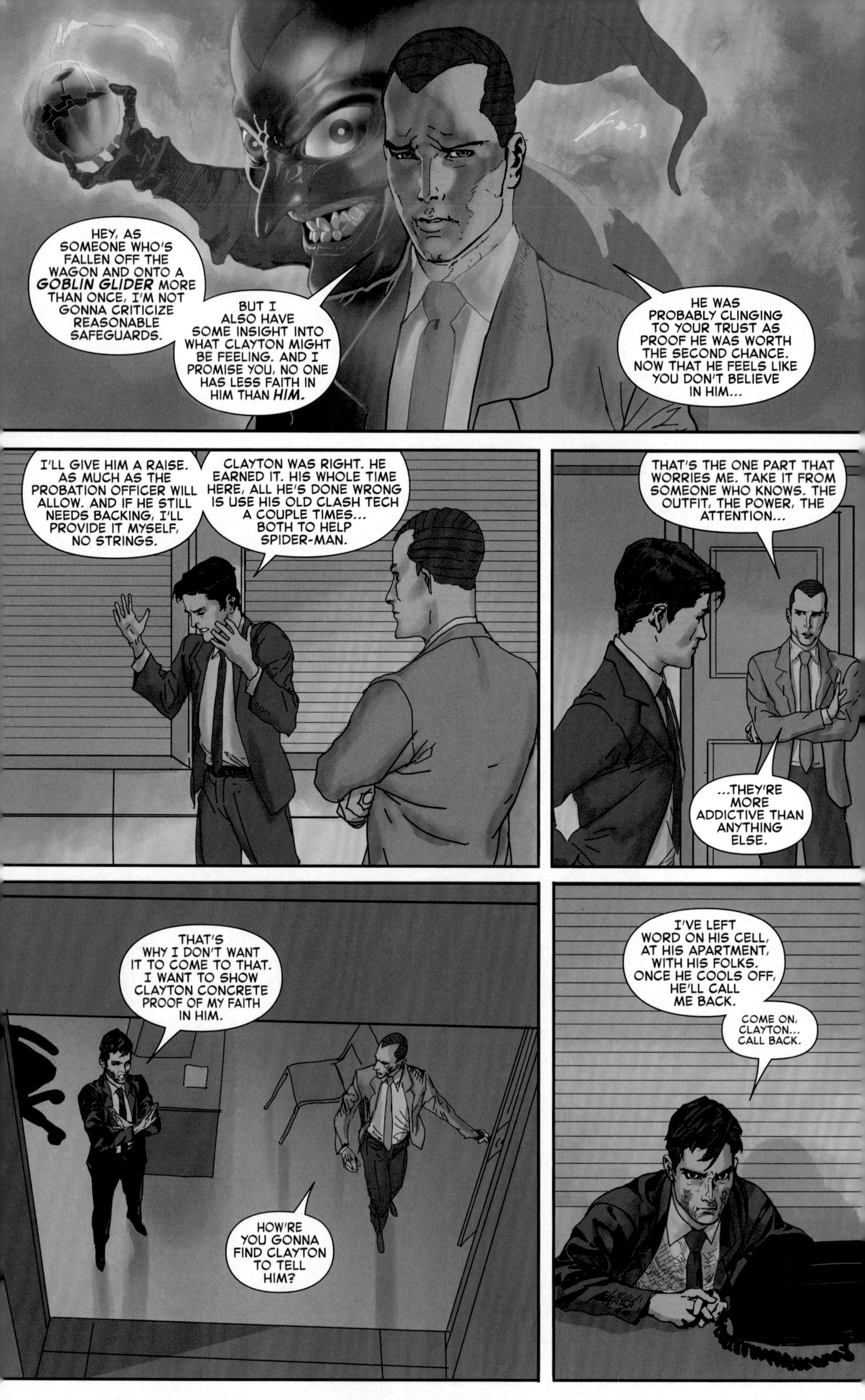
HEY, AS SOMEONE WHO'S FALLEN OFF THE WAGON AND ONTO A GOBLIN GLIDER MORE THAN ONCE, I'M NOT GONNA CRITICIZE REASONABLE SAFEGUARDS.
BUT I ALSO HAVE SOME INSIGHT INTO WHAT CLAYTON MIGHT BE FEELING. AND I PROMISE YOU, NO ONE HAS LESS FAITH IN HIM THAN HIM.
HE WAS PROBABLY CLINGING TO YOUR TRUST AS PROOF HE WAS WORTH THE SECOND CHANCE. NOW THAT HE FEELS LIKE YOU DON'T BELIEVE IN HIM...
I'LL GIVE HIM A RAISE. AS MUCH AS THE PROBATION OFFICER WILL ALLOW. AND IF HE STILL NEEDS BACKING, I'LL PROVIDE IT MYSELF, NO STRINGS.
CLAYTON WAS RIGHT. HE EARNED IT. HIS WHOLE TIME HERE, ALL HE'S DONE WRONG IS USE HIS OLD CLASH TECH A COUPLE TIMES... BOTH TO HELP SPIDER-MAN.
THAT'S THE ONE PART THAT WORRIES ME. TAKE IT FROM SOMEONE WHO KNOWS. THE OUTFIT, THE POWER, THE ATTENTION...
...THEY'RE MORE ADDICTIVE THAN ANYTHING ELSE.
THAT'S WHY I DON'T WANT IT TO COME TO THAT. I WANT TO SHOW CLAYTON CONCRETE PROOF OF MY FAITH IN HIM.
HOW'RE YOU GONNA FIND CLAYTON TO TELL HIM?
I'VE LEFT WORD ON HIS CELL, AT HIS APARTMENT, WITH HIS FOLKS. ONCE HE COOLS OFF, HE'LL CALL ME BACK.
COME ON, CLAYTON... CALL BACK.

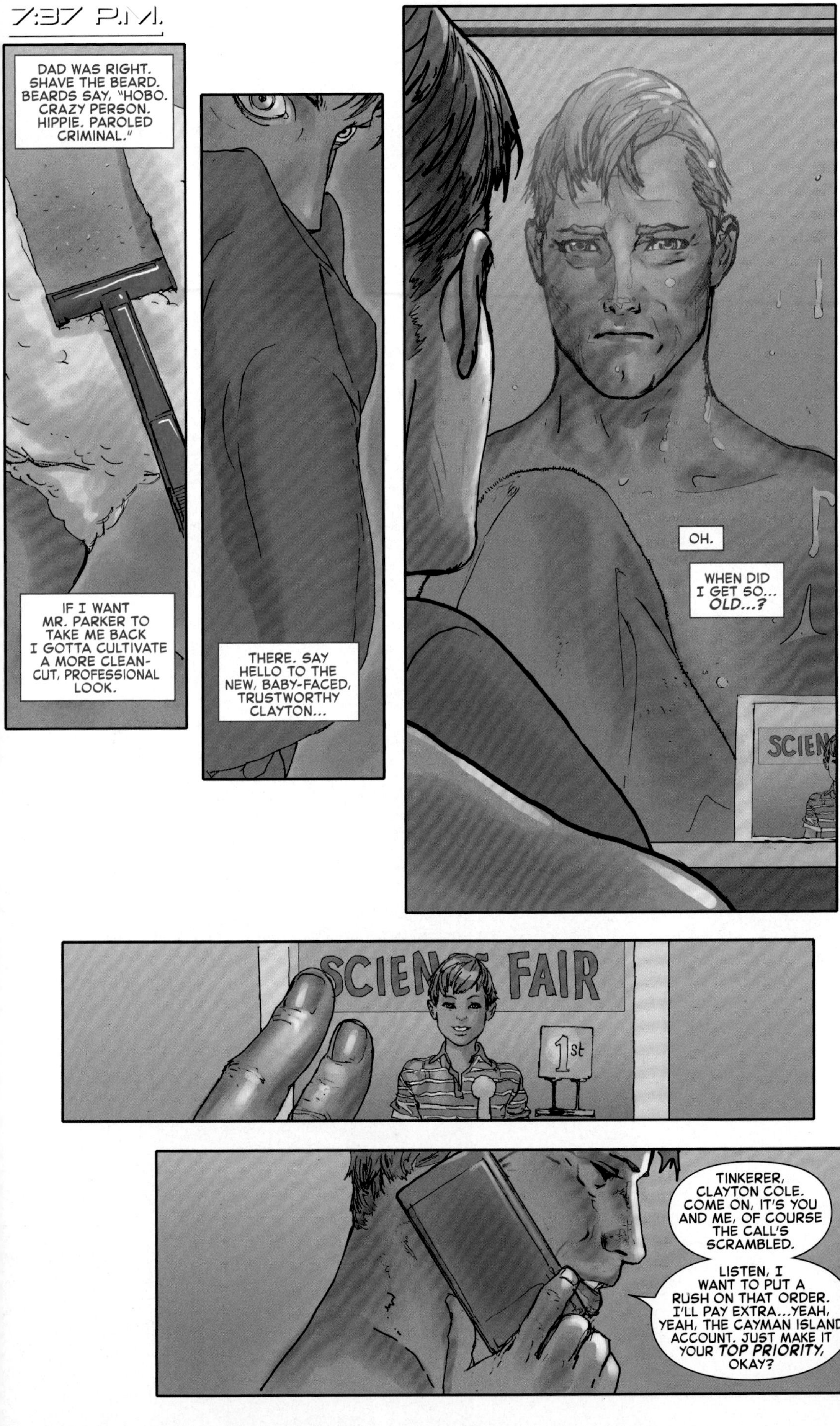
7:37 P.M.
DAD WAS RIGHT. SHAVE THE BEARD. BEARDS SAY, "HOBO. CRAZY PERSON. HIPPIE. PAROLED CRIMINAL."
IF I WANT MR. PARKER TO TAKE ME BACK I GOTTA CULTIVATE A MORE CLEAN-CUT, PROFESSIONAL LOOK.
THERE. SAY HELLO TO THE NEW, BABY-FACED, TRUSTWORTHY CLAYTON...
OH.
WHEN DID I GET SO... *OLD...?*
SCIEN
SCIEN FAIR
1st
TINKERER, CLAYTON COLE. COME ON, IT'S YOU AND ME, OF COURSE THE CALL'S SCRAMBLED.
LISTEN, I WANT TO PUT A RUSH ON THAT ORDER. I'LL PAY EXTRA...YEAH, YEAH, THE CAYMAN ISLAND ACCOUNT. JUST MAKE IT YOUR *TOP PRIORITY,* OKAY?

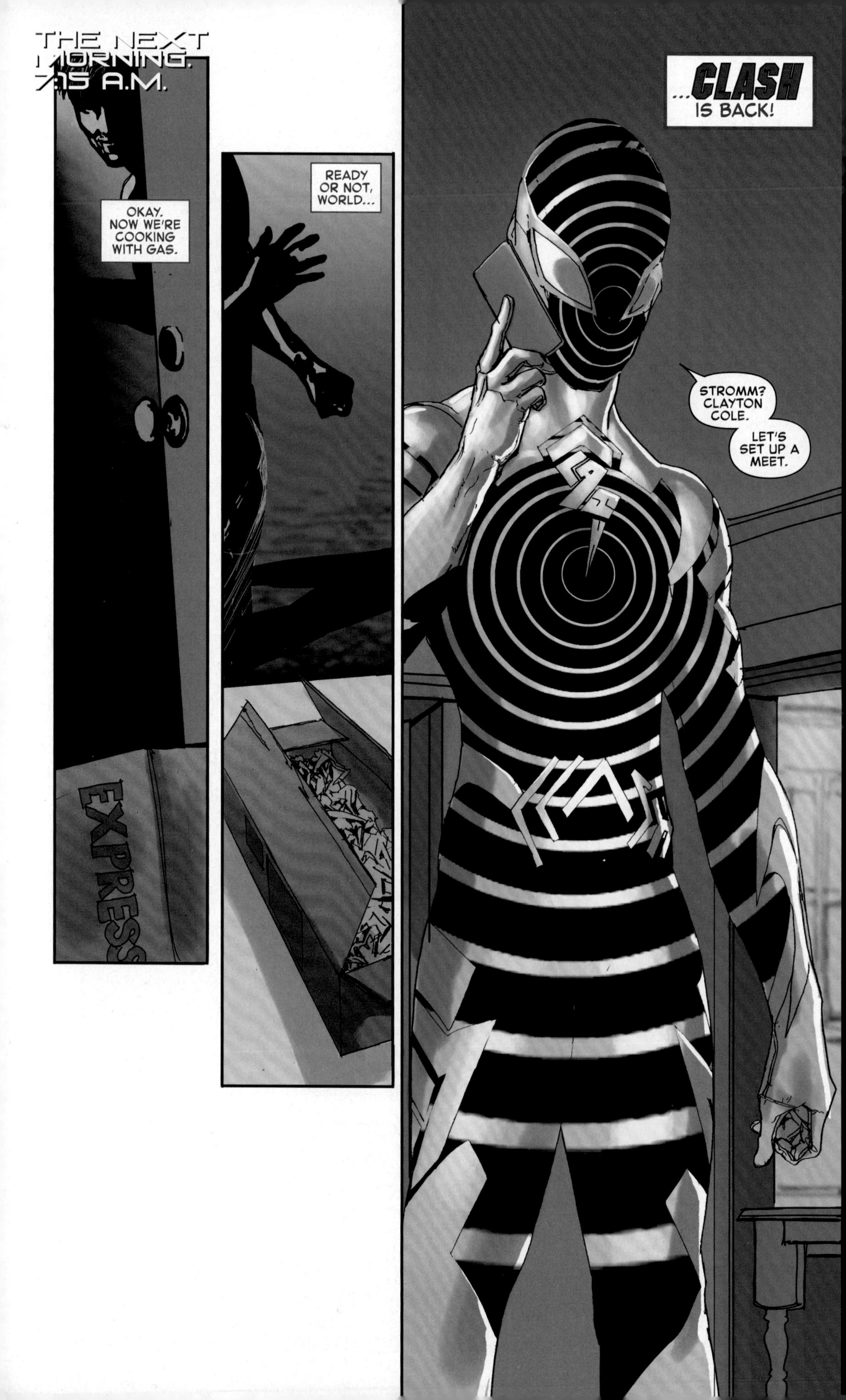
THE NEXT MORNING. 7:15 A.M.
OKAY. NOW WE'RE COOKING WITH GAS.
EXPRESS
READY OR NOT, WORLD...
...CLASH IS BACK!
STROMM? CLAYTON COLE.
LET'S SET UP A MEET.

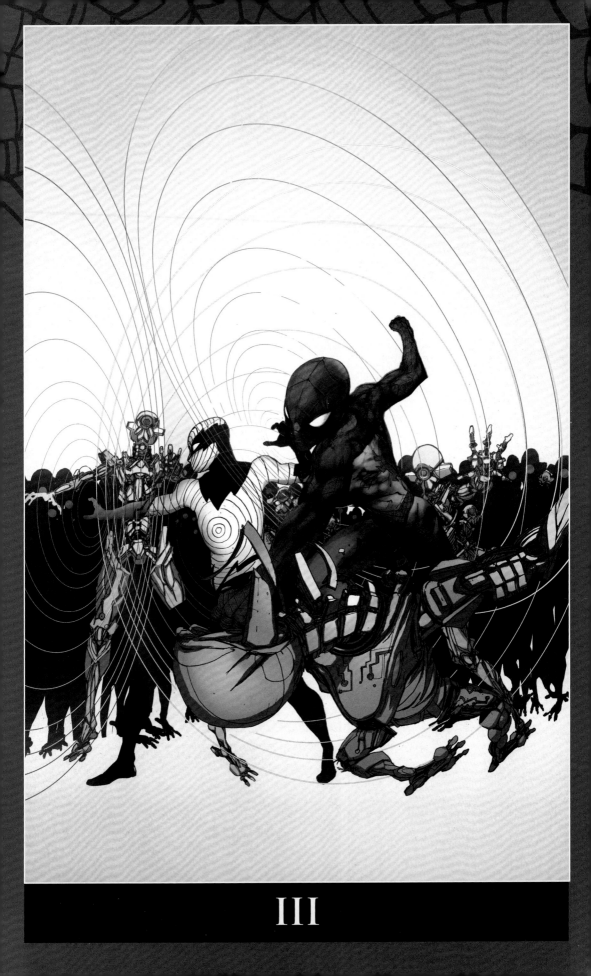

III

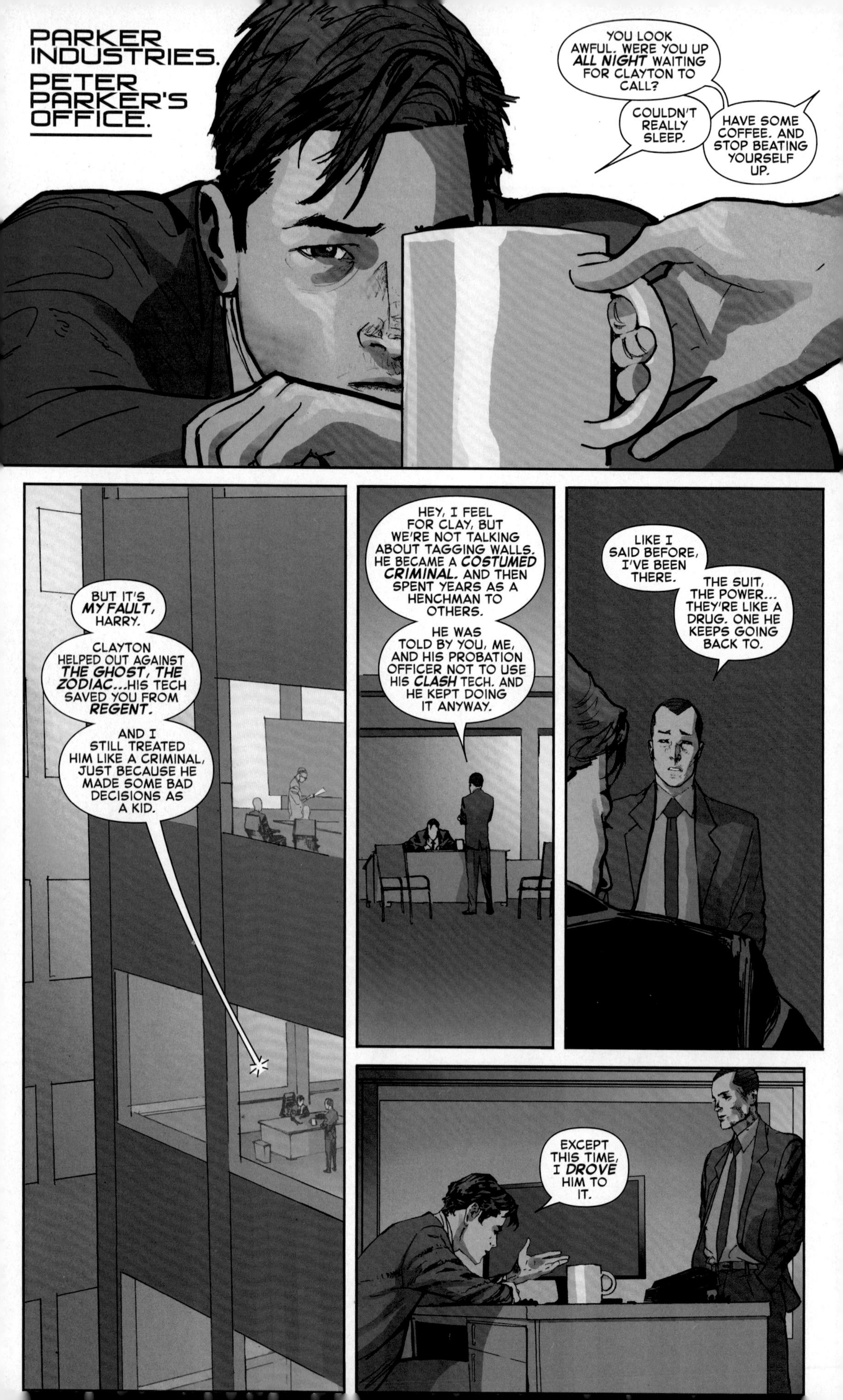
PARKER INDUSTRIES. PETER PARKER'S OFFICE.
YOU LOOK AWFUL. WERE YOU UP ALL NIGHT WAITING FOR CLAYTON TO CALL?
COULDN'T REALLY SLEEP.
HAVE SOME COFFEE. AND STOP BEATING YOURSELF UP.
BUT IT'S MY FAULT, HARRY.
CLAYTON HELPED OUT AGAINST THE GHOST, THE ZODIAC...HIS TECH SAVED YOU FROM REGENT.
AND I STILL TREATED HIM LIKE A CRIMINAL, JUST BECAUSE HE MADE SOME BAD DECISIONS AS A KID.
HEY, I FEEL FOR CLAY, BUT WE'RE NOT TALKING ABOUT TAGGING WALLS. HE BECAME A COSTUMED CRIMINAL. AND THEN SPENT YEARS AS A HENCHMAN TO OTHERS.
HE WAS TOLD BY YOU, ME, AND HIS PROBATION OFFICER NOT TO USE HIS CLASH TECH. AND HE KEPT DOING IT ANYWAY.
LIKE I SAID BEFORE, I'VE BEEN THERE.
THE SUIT, THE POWER... THEY'RE LIKE A DRUG. ONE HE KEEPS GOING BACK TO.
EXCEPT THIS TIME, I DROVE HIM TO IT.

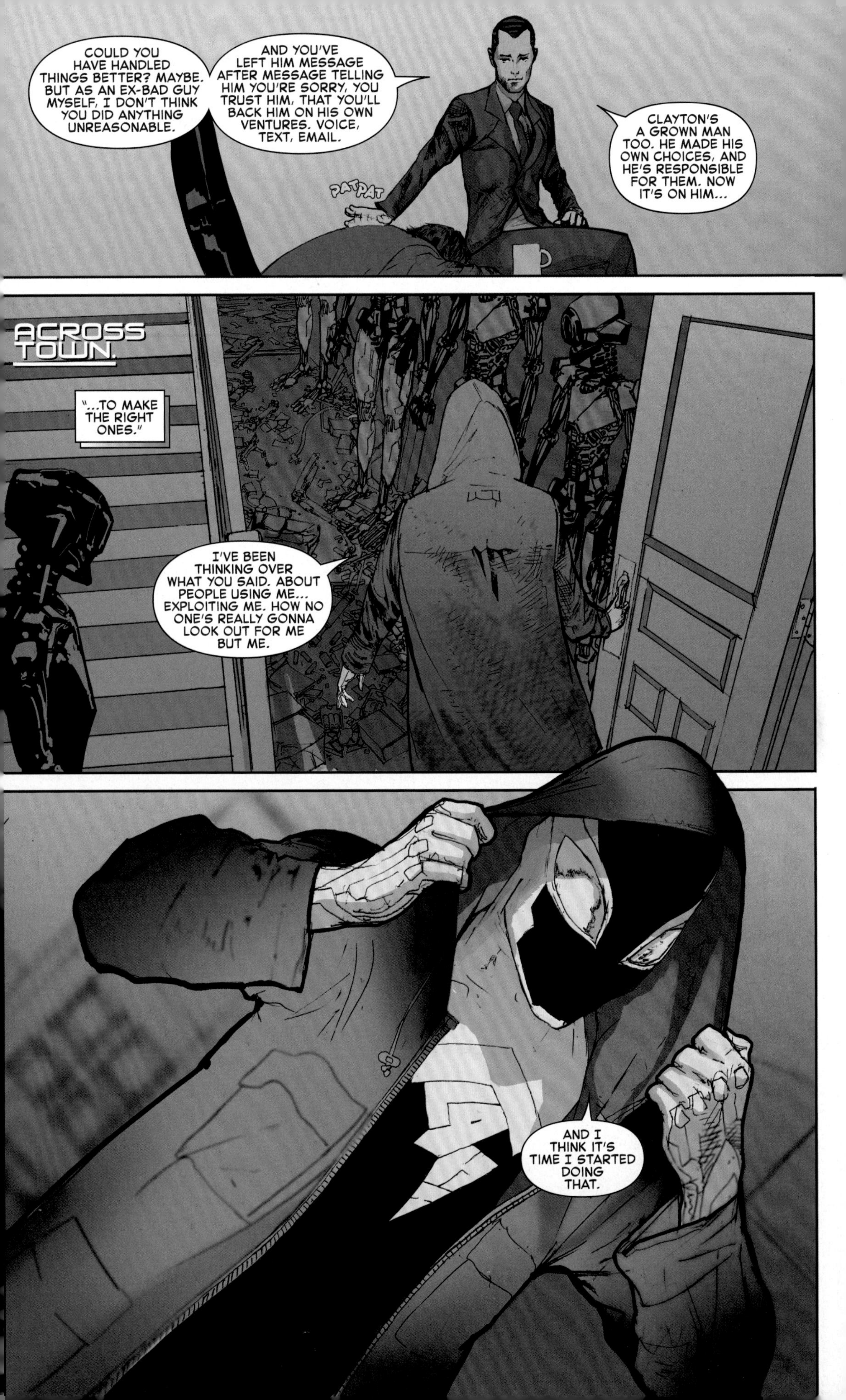
COULD YOU HAVE HANDLED THINGS BETTER? MAYBE. BUT AS AN EX-BAD GUY MYSELF, I DON'T THINK YOU DID ANYTHING UNREASONABLE.
AND YOU'VE LEFT HIM MESSAGE AFTER MESSAGE TELLING HIM YOU'RE SORRY, YOU TRUST HIM, THAT YOU'LL BACK HIM ON HIS OWN VENTURES. VOICE, TEXT, EMAIL.
PAT PAT
CLAYTON'S A GROWN MAN TOO. HE MADE HIS OWN CHOICES, AND HE'S RESPONSIBLE FOR THEM. NOW IT'S ON HIM...
ACROSS TOWN.
"...TO MAKE THE RIGHT ONES."
I'VE BEEN THINKING OVER WHAT YOU SAID. ABOUT PEOPLE USING ME... EXPLOITING ME. HOW NO ONE'S REALLY GONNA LOOK OUT FOR ME BUT ME.
AND I THINK IT'S TIME I STARTED DOING THAT.

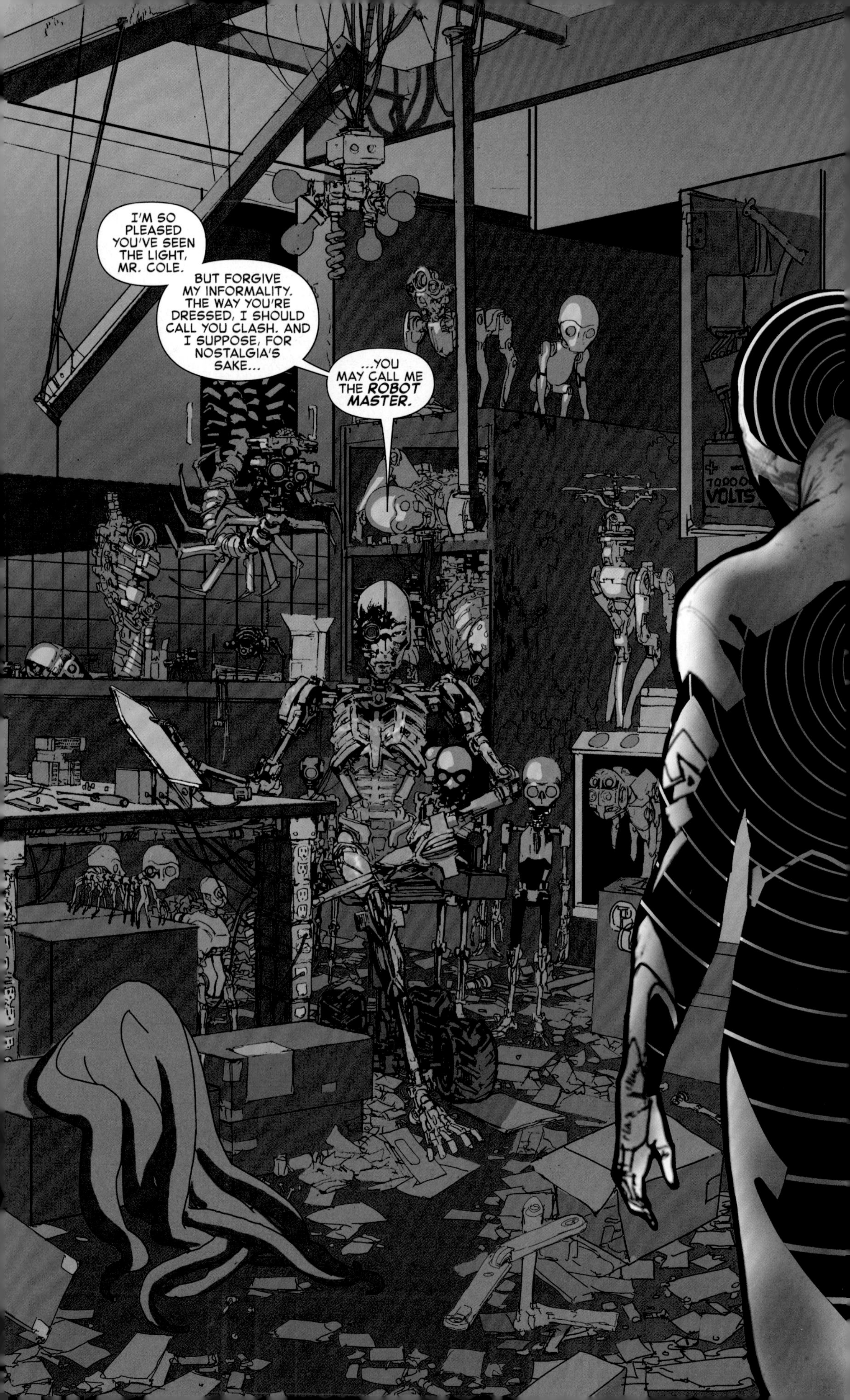
I'M SO PLEASED YOU'VE SEEN THE LIGHT, MR. COLE.
BUT FORGIVE MY INFORMALITY. THE WAY YOU'RE DRESSED, I SHOULD CALL YOU CLASH. AND I SUPPOSE, FOR NOSTALGIA'S SAKE...
...YOU MAY CALL ME THE ROBOT MASTER.
VOLTS

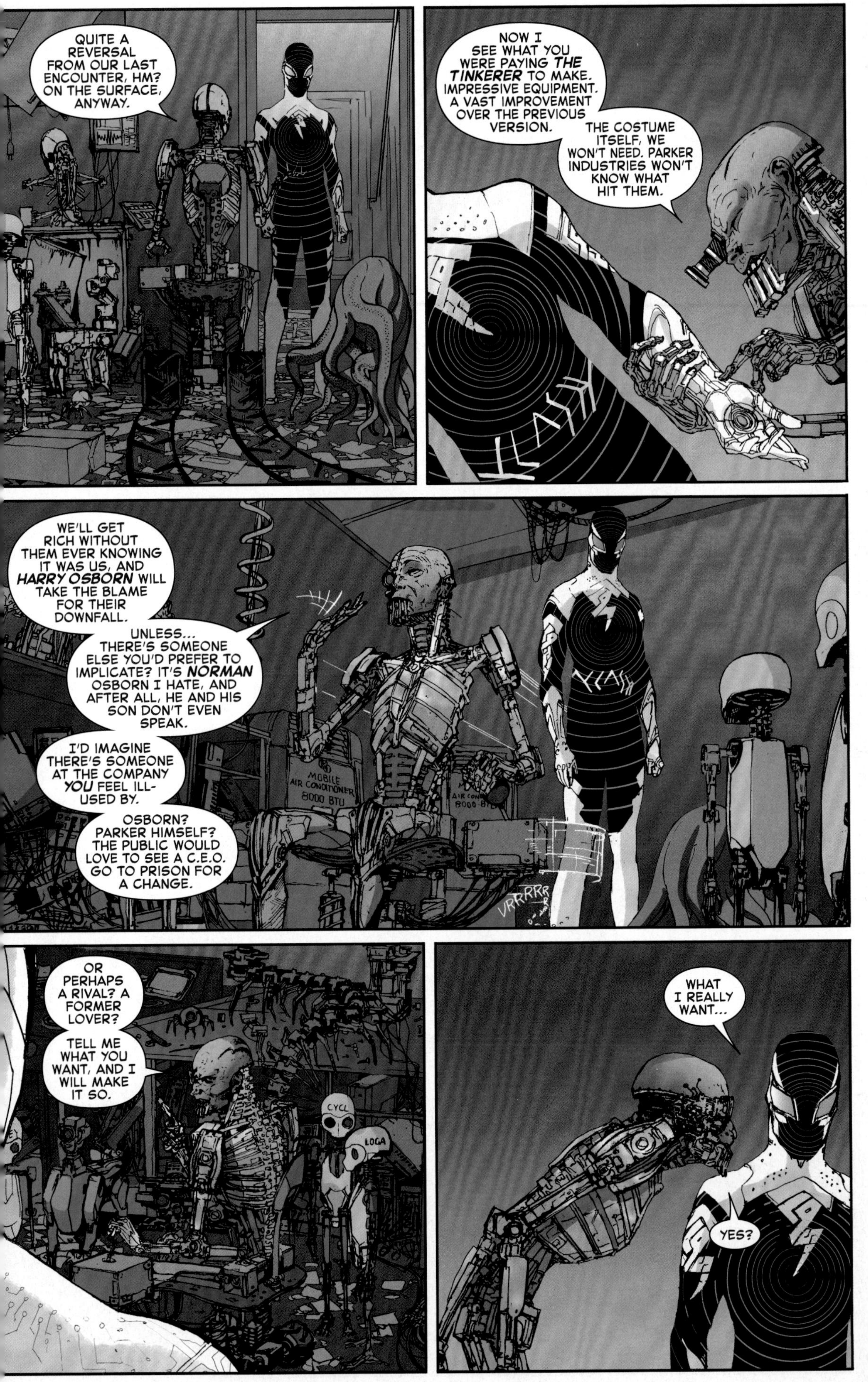
QUITE A REVERSAL FROM OUR LAST ENCOUNTER, HM? ON THE SURFACE, ANYWAY.
NOW I SEE WHAT YOU WERE PAYING THE TINKERER TO MAKE. IMPRESSIVE EQUIPMENT. A VAST IMPROVEMENT OVER THE PREVIOUS VERSION.
THE COSTUME ITSELF, WE WON'T NEED. PARKER INDUSTRIES WON'T KNOW WHAT HIT THEM.
WE'LL GET RICH WITHOUT THEM EVER KNOWING IT WAS US, AND HARRY OSBORN WILL TAKE THE BLAME FOR THEIR DOWNFALL.
UNLESS... THERE'S SOMEONE ELSE YOU'D PREFER TO IMPLICATE? IT'S NORMAN OSBORN I HATE, AND AFTER ALL, HE AND HIS SON DON'T EVEN SPEAK.
I'D IMAGINE THERE'S SOMEONE AT THE COMPANY YOU FEEL ILL-USED BY.
OSBORN? PARKER HIMSELF? THE PUBLIC WOULD LOVE TO SEE A C.E.O. GO TO PRISON FOR A CHANGE.
MOBILE AIR CONDITIONER 8000 BTU
VRRRRR
OR PERHAPS A RIVAL? A FORMER LOVER?
TELL ME WHAT YOU WANT, AND I WILL MAKE IT SO.
CYCL
LOGA
WHAT I REALLY WANT...
YES?

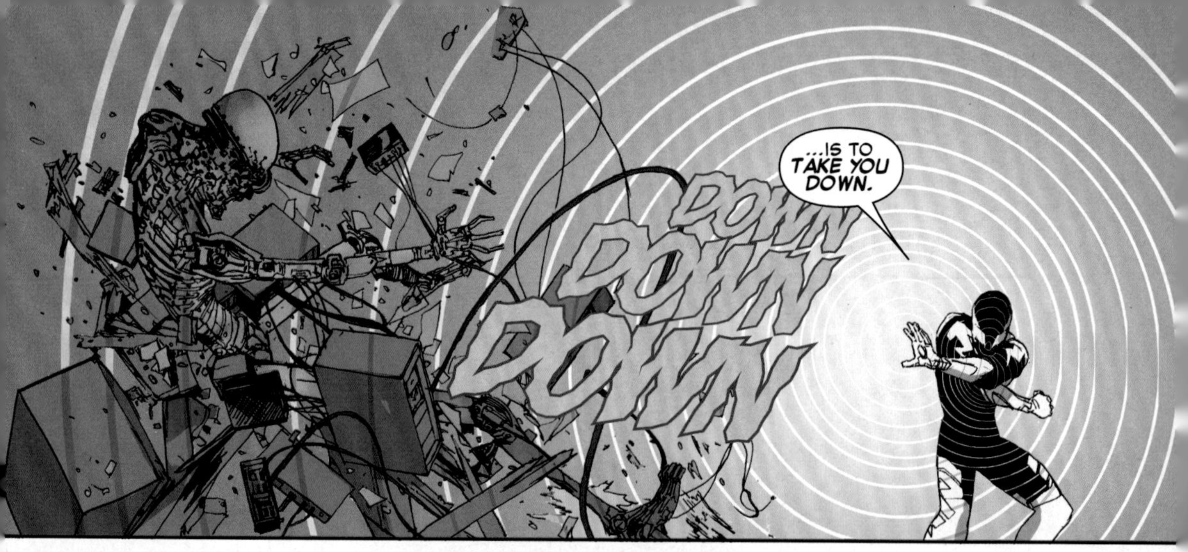
...IS TO *TAKE YOU* DOWN.
DOWN
DOWN
DOWN

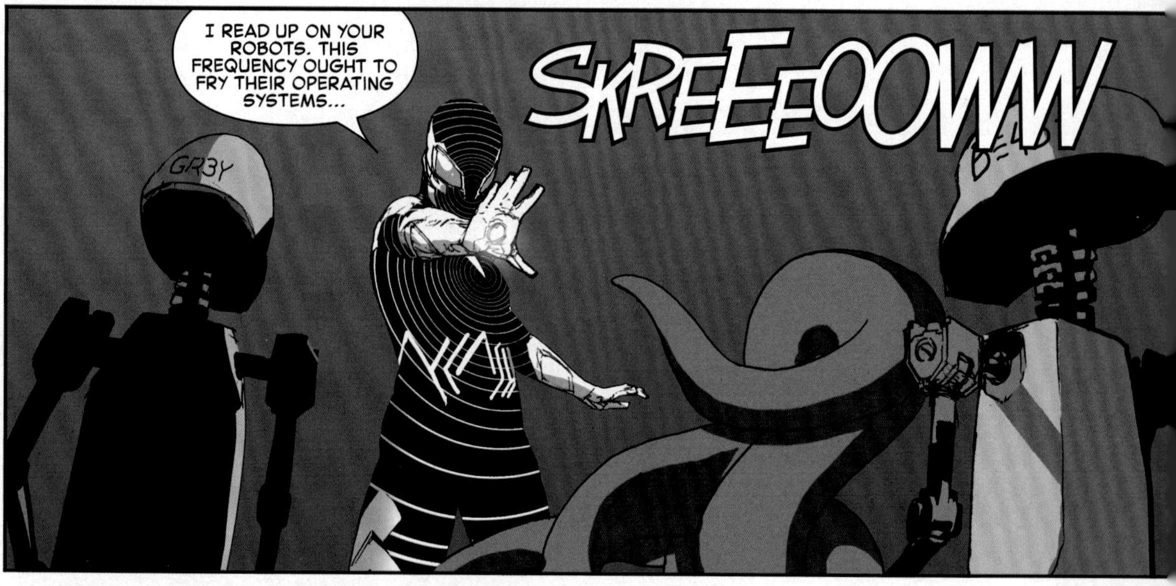
I READ UP ON YOUR ROBOTS. THIS FREQUENCY OUGHT TO FRY THEIR OPERATING SYSTEMS...
SKREEEEOOWWN
GR3Y

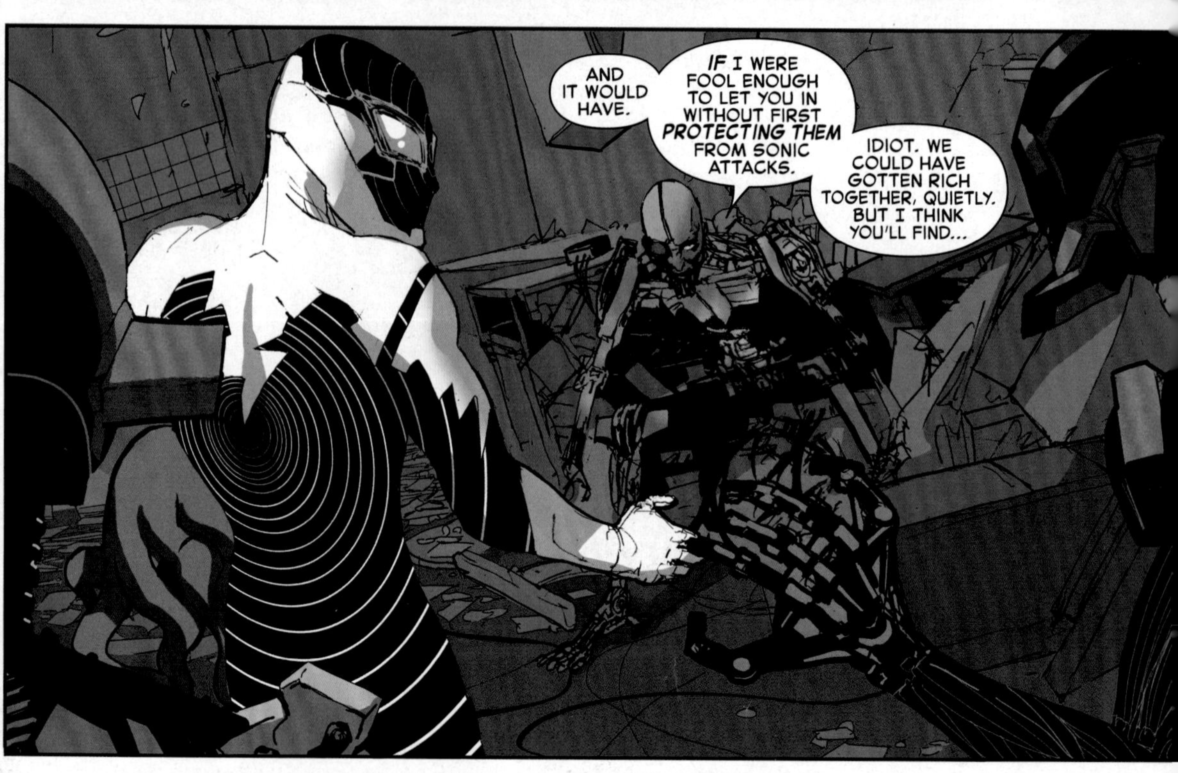
AND IT WOULD HAVE.
IF I WERE FOOL ENOUGH TO LET YOU IN WITHOUT FIRST *PROTECTING THEM* FROM SONIC ATTACKS.
IDIOT. WE COULD HAVE GOTTEN RICH TOGETHER, QUIETLY. BUT I THINK YOU'LL FIND...

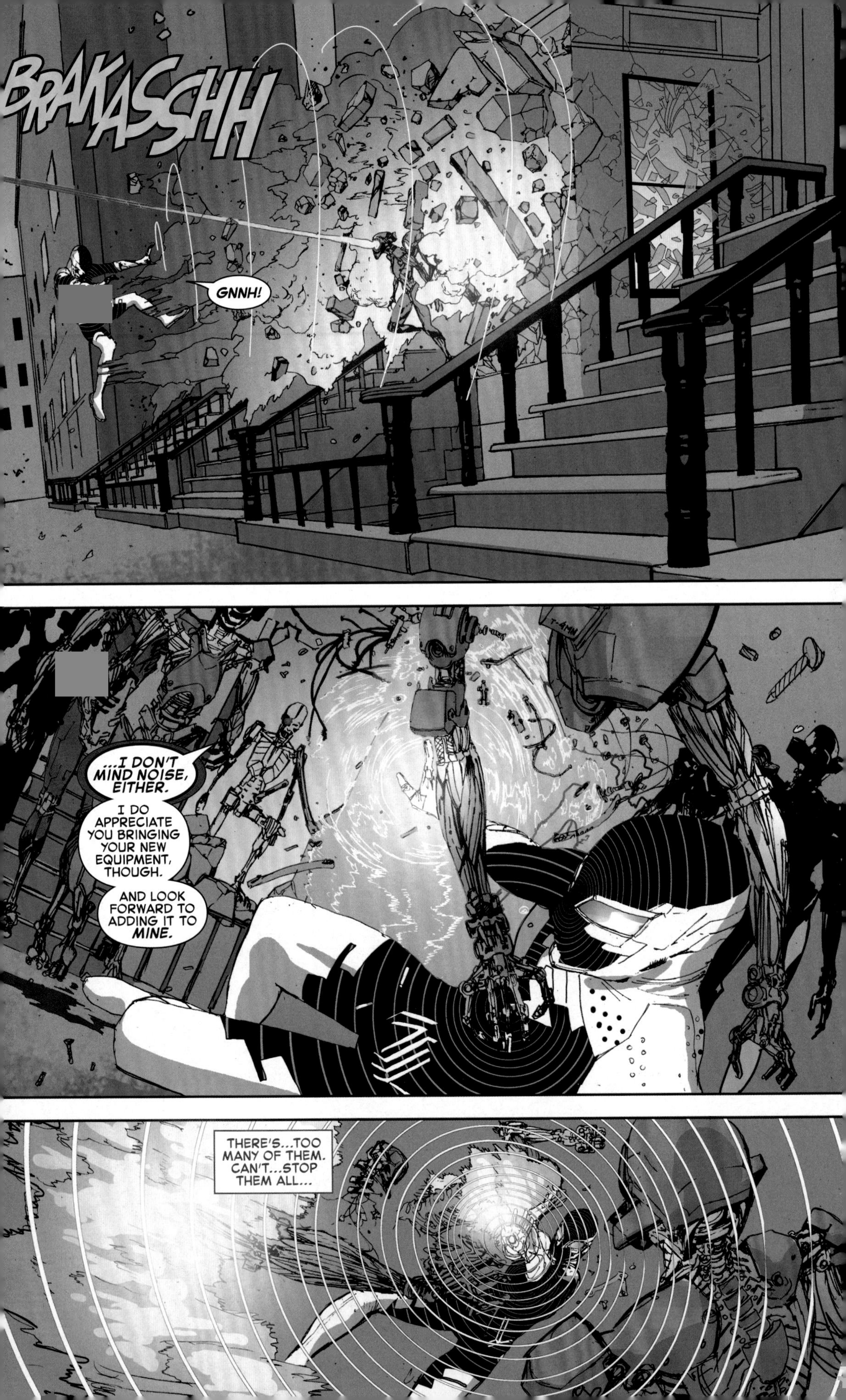
BRAKASSHH
GNNH!
...I DON'T MIND NOISE, EITHER.
I DO APPRECIATE YOU BRINGING YOUR NEW EQUIPMENT, THOUGH.
AND LOOK FORWARD TO ADDING IT TO MINE.
THERE'S...TOO MANY OF THEM. CAN'T...STOP THEM ALL...

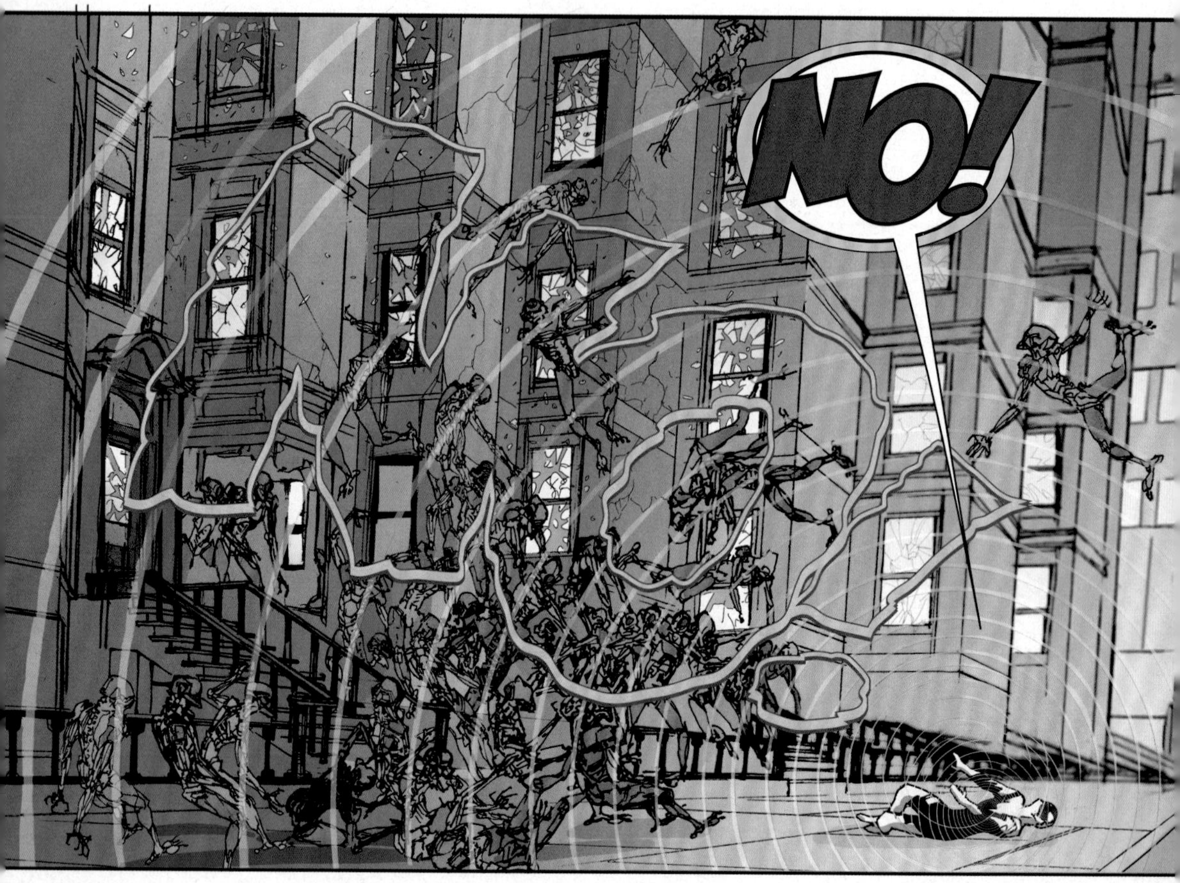
NO!

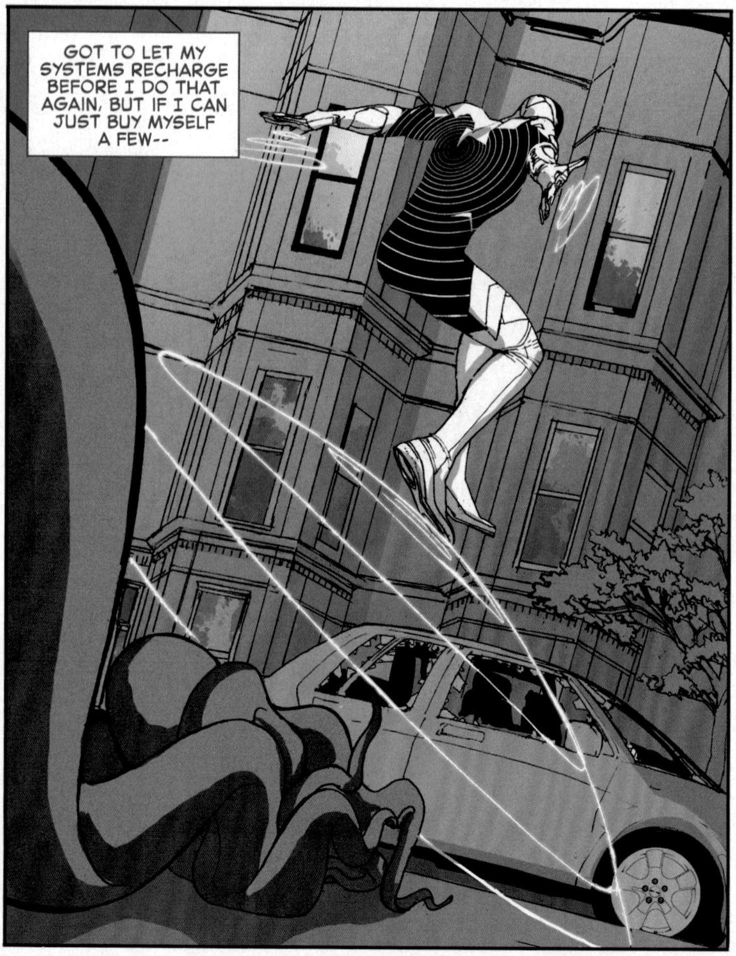
GOT TO LET MY SYSTEMS RECHARGE BEFORE I DO THAT AGAIN, BUT IF I CAN JUST BUY MYSELF A FEW--

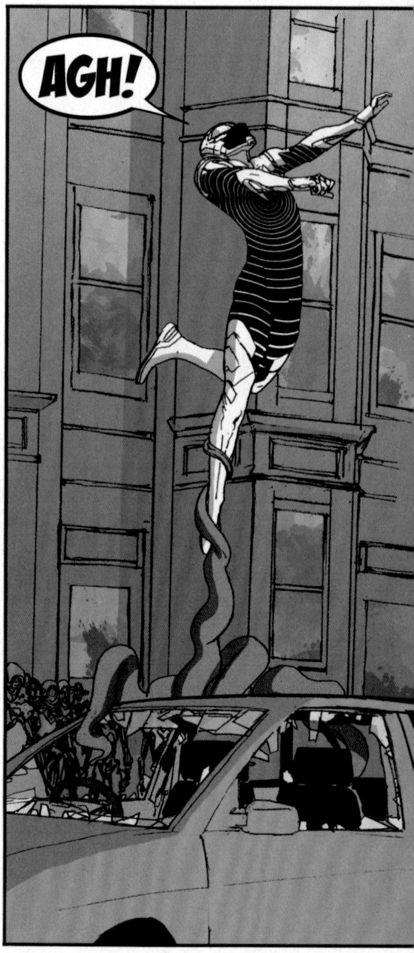
AGH!

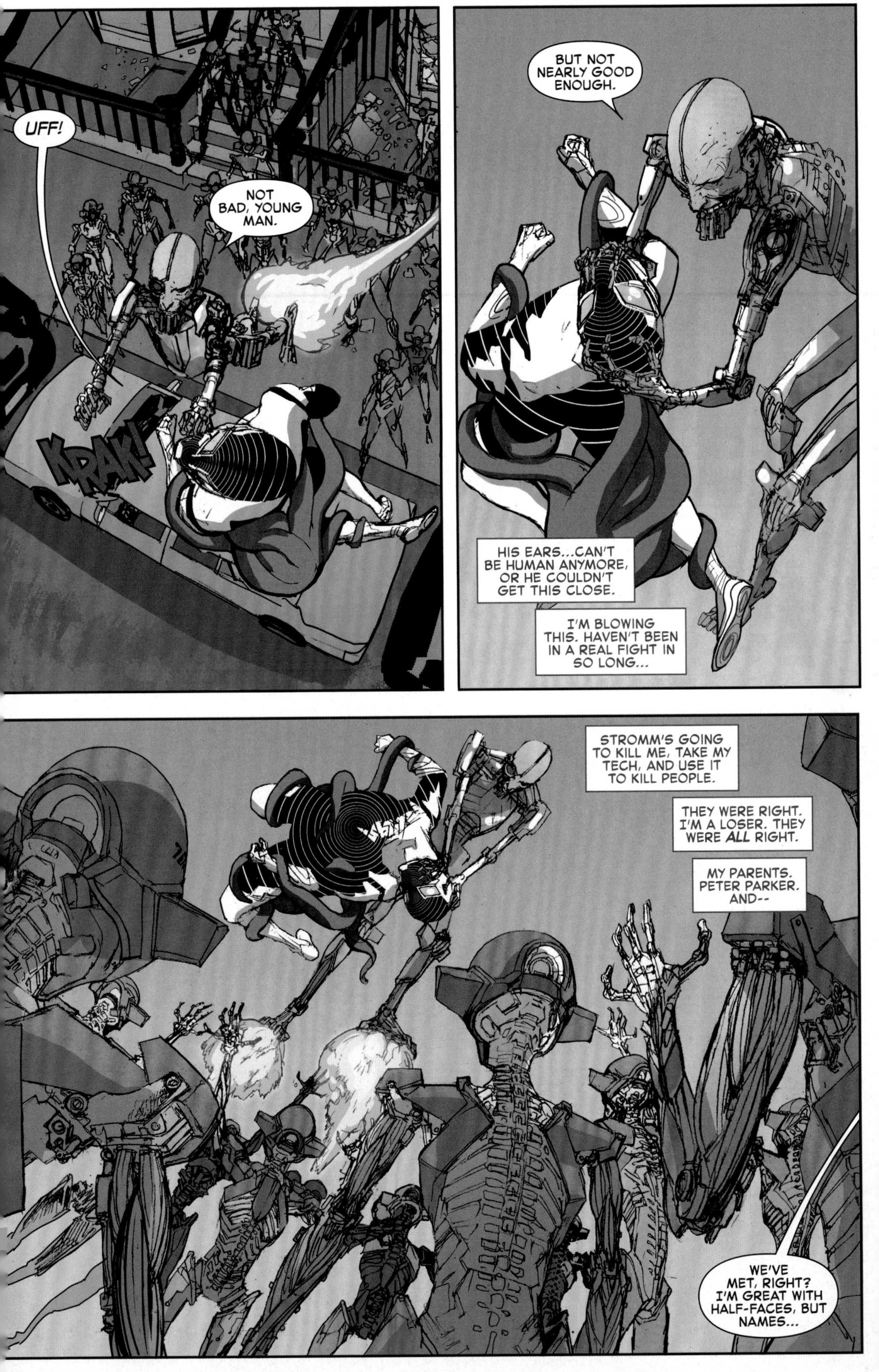
UFF!
NOT BAD, YOUNG MAN.
KRAK!
BUT NOT NEARLY GOOD ENOUGH.
HIS EARS...CAN'T BE HUMAN ANYMORE, OR HE COULDN'T GET THIS CLOSE.
I'M BLOWING THIS. HAVEN'T BEEN IN A REAL FIGHT IN SO LONG...
STROMM'S GOING TO KILL ME, TAKE MY TECH, AND USE IT TO KILL PEOPLE.
THEY WERE RIGHT. I'M A LOSER. THEY WERE ALL RIGHT.
MY PARENTS. PETER PARKER. AND--
WE'VE MET, RIGHT? I'M GREAT WITH HALF-FACES, BUT NAMES...

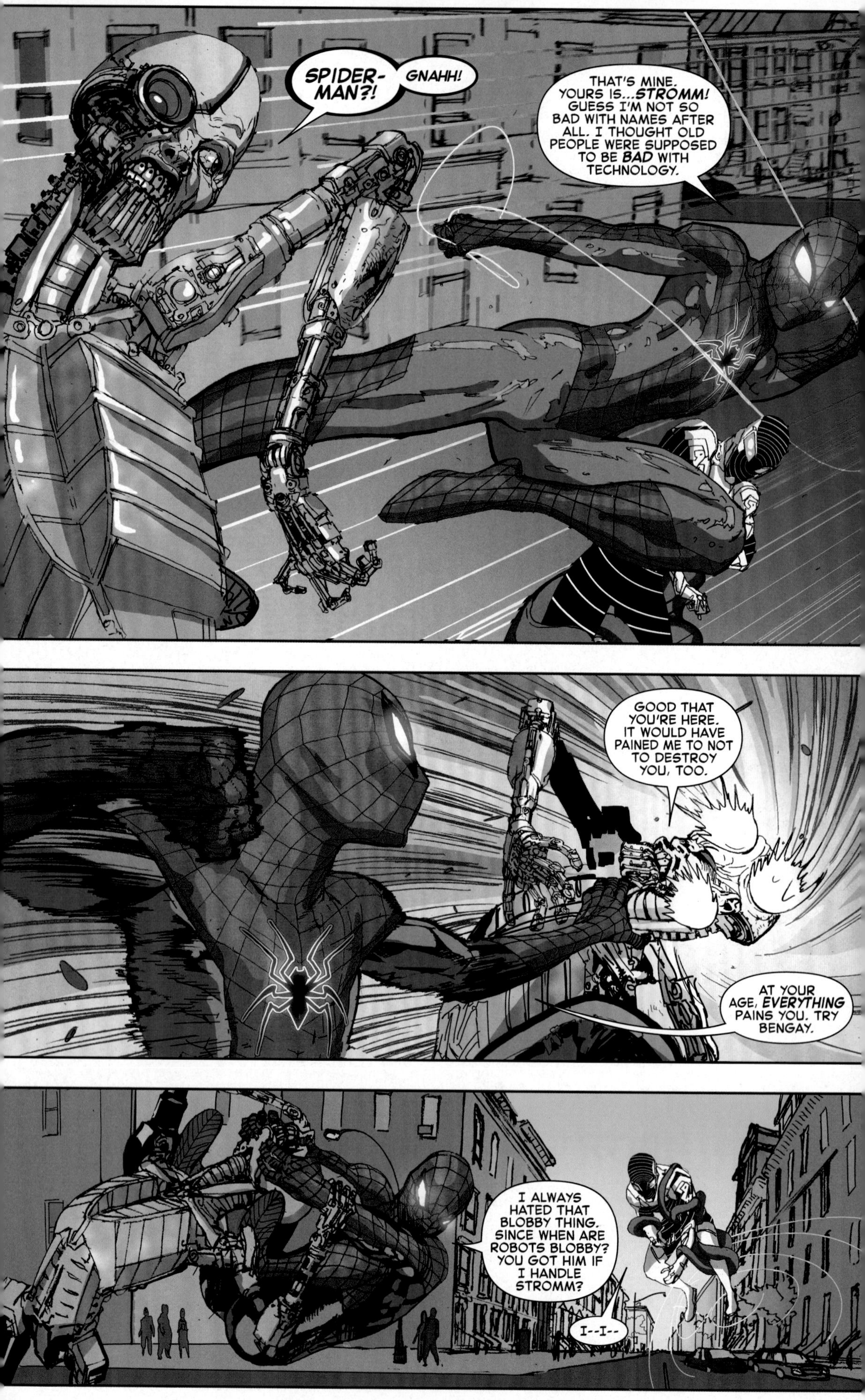
SPIDER-MAN?!
GNAHH!
THAT'S MINE. YOURS IS...STROMM! GUESS I'M NOT SO BAD WITH NAMES AFTER ALL. I THOUGHT OLD PEOPLE WERE SUPPOSED TO BE BAD WITH TECHNOLOGY.
GOOD THAT YOU'RE HERE. IT WOULD HAVE PAINED ME TO NOT TO DESTROY YOU, TOO.
AT YOUR AGE, EVERYTHING PAINS YOU. TRY BENGAY.
I ALWAYS HATED THAT BLOBBY THING. SINCE WHEN ARE ROBOTS BLOBBY? YOU GOT HIM IF I HANDLE STROMM?
I--I--

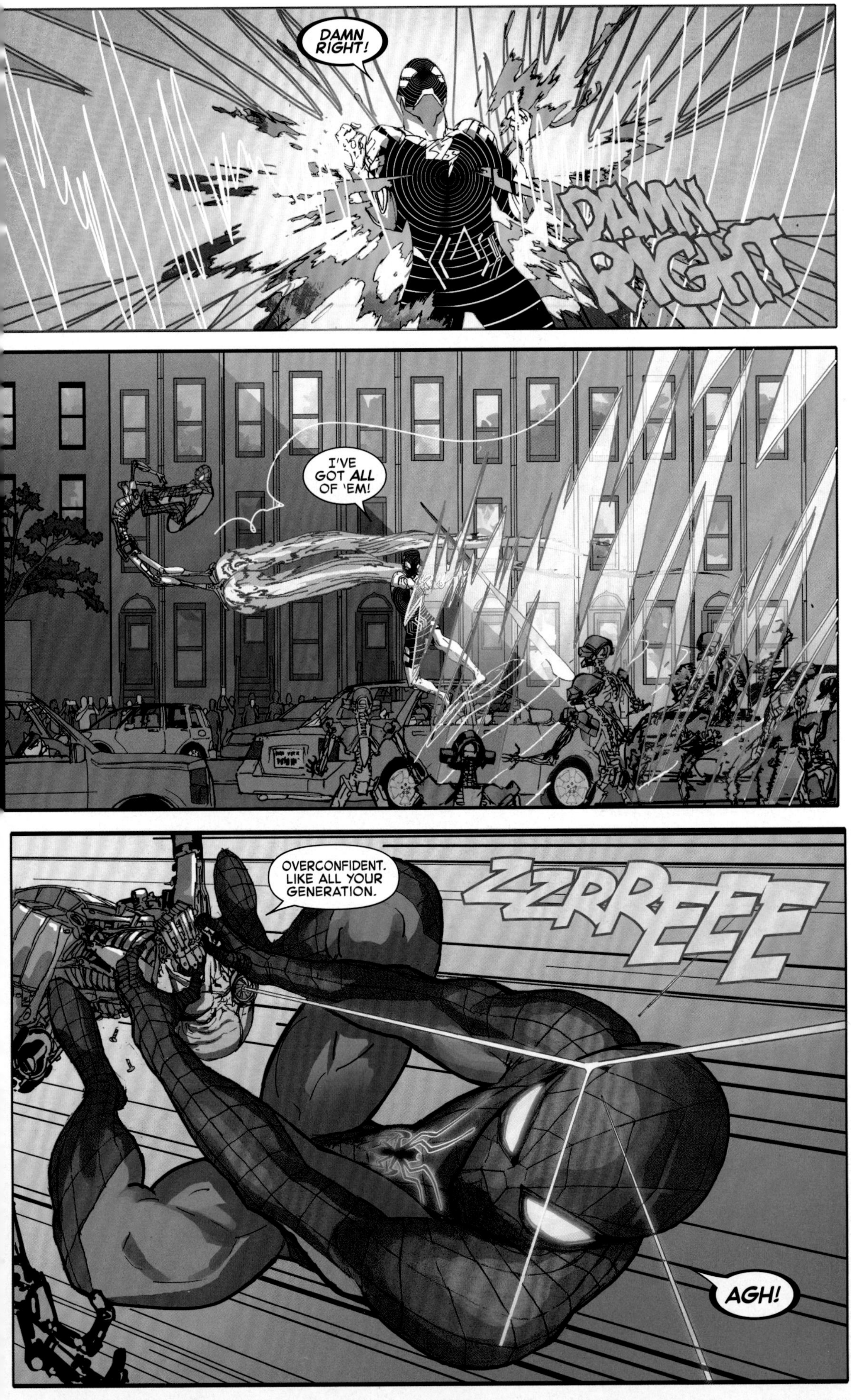
DAMN RIGHT!
DAMN RIGHT!
I'VE GOT ALL OF 'EM!
OVERCONFIDENT. LIKE ALL YOUR GENERATION.
ZZRRREEE
AGH!

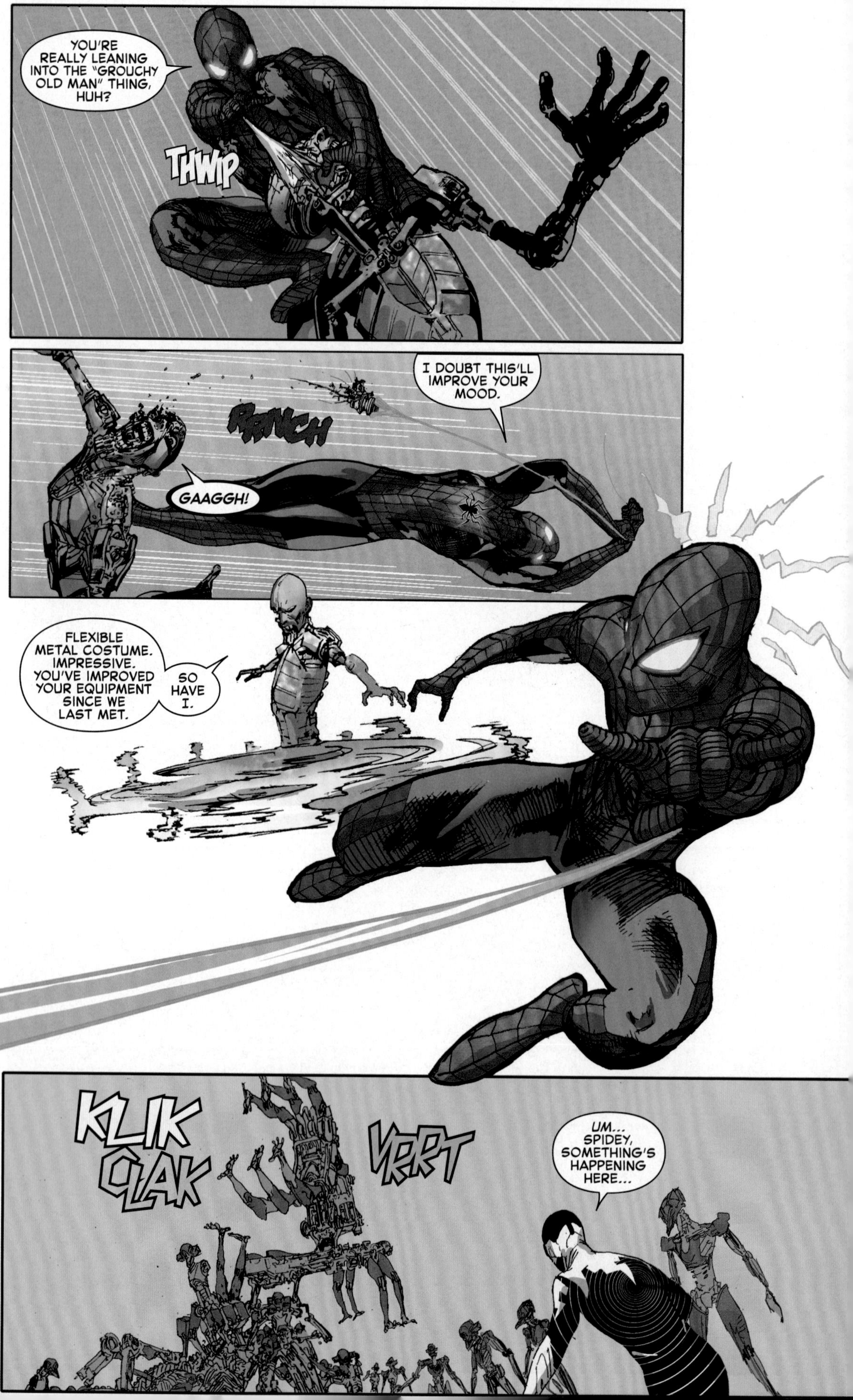

YOU'RE REALLY LEANING INTO THE "GROUCHY OLD MAN" THING, HUH?
THWIP
I DOUBT THIS'LL IMPROVE YOUR MOOD.
RRNCH
GAAGGH!
FLEXIBLE METAL COSTUME. IMPRESSIVE. YOU'VE IMPROVED YOUR EQUIPMENT SINCE WE LAST MET.
SO HAVE I.
KLIK
CLAK
VRRT
UM... SPIDEY, SOMETHING'S HAPPENING HERE...

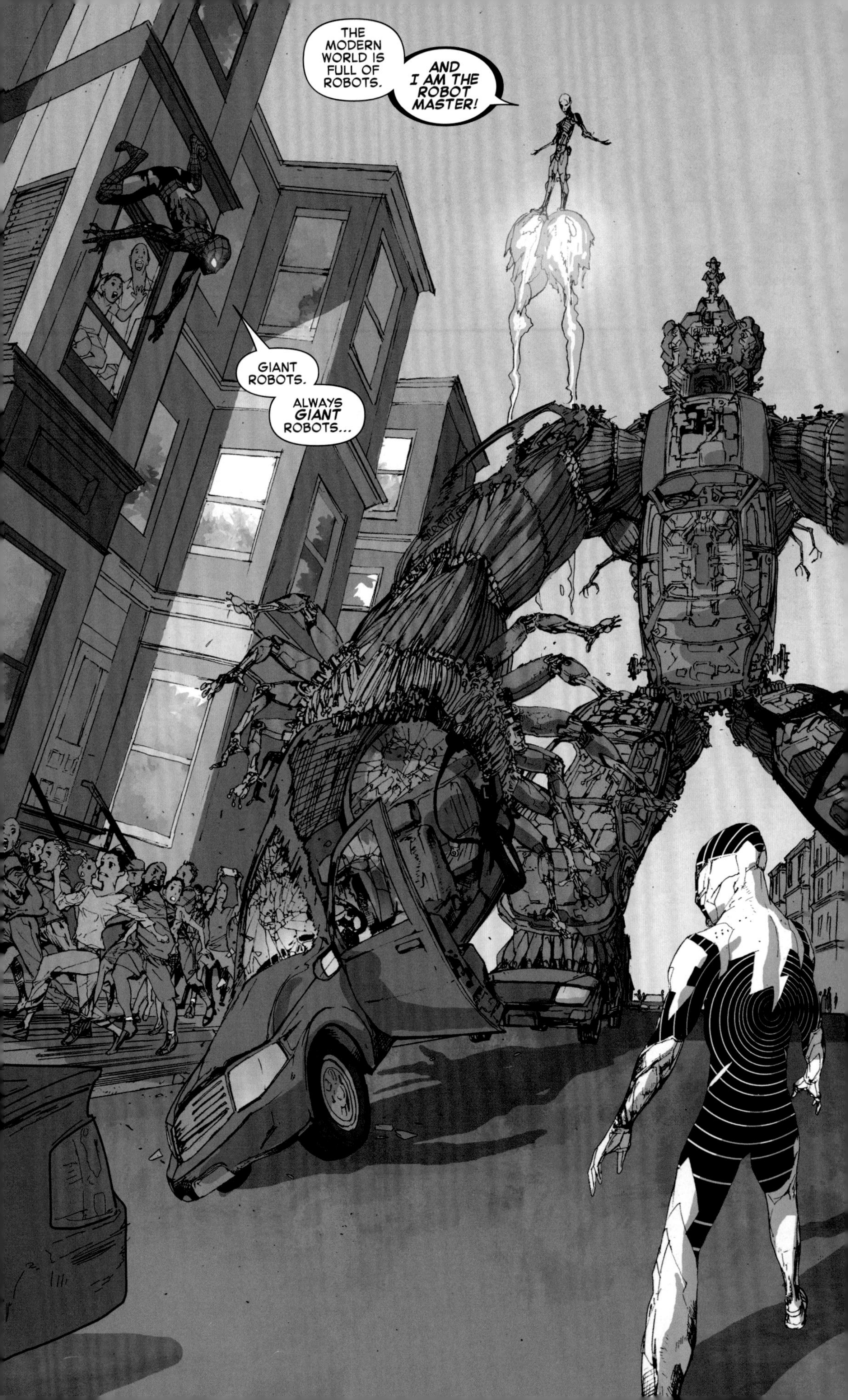
THE MODERN WORLD IS FULL OF ROBOTS.
AND I AM THE ROBOT MASTER!
GIANT ROBOTS.
ALWAYS GIANT ROBOTS...

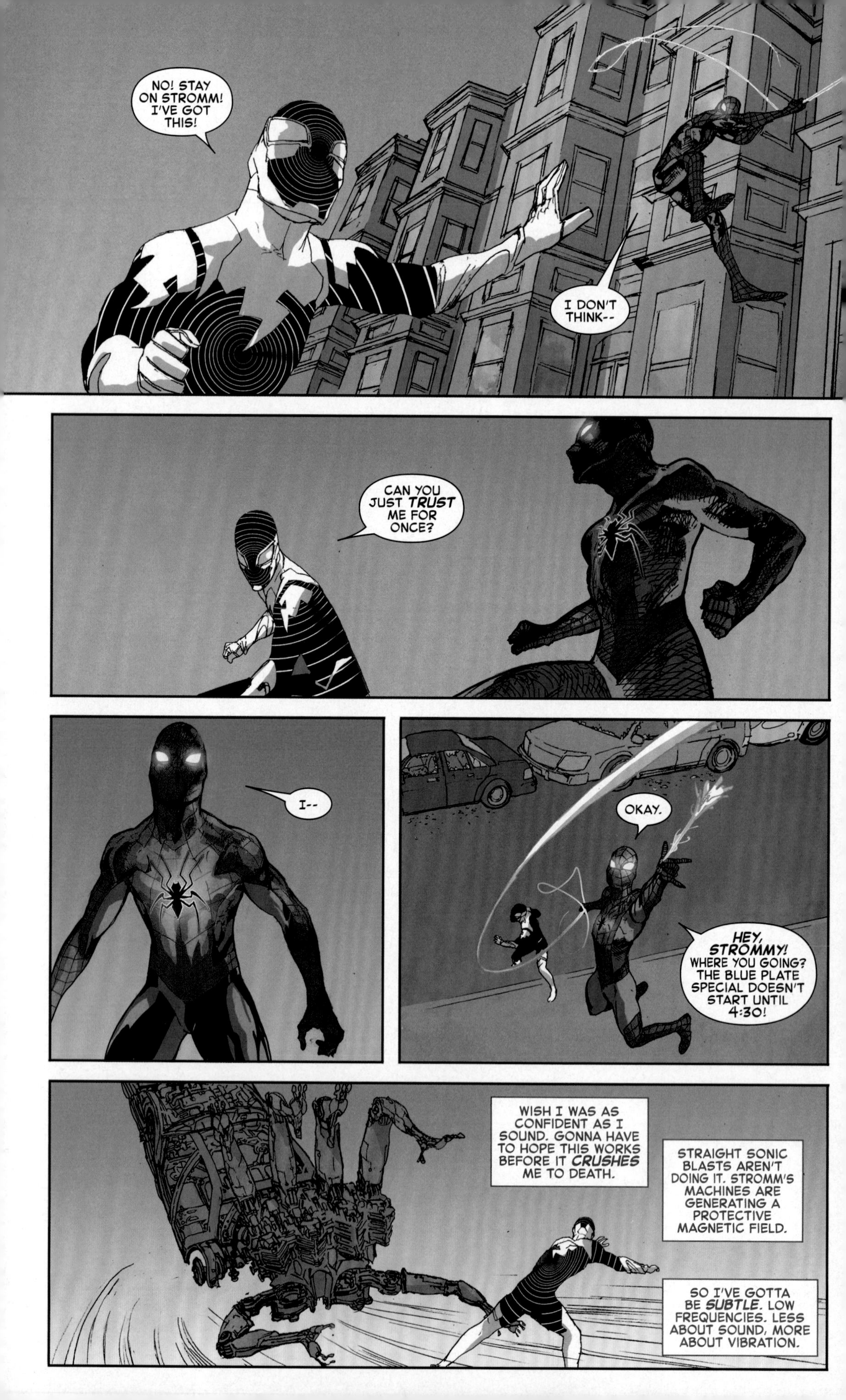
NO! STAY ON STROMM! I'VE GOT THIS!
I DON'T THINK--
CAN YOU JUST TRUST ME FOR ONCE?
I--
OKAY.
HEY, STROMMY! WHERE YOU GOING? THE BLUE PLATE SPECIAL DOESN'T START UNTIL 4:30!
WISH I WAS AS CONFIDENT AS I SOUND. GONNA HAVE TO HOPE THIS WORKS BEFORE IT CRUSHES ME TO DEATH.
STRAIGHT SONIC BLASTS AREN'T DOING IT. STROMM'S MACHINES ARE GENERATING A PROTECTIVE MAGNETIC FIELD.
SO I'VE GOTTA BE SUBTLE. LOW FREQUENCIES. LESS ABOUT SOUND, MORE ABOUT VIBRATION.

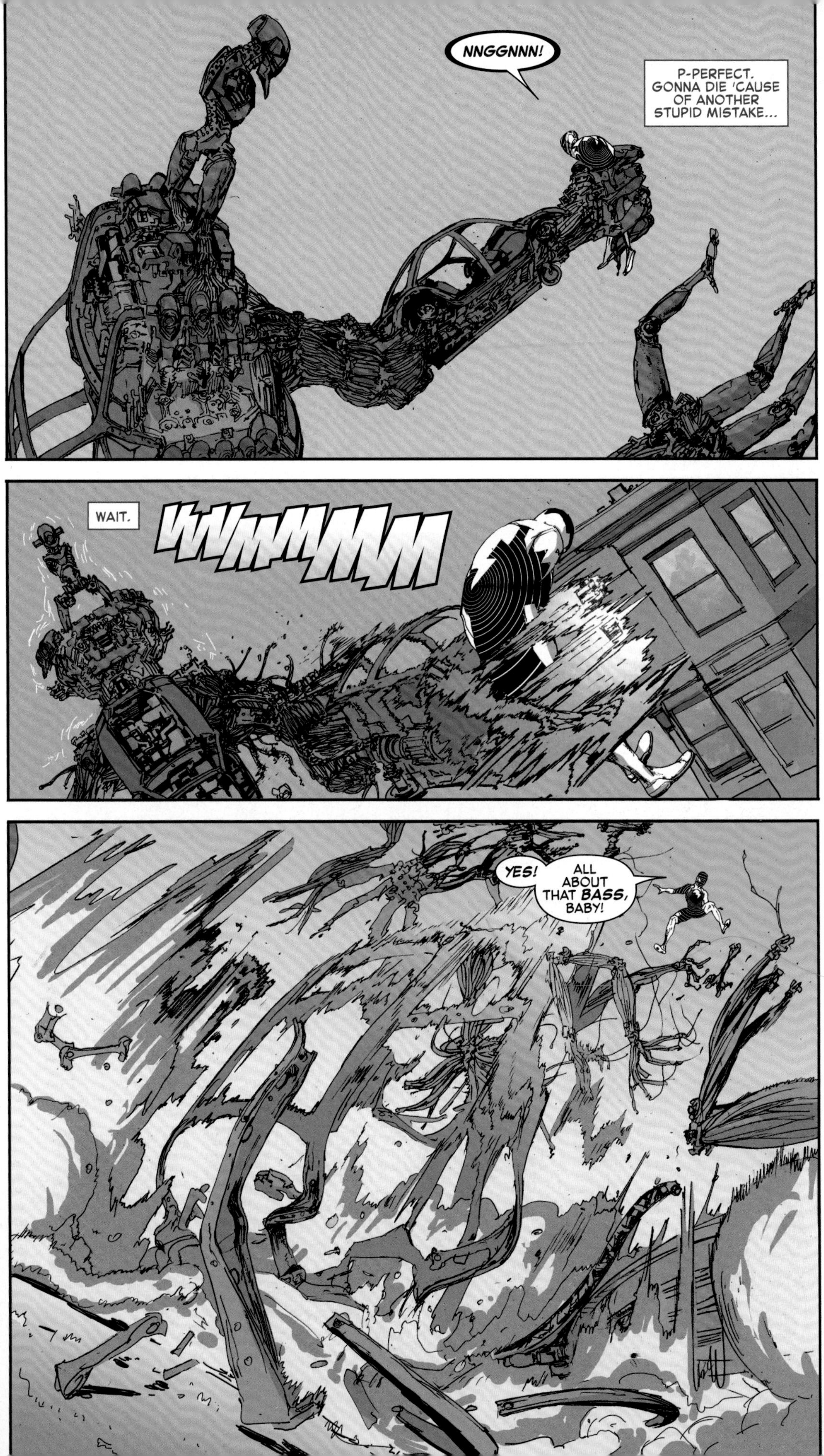
NNGGNNN!
P-PERFECT. GONNA DIE 'CAUSE OF ANOTHER STUPID MISTAKE...
WAIT.
VVMMMMM
YES!
ALL ABOUT THAT BASS, BABY!

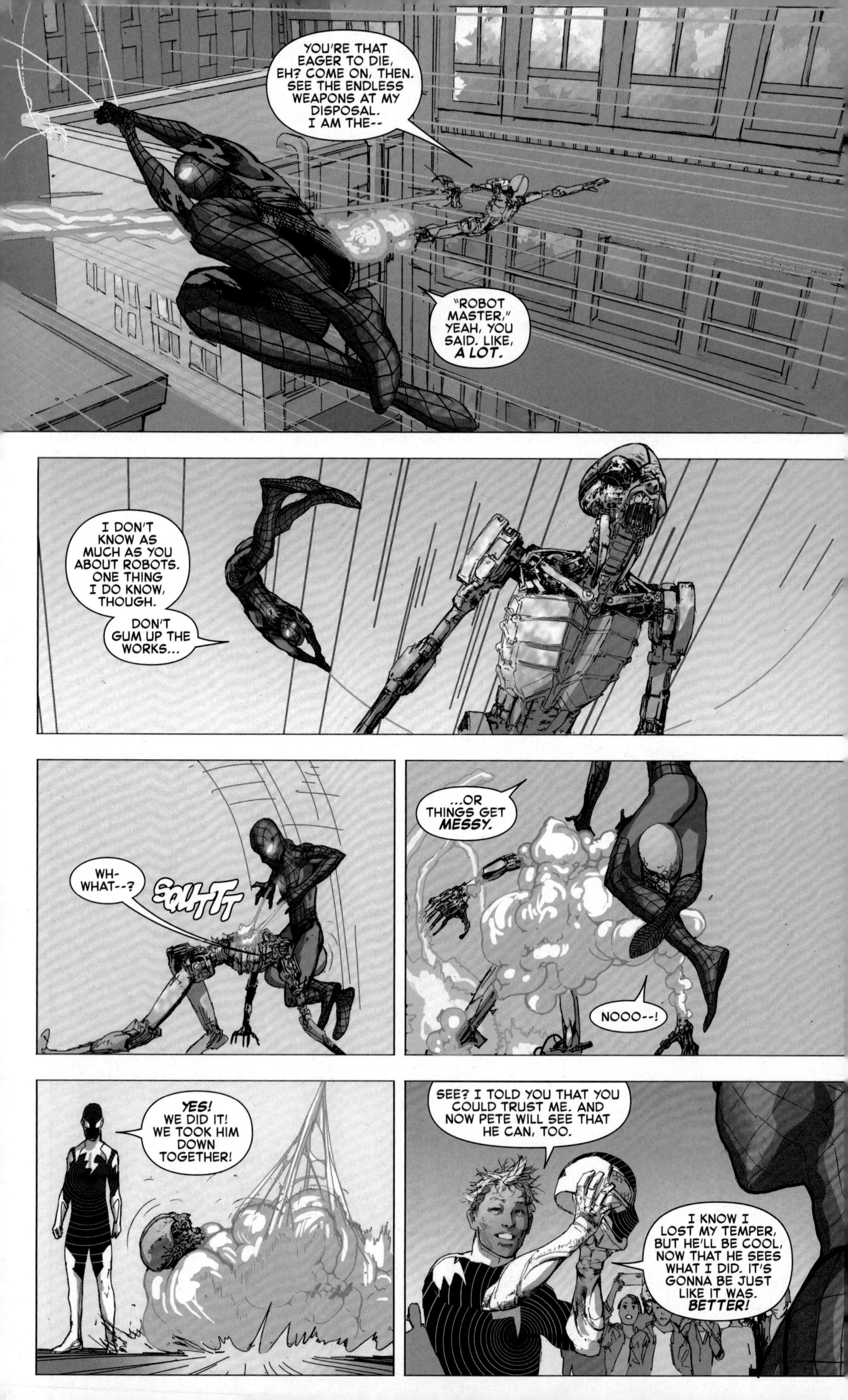
YOU'RE THAT EAGER TO DIE, EH? COME ON, THEN. SEE THE ENDLESS WEAPONS AT MY DISPOSAL. I AM THE--
"ROBOT MASTER," YEAH, YOU SAID. LIKE, A LOT.
I DON'T KNOW AS MUCH AS YOU ABOUT ROBOTS. ONE THING I DO KNOW, THOUGH.
DON'T GUM UP THE WORKS...
WH-WHAT--?
SQUTTT
...OR THINGS GET MESSY.
NOOO--!
YES! WE DID IT! WE TOOK HIM DOWN TOGETHER!
SEE? I TOLD YOU THAT YOU COULD TRUST ME. AND NOW PETE WILL SEE THAT HE CAN, TOO.
I KNOW I LOST MY TEMPER, BUT HE'LL BE COOL, NOW THAT HE SEES WHAT I DID. IT'S GONNA BE JUST LIKE IT WAS. BETTER!

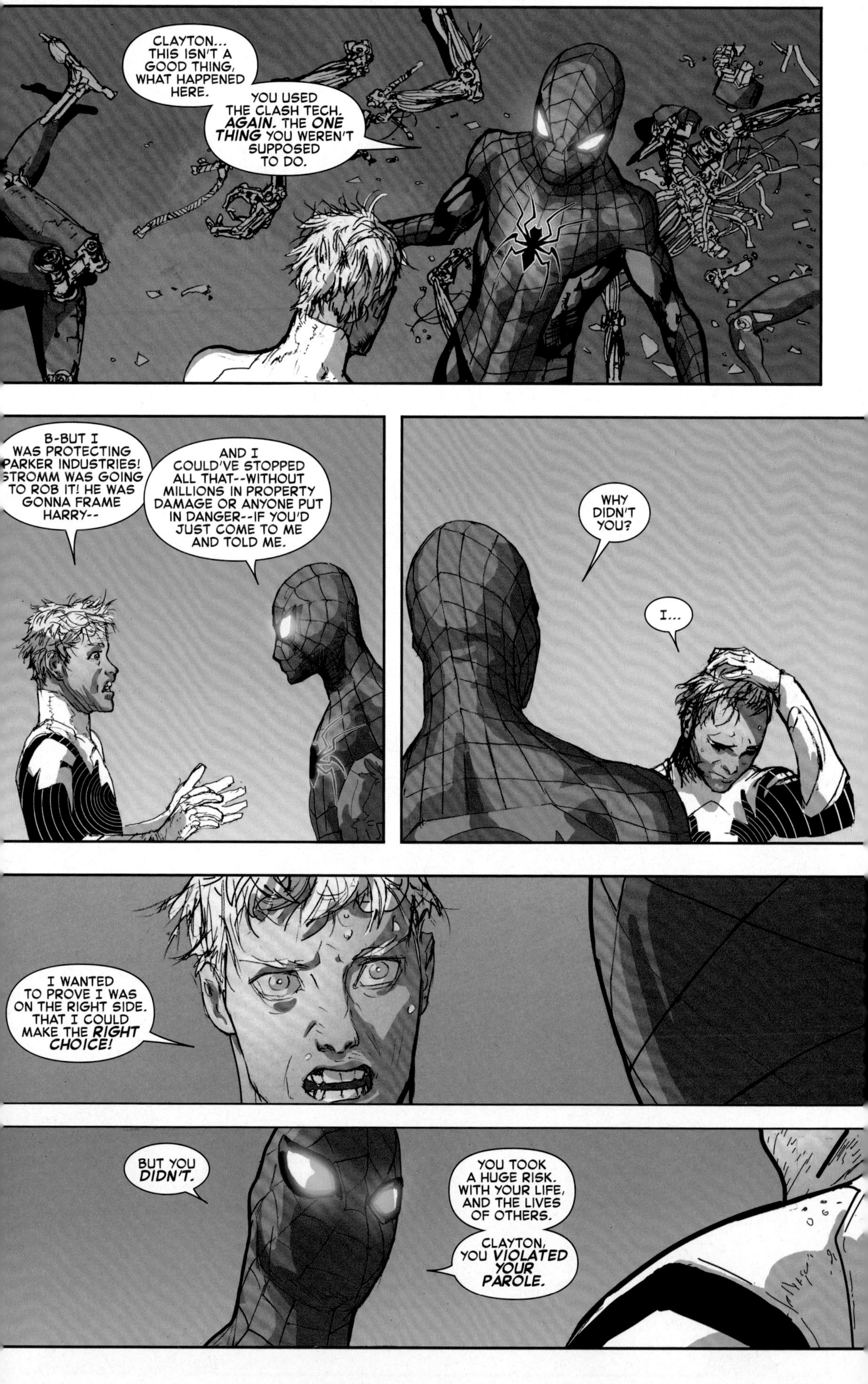
CLAYTON... THIS ISN'T A GOOD THING, WHAT HAPPENED HERE.
YOU USED THE CLASH TECH. AGAIN. THE ONE THING YOU WEREN'T SUPPOSED TO DO.
B-BUT I WAS PROTECTING PARKER INDUSTRIES! STROMM WAS GOING TO ROB IT! HE WAS GONNA FRAME HARRY--
AND I COULD'VE STOPPED ALL THAT--WITHOUT MILLIONS IN PROPERTY DAMAGE OR ANYONE PUT IN DANGER--IF YOU'D JUST COME TO ME AND TOLD ME.
WHY DIDN'T YOU?
I...
I WANTED TO PROVE I WAS ON THE RIGHT SIDE. THAT I COULD MAKE THE RIGHT CHOICE!
BUT YOU DIDN'T.
YOU TOOK A HUGE RISK. WITH YOUR LIFE, AND THE LIVES OF OTHERS.
CLAYTON, YOU VIOLATED YOUR PAROLE.

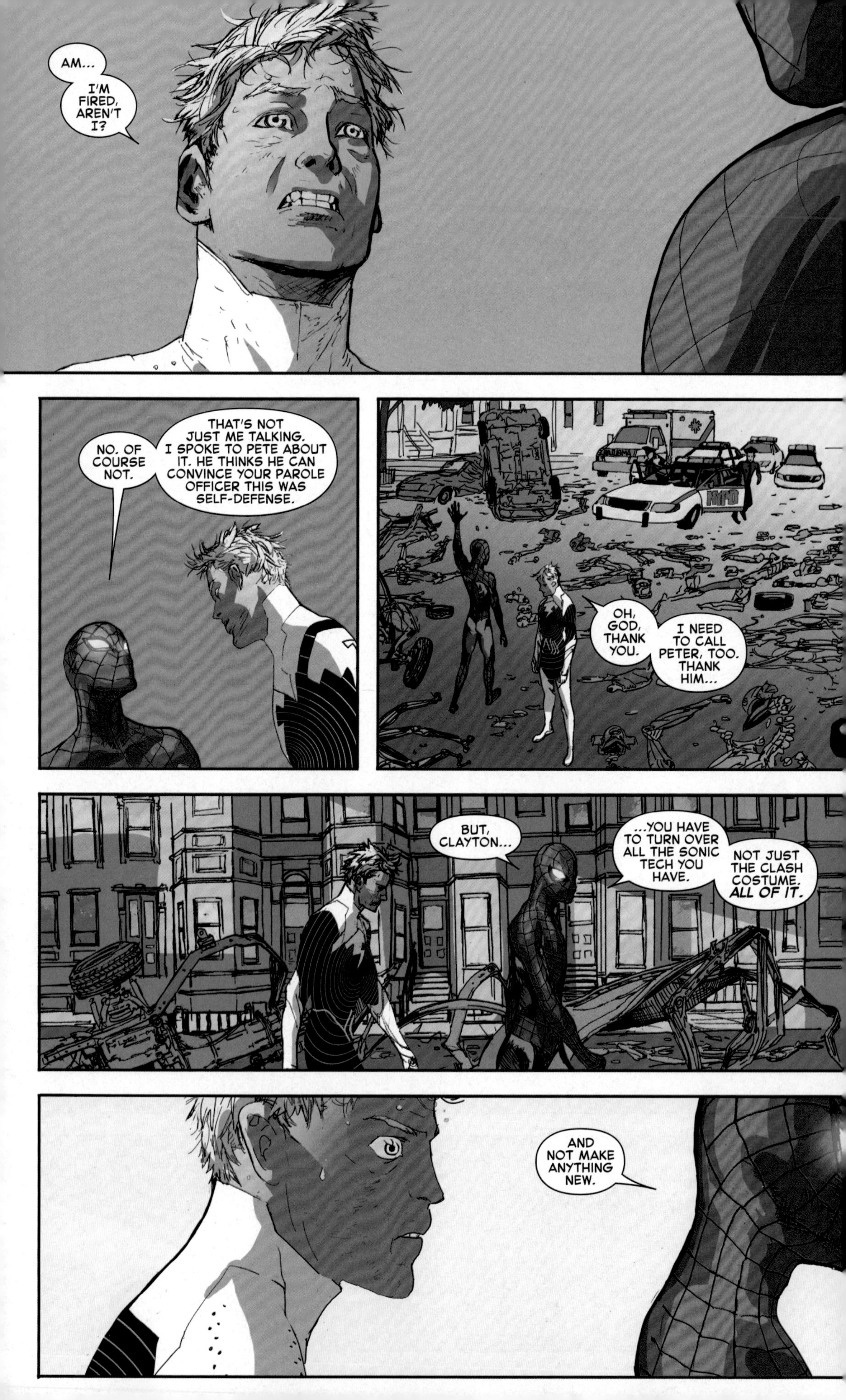
AM...
I'M FIRED, AREN'T I?
NO. OF COURSE NOT.
THAT'S NOT JUST ME TALKING. I SPOKE TO PETE ABOUT IT. HE THINKS HE CAN CONVINCE YOUR PAROLE OFFICER THIS WAS SELF-DEFENSE.
NYPD
OH, GOD, THANK YOU.
I NEED TO CALL PETER, TOO. THANK HIM...
BUT, CLAYTON...
...YOU HAVE TO TURN OVER ALL THE SONIC TECH YOU HAVE.
NOT JUST THE CLASH COSTUME. ALL OF IT.
AND NOT MAKE ANYTHING NEW.

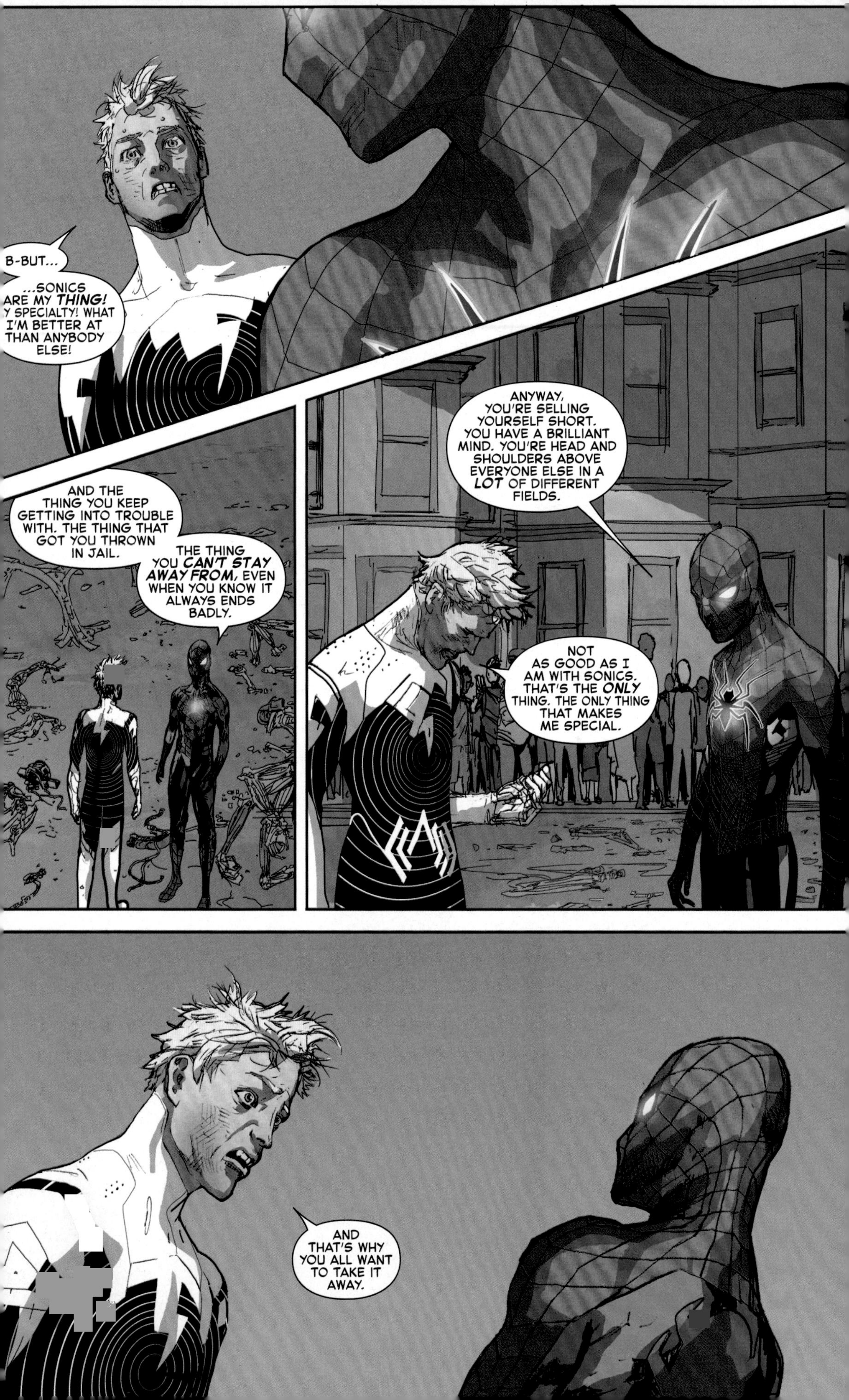
B-BUT...
...SONICS ARE MY THING! Y SPECIALTY! WHAT I'M BETTER AT THAN ANYBODY ELSE!
AND THE THING YOU KEEP GETTING INTO TROUBLE WITH. THE THING THAT GOT YOU THROWN IN JAIL.
THE THING YOU CAN'T STAY AWAY FROM, EVEN WHEN YOU KNOW IT ALWAYS ENDS BADLY.
ANYWAY, YOU'RE SELLING YOURSELF SHORT. YOU HAVE A BRILLIANT MIND. YOU'RE HEAD AND SHOULDERS ABOVE EVERYONE ELSE IN A LOT OF DIFFERENT FIELDS.
NOT AS GOOD AS I AM WITH SONICS. THAT'S THE ONLY THING. THE ONLY THING THAT MAKES ME SPECIAL.
AND THAT'S WHY YOU ALL WANT TO TAKE IT AWAY.

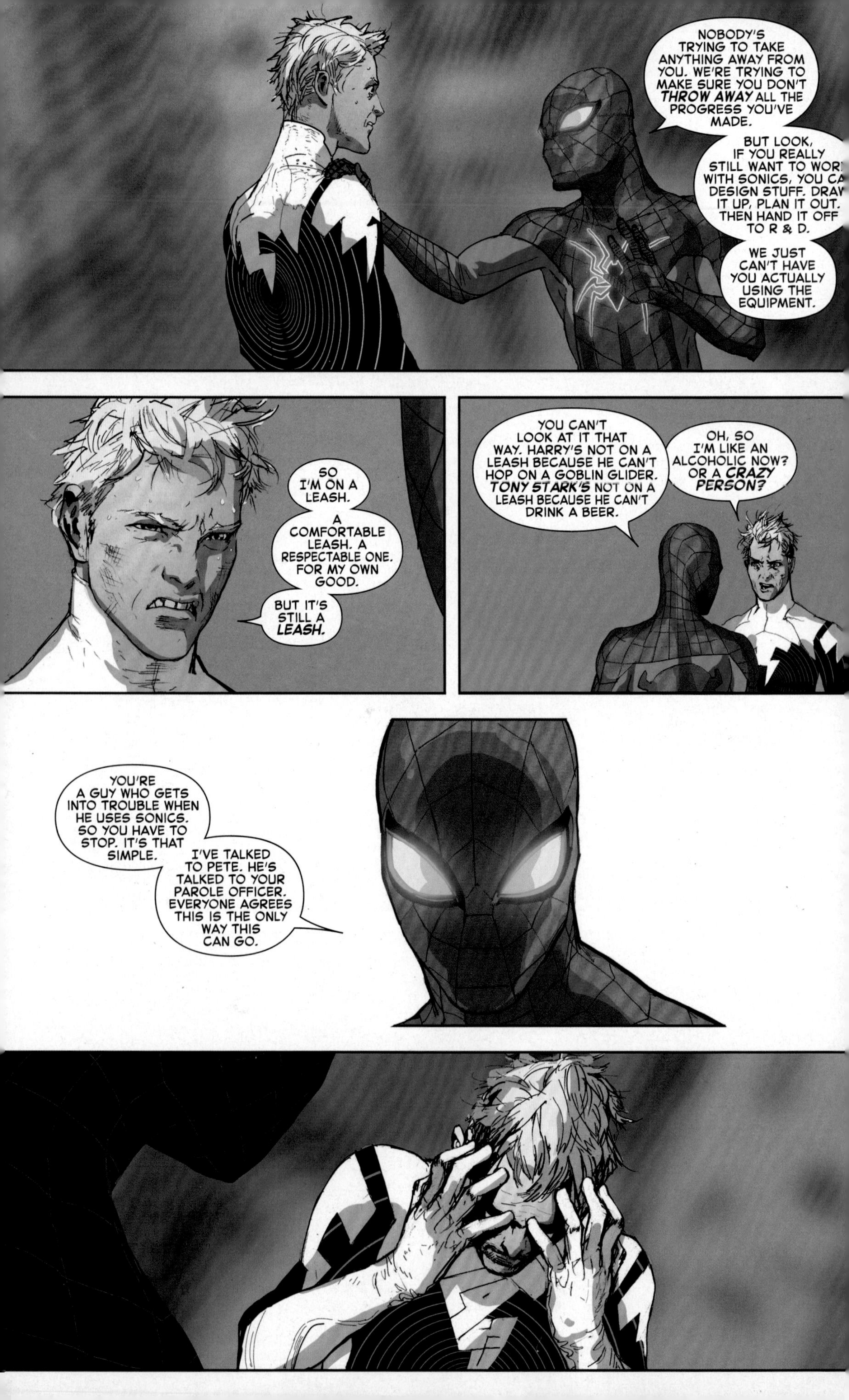
NOBODY'S TRYING TO TAKE ANYTHING AWAY FROM YOU. WE'RE TRYING TO MAKE SURE YOU DON'T THROW AWAY ALL THE PROGRESS YOU'VE MADE.
BUT LOOK, IF YOU REALLY STILL WANT TO WOR WITH SONICS, YOU CA DESIGN STUFF. DRAV IT UP, PLAN IT OUT. THEN HAND IT OFF TO R & D.
WE JUST CAN'T HAVE YOU ACTUALLY USING THE EQUIPMENT.
SO I'M ON A LEASH.
A COMFORTABLE LEASH. A RESPECTABLE ONE. FOR MY OWN GOOD.
BUT IT'S STILL A LEASH.
YOU CAN'T LOOK AT IT THAT WAY. HARRY'S NOT ON A LEASH BECAUSE HE CAN'T HOP ON A GOBLIN GLIDER. TONY STARK'S NOT ON A LEASH BECAUSE HE CAN'T DRINK A BEER.
OH, SO I'M LIKE AN ALCOHOLIC NOW? OR A CRAZY PERSON?
YOU'RE A GUY WHO GETS INTO TROUBLE WHEN HE USES SONICS. SO YOU HAVE TO STOP. IT'S THAT SIMPLE.
I'VE TALKED TO PETE. HE'S TALKED TO YOUR PAROLE OFFICER. EVERYONE AGREES THIS IS THE ONLY WAY THIS CAN GO.

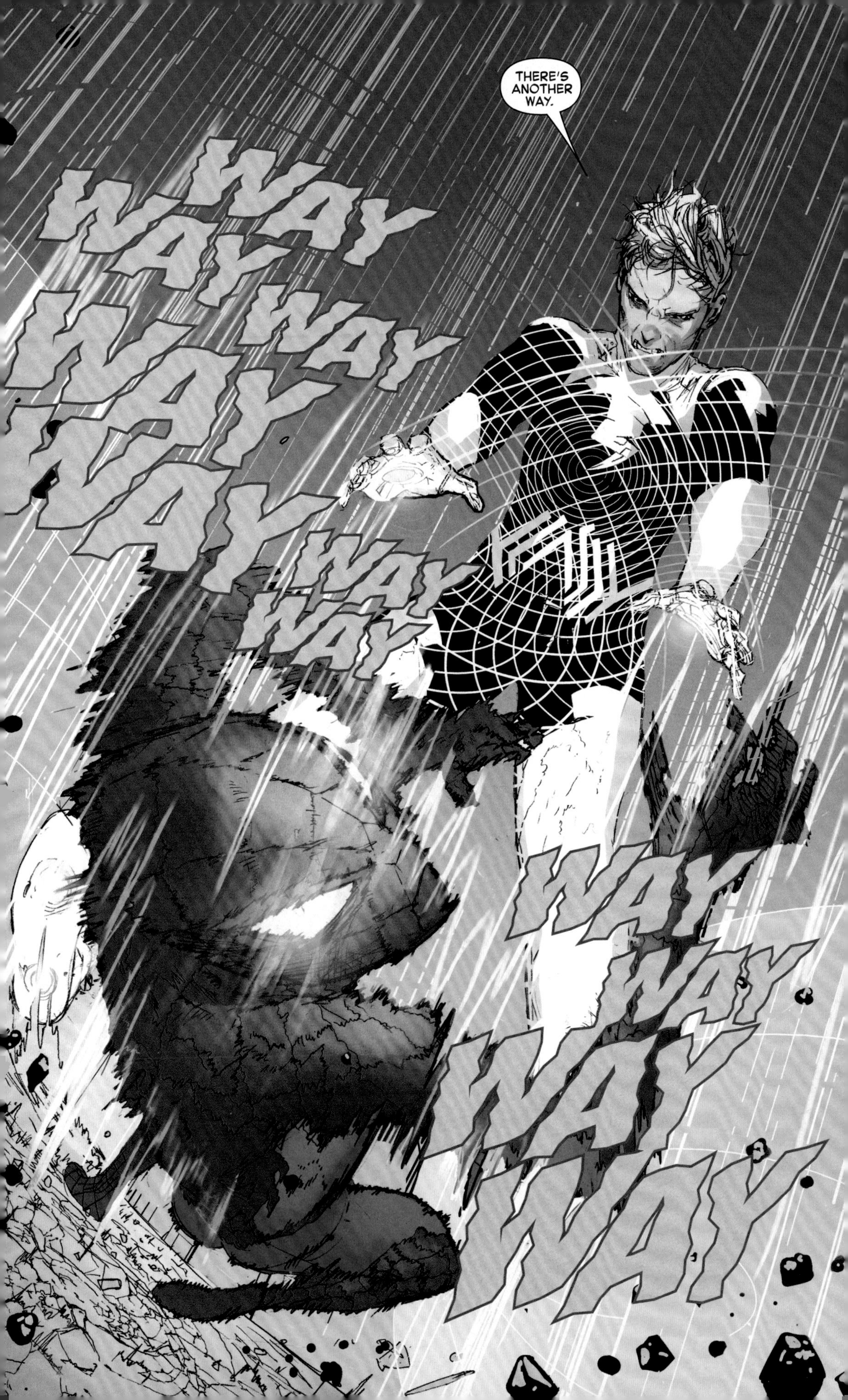
THERE'S ANOTHER WAY.
WAY WAY WAY WAY WAY WAY WAY WAY
WAY WAY WAY WAY

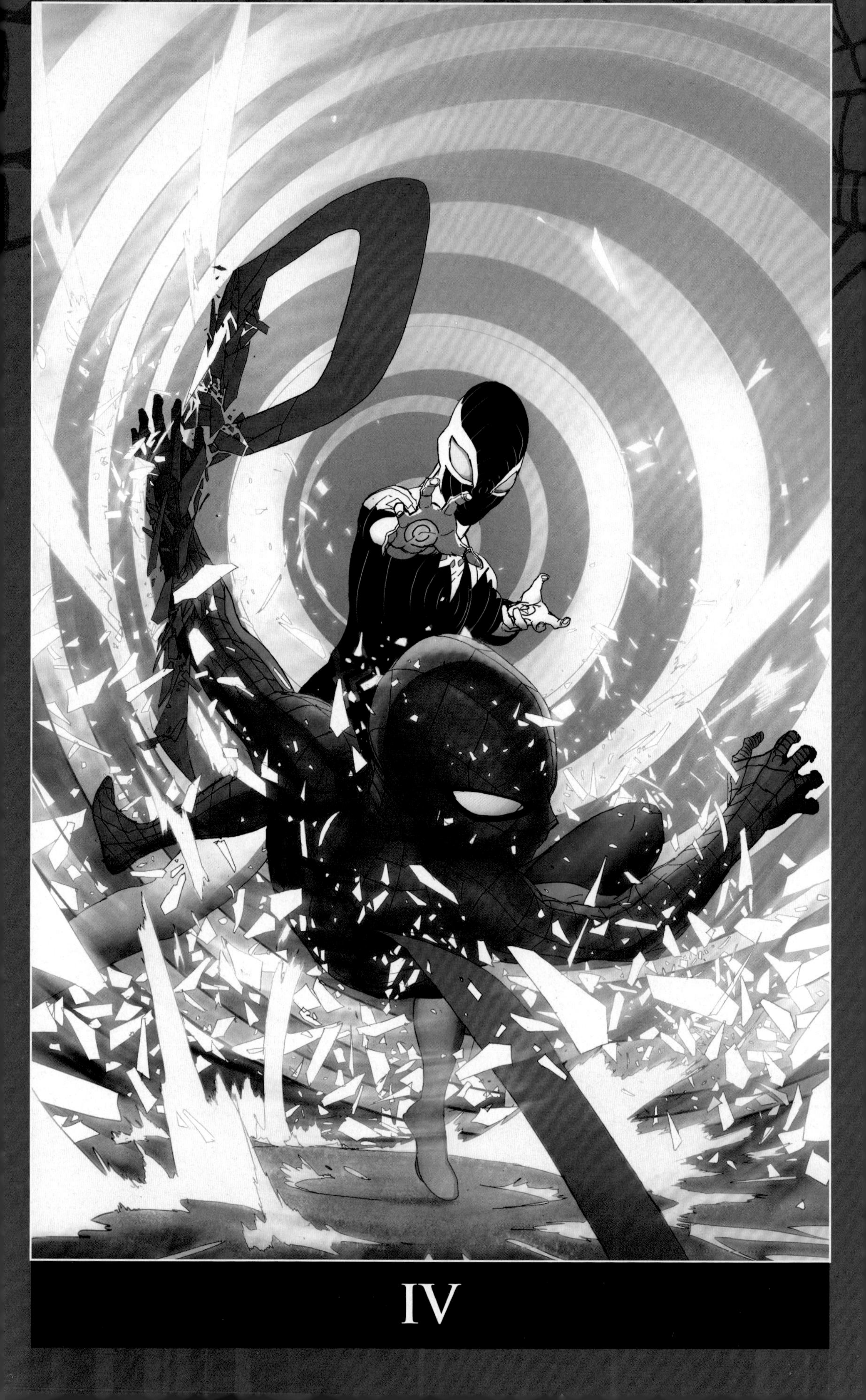

IV

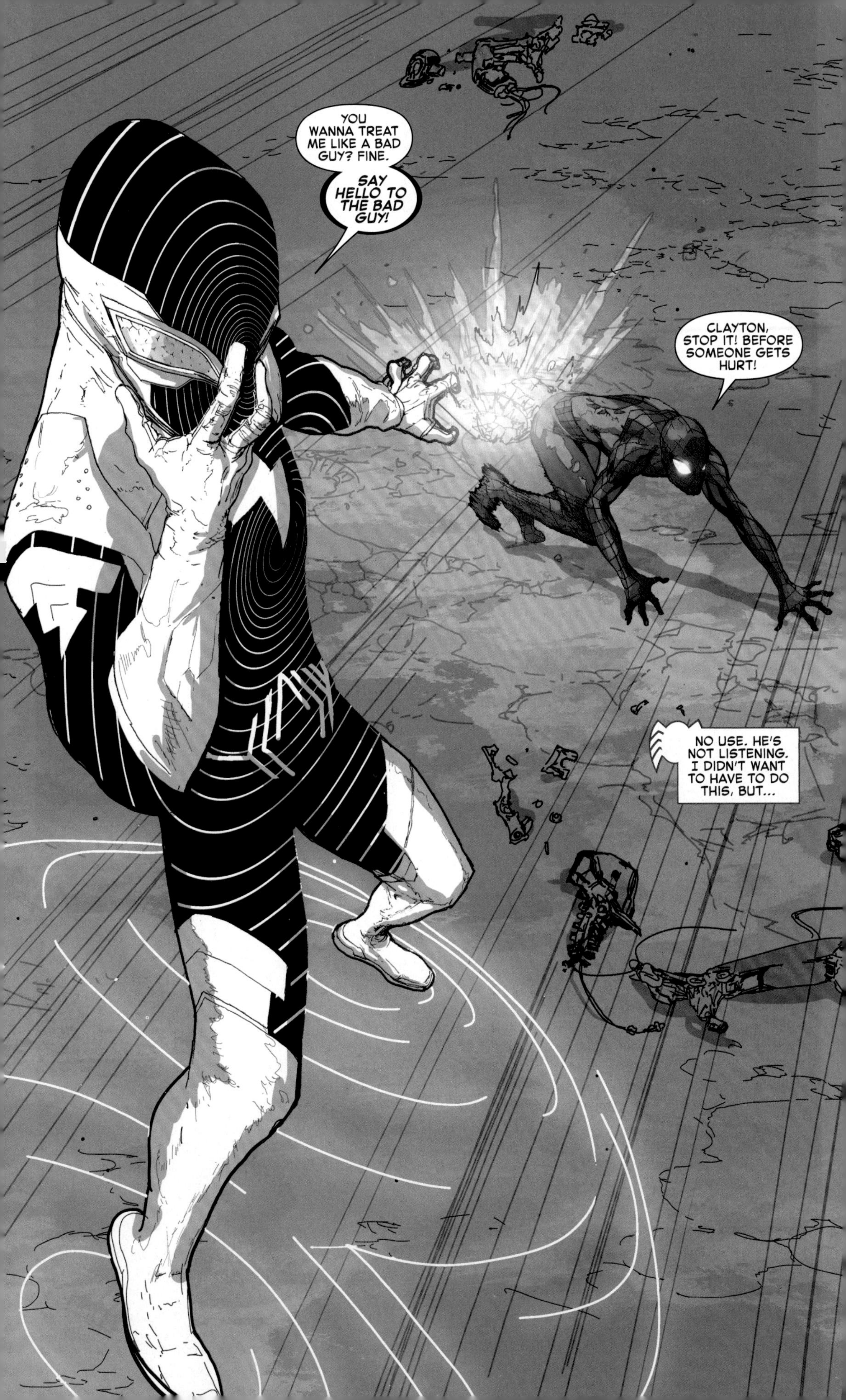
YOU WANNA TREAT ME LIKE A BAD GUY? FINE.
SAY HELLO TO THE BAD GUY!
CLAYTON, STOP IT! BEFORE SOMEONE GETS HURT!
NO USE. HE'S NOT LISTENING. I DIDN'T WANT TO HAVE TO DO THIS, BUT...

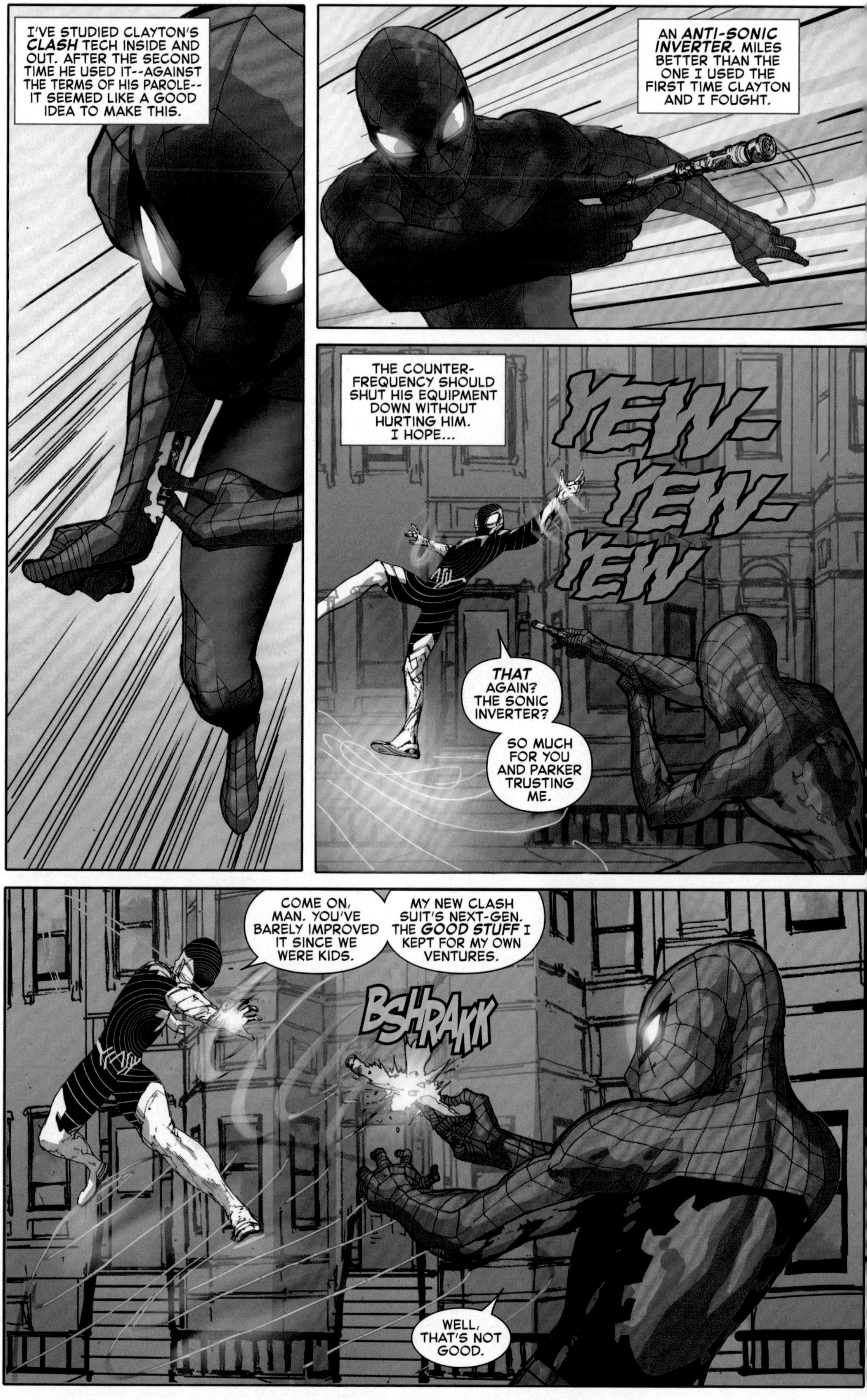
I'VE STUDIED CLAYTON'S CLASH TECH INSIDE AND OUT. AFTER THE SECOND TIME HE USED IT--AGAINST THE TERMS OF HIS PAROLE--IT SEEMED LIKE A GOOD IDEA TO MAKE THIS.
AN ANTI-SONIC INVERTER. MILES BETTER THAN THE ONE I USED THE FIRST TIME CLAYTON AND I FOUGHT.
THE COUNTER-FREQUENCY SHOULD SHUT HIS EQUIPMENT DOWN WITHOUT HURTING HIM. I HOPE...
YEW-YEW-YEW
THAT AGAIN? THE SONIC INVERTER?
SO MUCH FOR YOU AND PARKER TRUSTING ME.
COME ON, MAN. YOU'VE BARELY IMPROVED IT SINCE WE WERE KIDS.
MY NEW CLASH SUIT'S NEXT-GEN. THE GOOD STUFF I KEPT FOR MY OWN VENTURES.
BSHRAKK
WELL, THAT'S NOT GOOD.

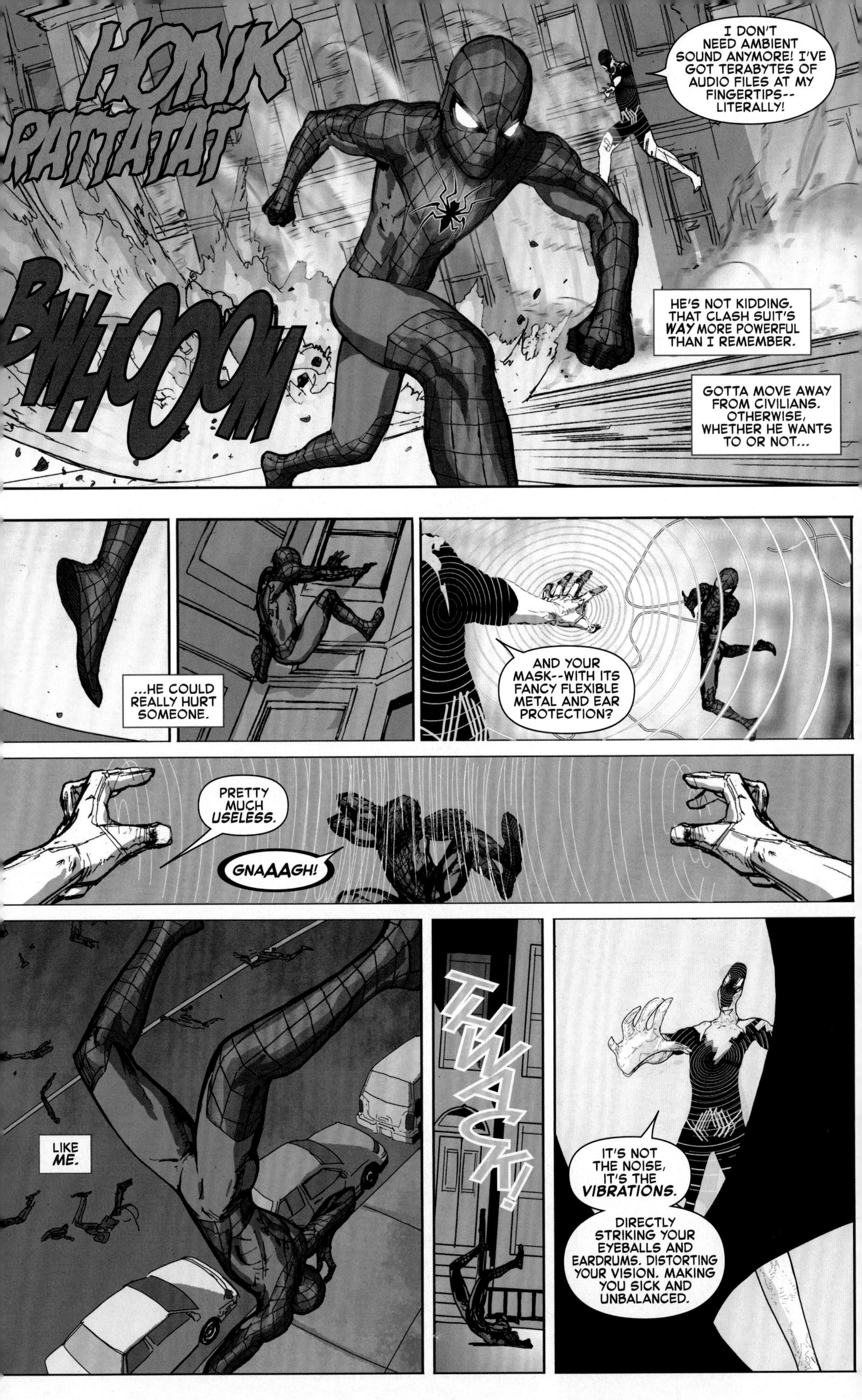
HONK
RATTATAT
I DON'T NEED AMBIENT SOUND ANYMORE! I'VE GOT TERABYTES OF AUDIO FILES AT MY FINGERTIPS-- LITERALLY!
BWHOOOM
HE'S NOT KIDDING. THAT CLASH SUIT'S WAY MORE POWERFUL THAN I REMEMBER.
GOTTA MOVE AWAY FROM CIVILIANS. OTHERWISE, WHETHER HE WANTS TO OR NOT...
...HE COULD REALLY HURT SOMEONE.
AND YOUR MASK--WITH ITS FANCY FLEXIBLE METAL AND EAR PROTECTION?
PRETTY MUCH USELESS.
GNAAAGH!
LIKE ME.
THWACK!
IT'S NOT THE NOISE, IT'S THE VIBRATIONS.
DIRECTLY STRIKING YOUR EYEBALLS AND EARDRUMS. DISTORTING YOUR VISION. MAKING YOU SICK AND UNBALANCED.

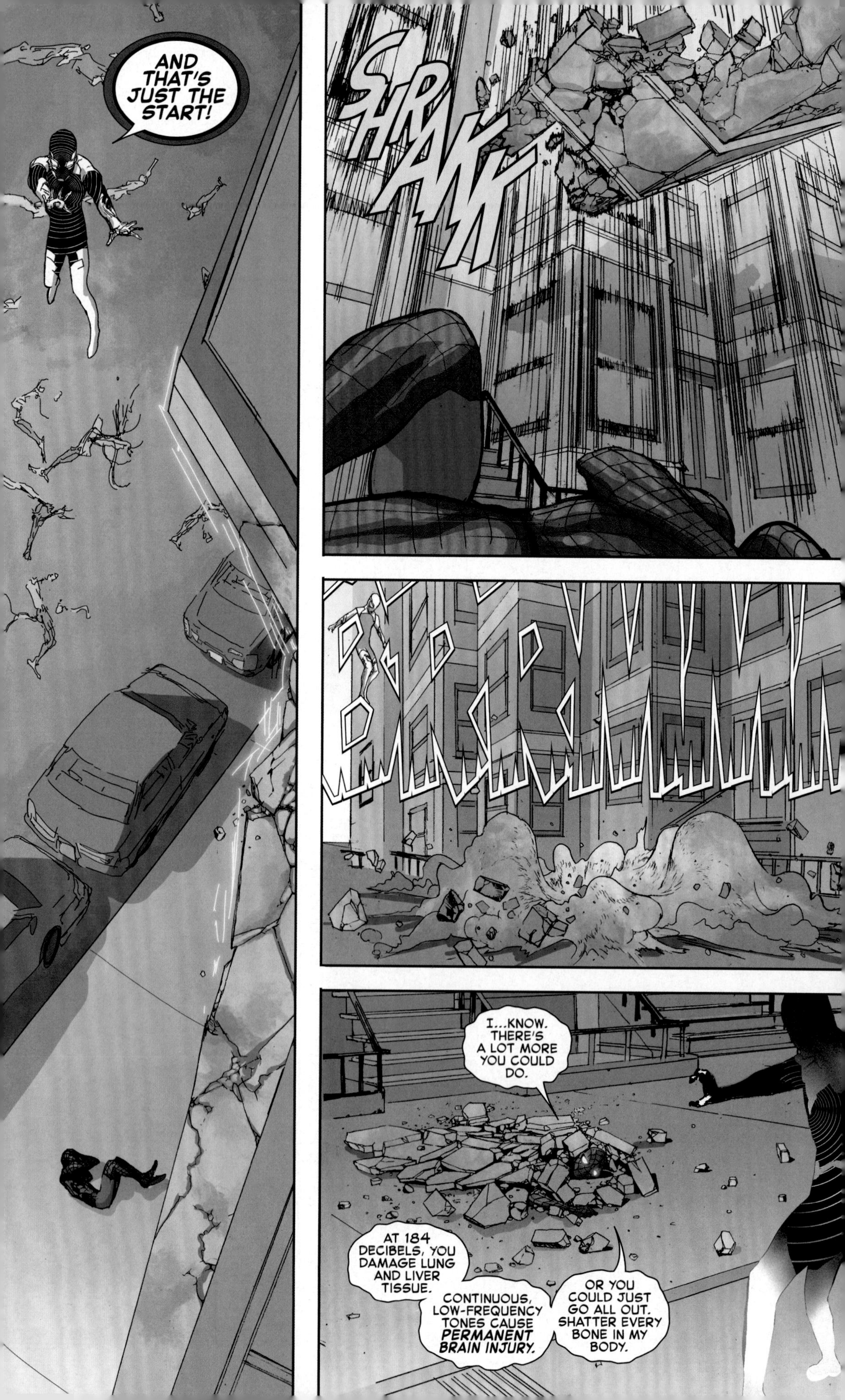
AND THAT'S JUST THE START!
SHRAKK
I...KNOW. THERE'S A LOT MORE YOU COULD DO.
AT 184 DECIBELS, YOU DAMAGE LUNG AND LIVER TISSUE.
CONTINUOUS, LOW-FREQUENCY TONES CAUSE PERMANENT BRAIN INJURY.
OR YOU COULD JUST GO ALL OUT. SHATTER EVERY BONE IN MY BODY.

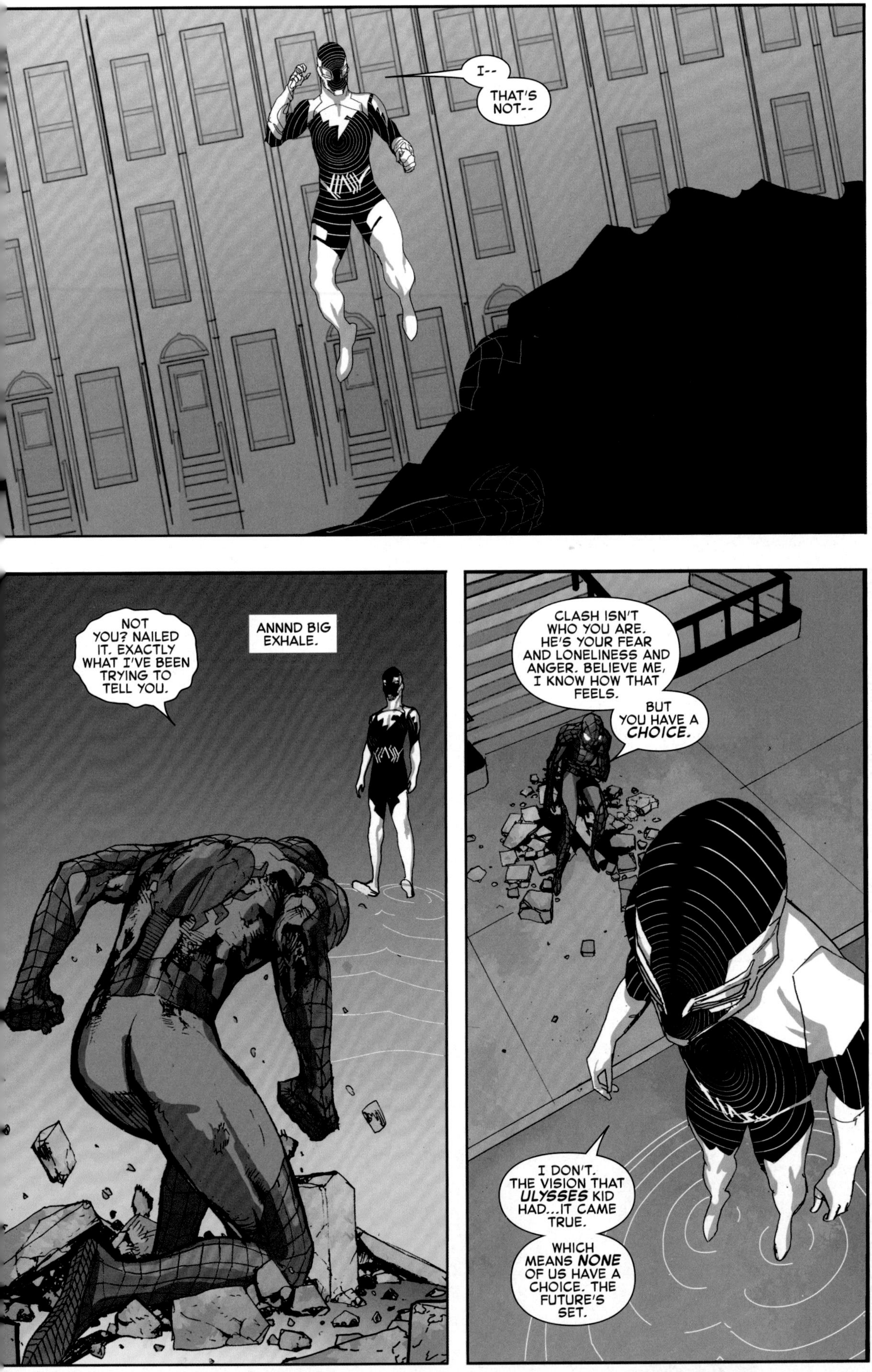
I--
THAT'S NOT--
NOT YOU? NAILED IT. EXACTLY WHAT I'VE BEEN TRYING TO TELL YOU.
ANNND BIG EXHALE.
CLASH ISN'T WHO YOU ARE. HE'S YOUR FEAR AND LONELINESS AND ANGER. BELIEVE ME, I KNOW HOW THAT FEELS.
BUT YOU HAVE A CHOICE.
I DON'T. THE VISION THAT ULYSSES KID HAD...IT CAME TRUE.
WHICH MEANS NONE OF US HAVE A CHOICE. THE FUTURE'S SET.

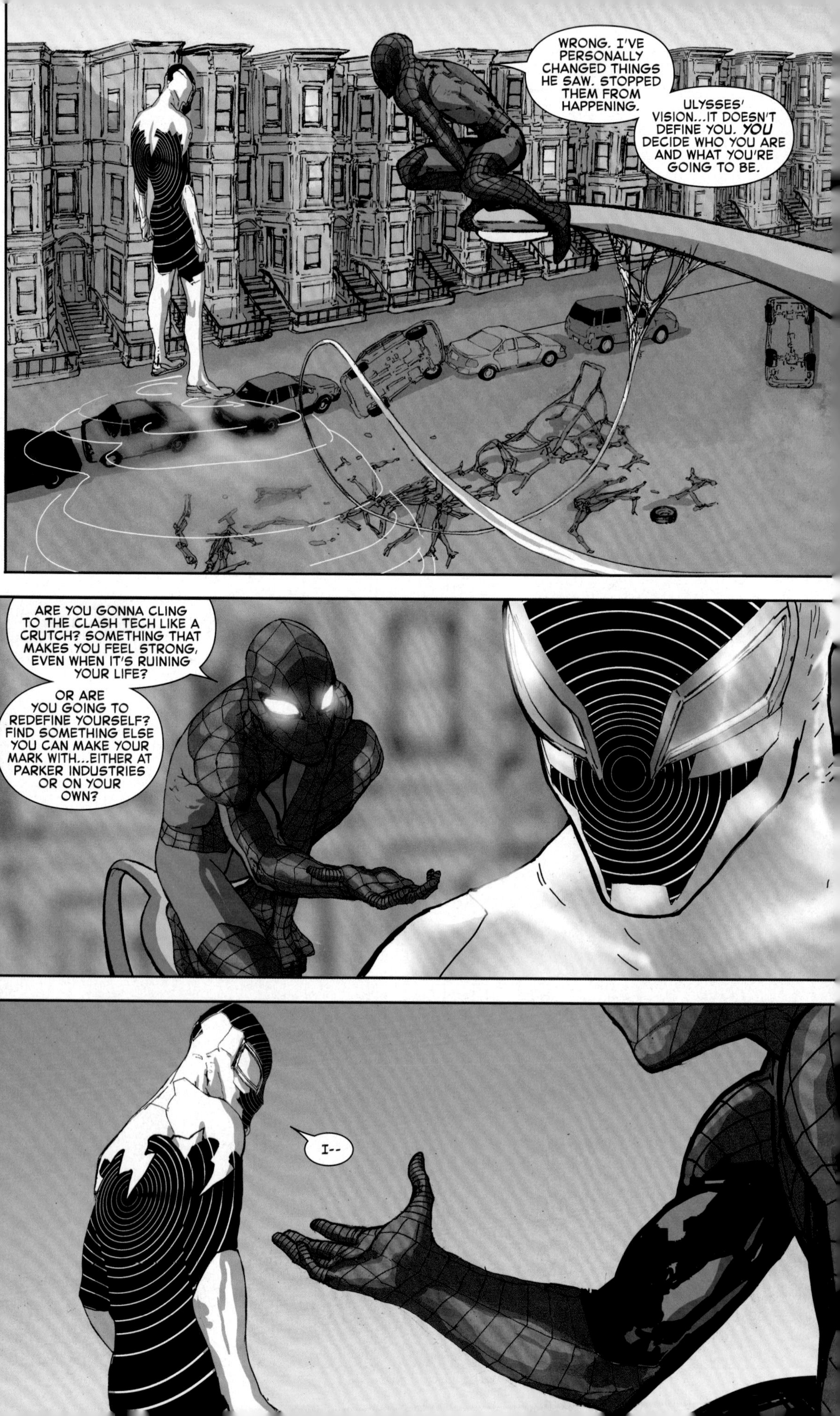
WRONG. I'VE PERSONALLY CHANGED THINGS HE SAW. STOPPED THEM FROM HAPPENING.
ULYSSES' VISION...IT DOESN'T DEFINE YOU. *YOU* DECIDE WHO YOU ARE AND WHAT YOU'RE GOING TO BE.
ARE YOU GONNA CLING TO THE CLASH TECH LIKE A CRUTCH? SOMETHING THAT MAKES YOU FEEL STRONG, EVEN WHEN IT'S RUINING YOUR LIFE?
OR ARE YOU GOING TO REDEFINE YOURSELF? FIND SOMETHING ELSE YOU CAN MAKE YOUR MARK WITH...EITHER AT PARKER INDUSTRIES OR ON YOUR OWN?
I--

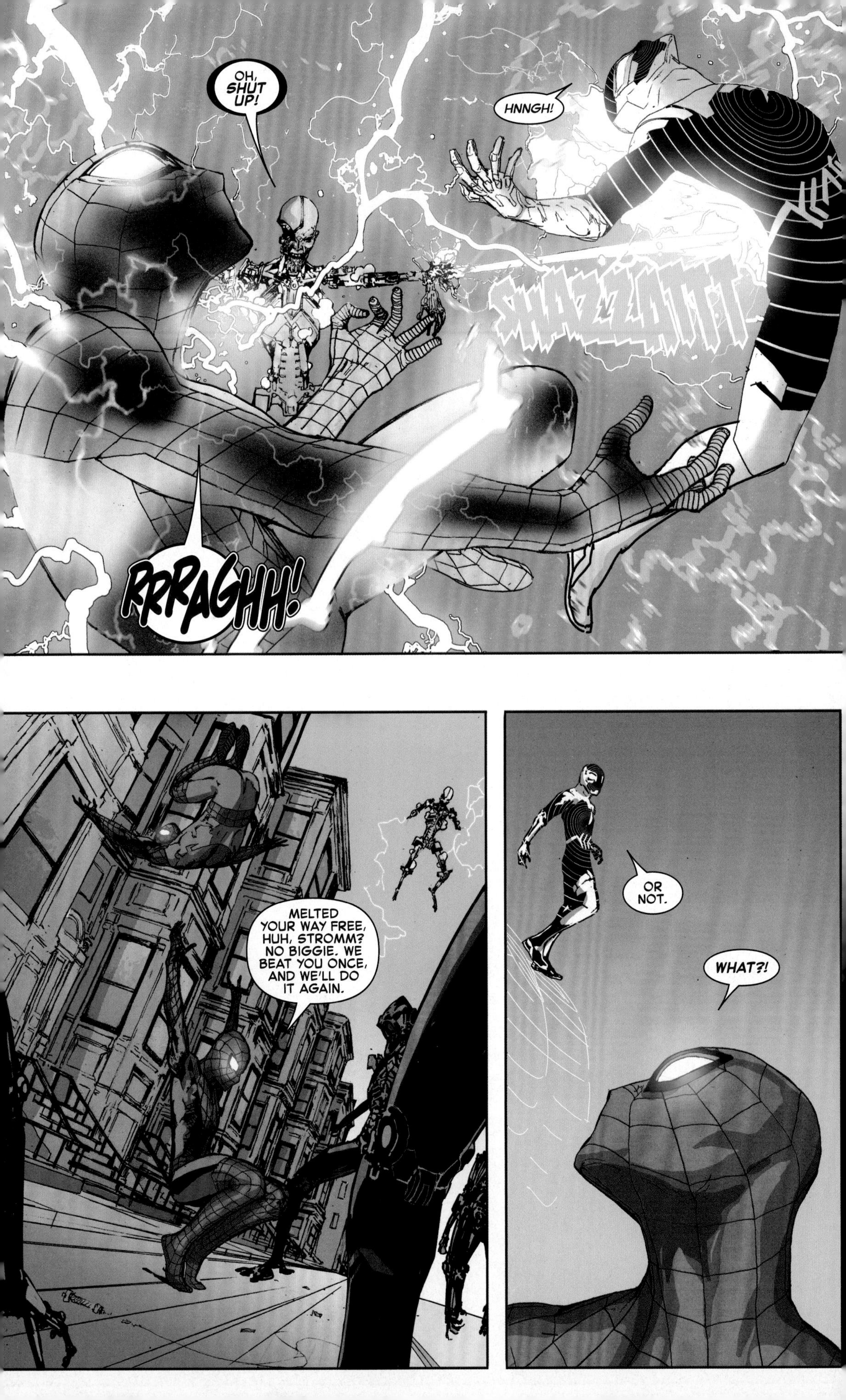
OH, SHUT UP!
HNNGH!
RRRAGHH!
MELTED YOUR WAY FREE, HUH, STROMM? NO BIGGIE. WE BEAT YOU ONCE, AND WE'LL DO IT AGAIN.
OR NOT.
WHAT?!

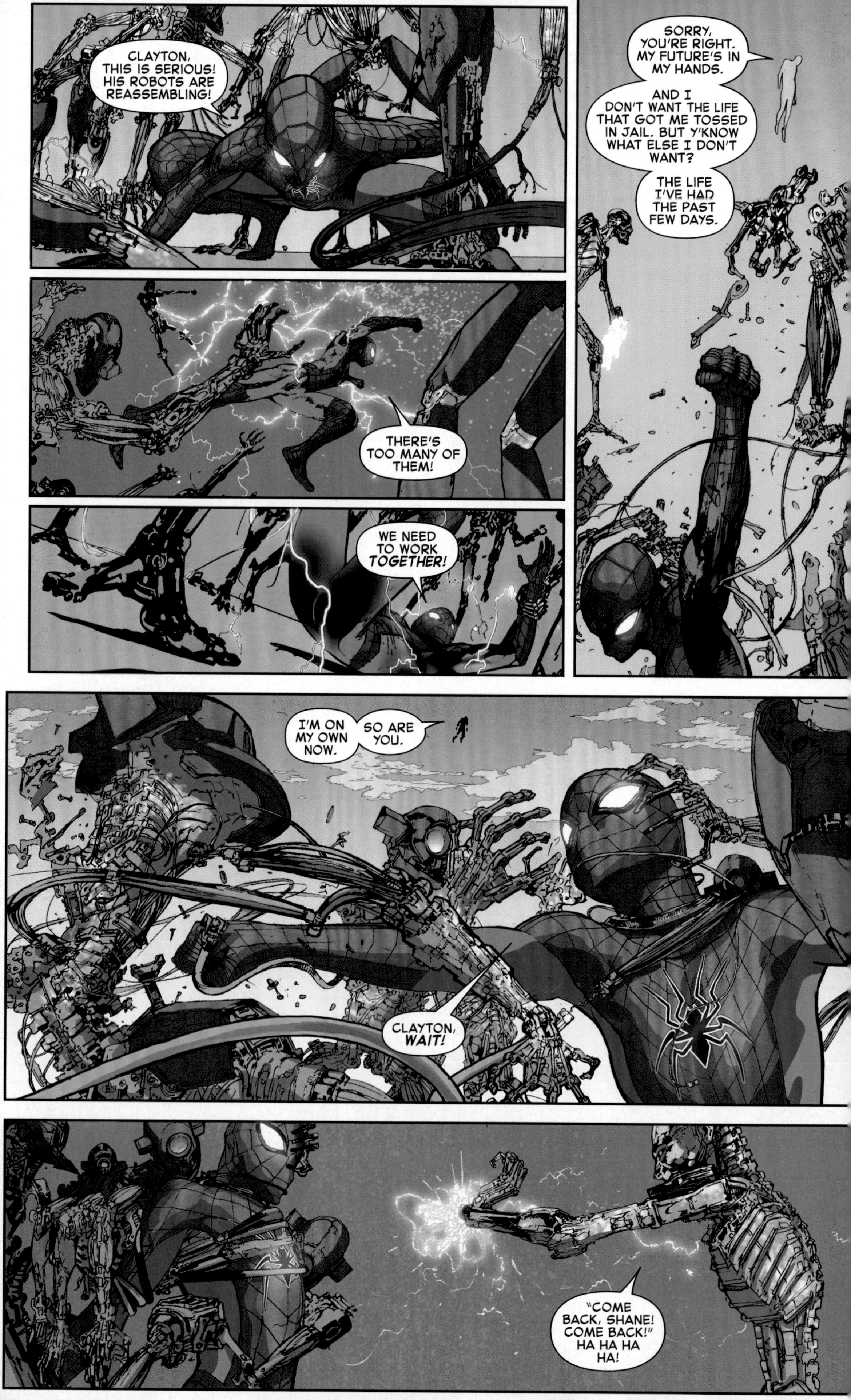
CLAYTON, THIS IS SERIOUS! HIS ROBOTS ARE REASSEMBLING!
SORRY, YOU'RE RIGHT. MY FUTURE'S IN MY HANDS.
AND I DON'T WANT THE LIFE THAT GOT ME TOSSED IN JAIL. BUT Y'KNOW WHAT ELSE I DON'T WANT?
THE LIFE I'VE HAD THE PAST FEW DAYS.
THERE'S TOO MANY OF THEM!
WE NEED TO WORK *TOGETHER!*
I'M ON MY OWN NOW.
SO ARE YOU.
CLAYTON, *WAIT!*
"COME BACK, SHANE! COME BACK!" HA HA HA HA!

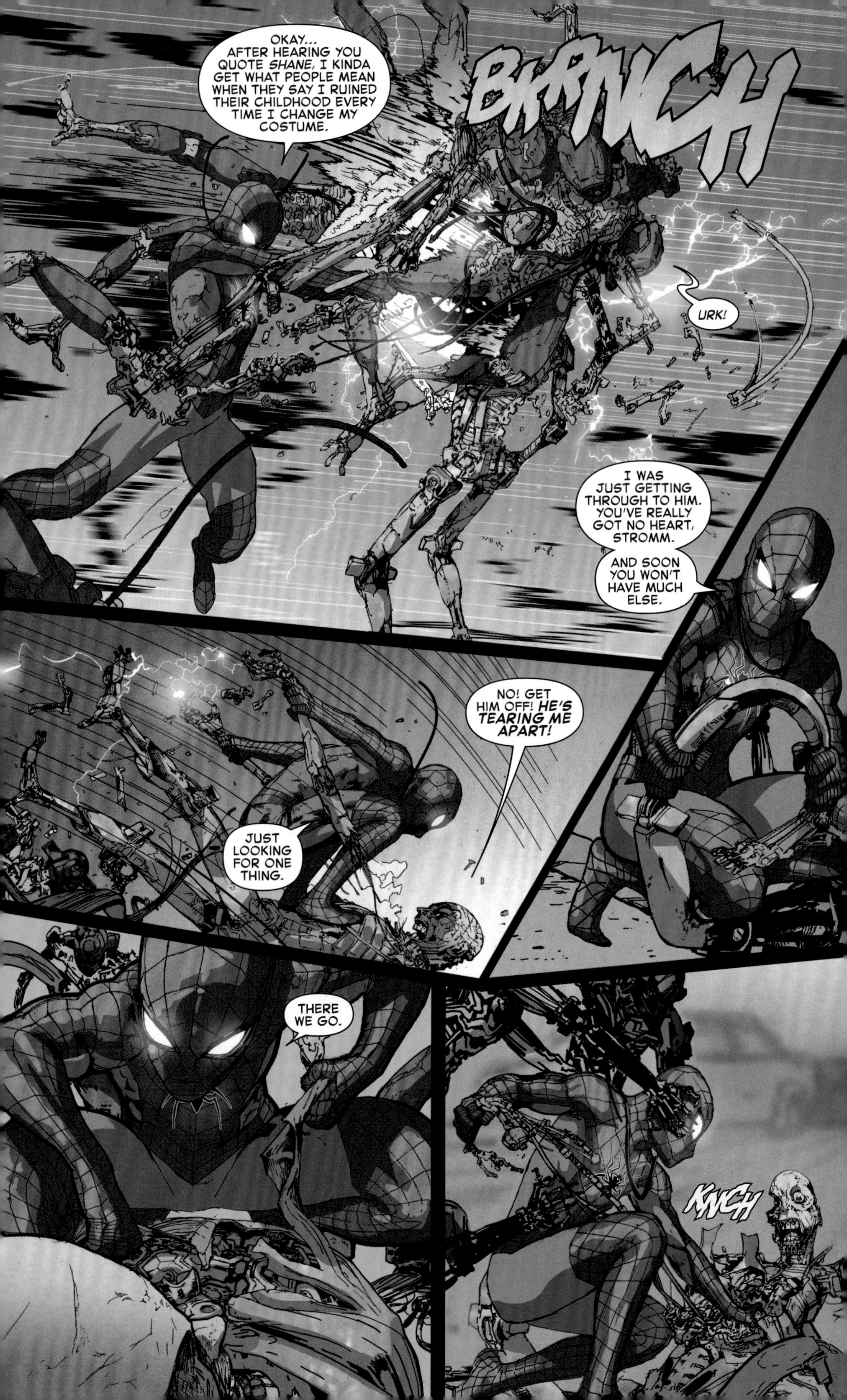
OKAY... AFTER HEARING YOU QUOTE SHANE, I KINDA GET WHAT PEOPLE MEAN WHEN THEY SAY I RUINED THEIR CHILDHOOD EVERY TIME I CHANGE MY COSTUME.
BKRNCH
URK!
I WAS JUST GETTING THROUGH TO HIM. YOU'VE REALLY GOT NO HEART, STROMM.
AND SOON YOU WON'T HAVE MUCH ELSE.
NO! GET HIM OFF! HE'S TEARING ME APART!
JUST LOOKING FOR ONE THING.
THERE WE GO.
KNCH

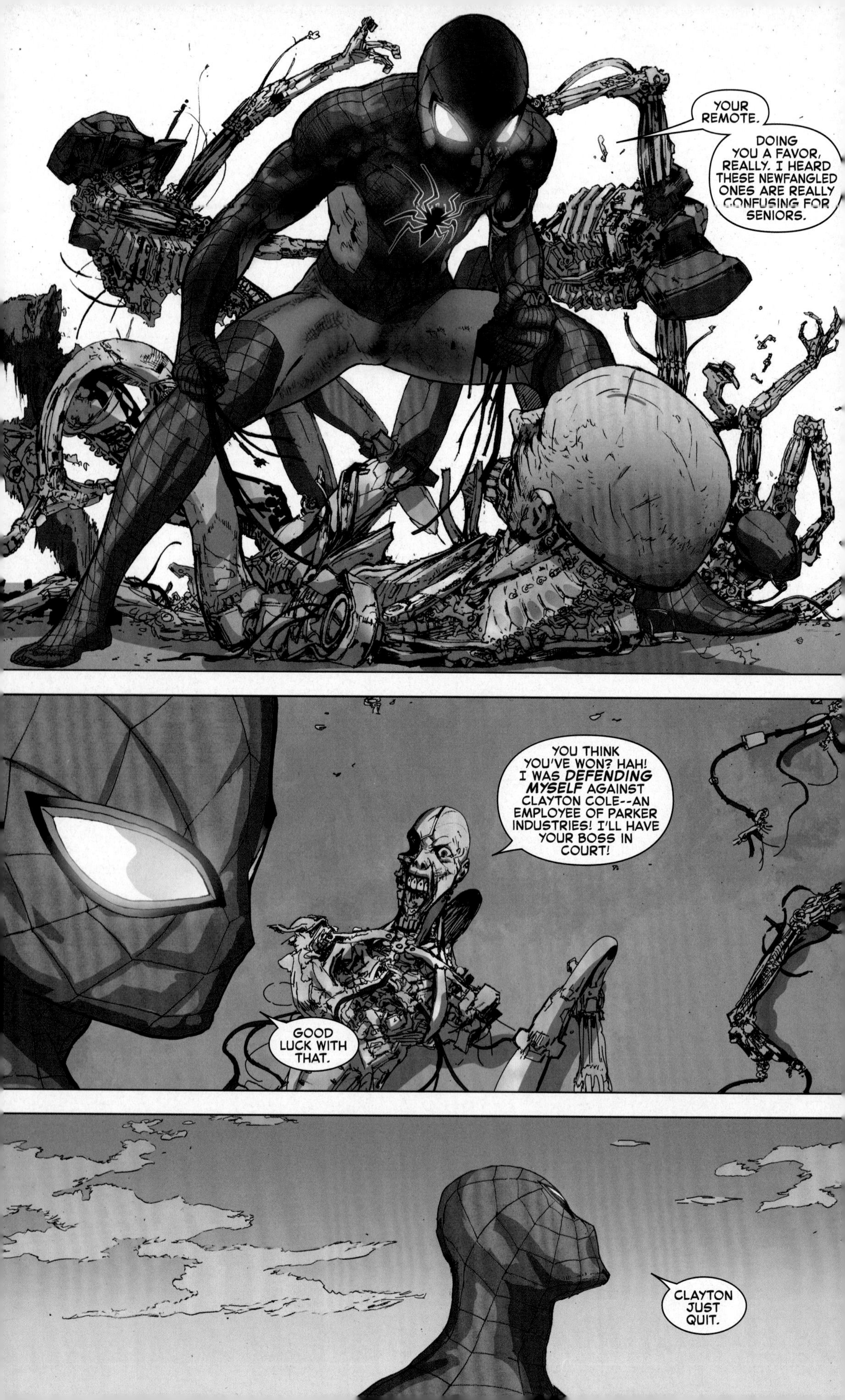
YOUR REMOTE.
DOING YOU A FAVOR, REALLY. I HEARD THESE NEWFANGLED ONES ARE REALLY CONFUSING FOR SENIORS.
YOU THINK YOU'VE WON? HAH! I WAS DEFENDING MYSELF AGAINST CLAYTON COLE--AN EMPLOYEE OF PARKER INDUSTRIES! I'LL HAVE YOUR BOSS IN COURT!
GOOD LUCK WITH THAT.
CLAYTON JUST QUIT.

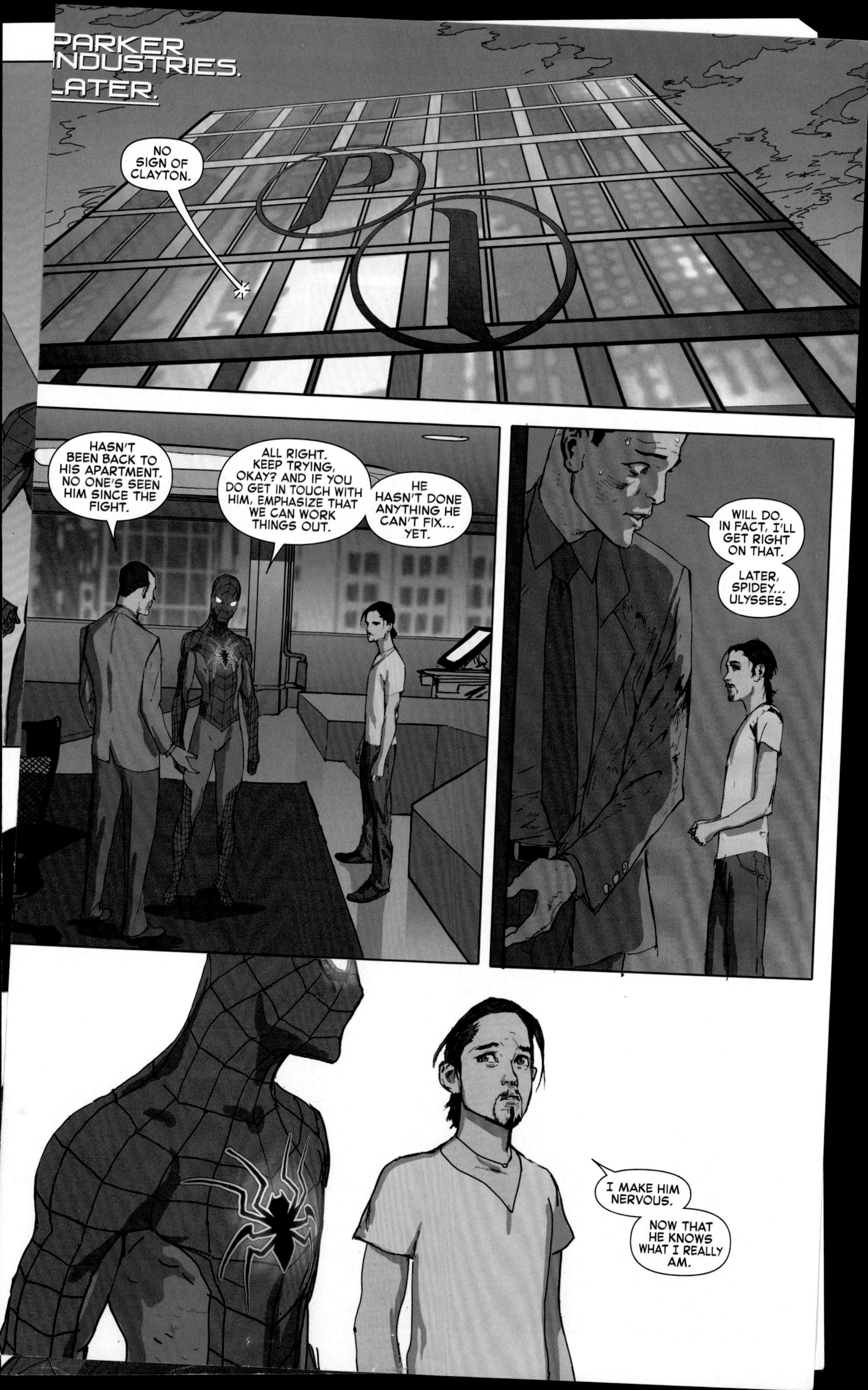

PARKER INDUSTRIES. LATER.
NO SIGN OF CLAYTON.
HASN'T BEEN BACK TO HIS APARTMENT. NO ONE'S SEEN HIM SINCE THE FIGHT.
ALL RIGHT. KEEP TRYING, OKAY? AND IF YOU DO GET IN TOUCH WITH HIM, EMPHASIZE THAT WE CAN WORK THINGS OUT.
HE HASN'T DONE ANYTHING HE CAN'T FIX... YET.
WILL DO. IN FACT, I'LL GET RIGHT ON THAT.
LATER, SPIDEY... ULYSSES.
I MAKE HIM NERVOUS.
NOW THAT HE KNOWS WHAT I REALLY AM.

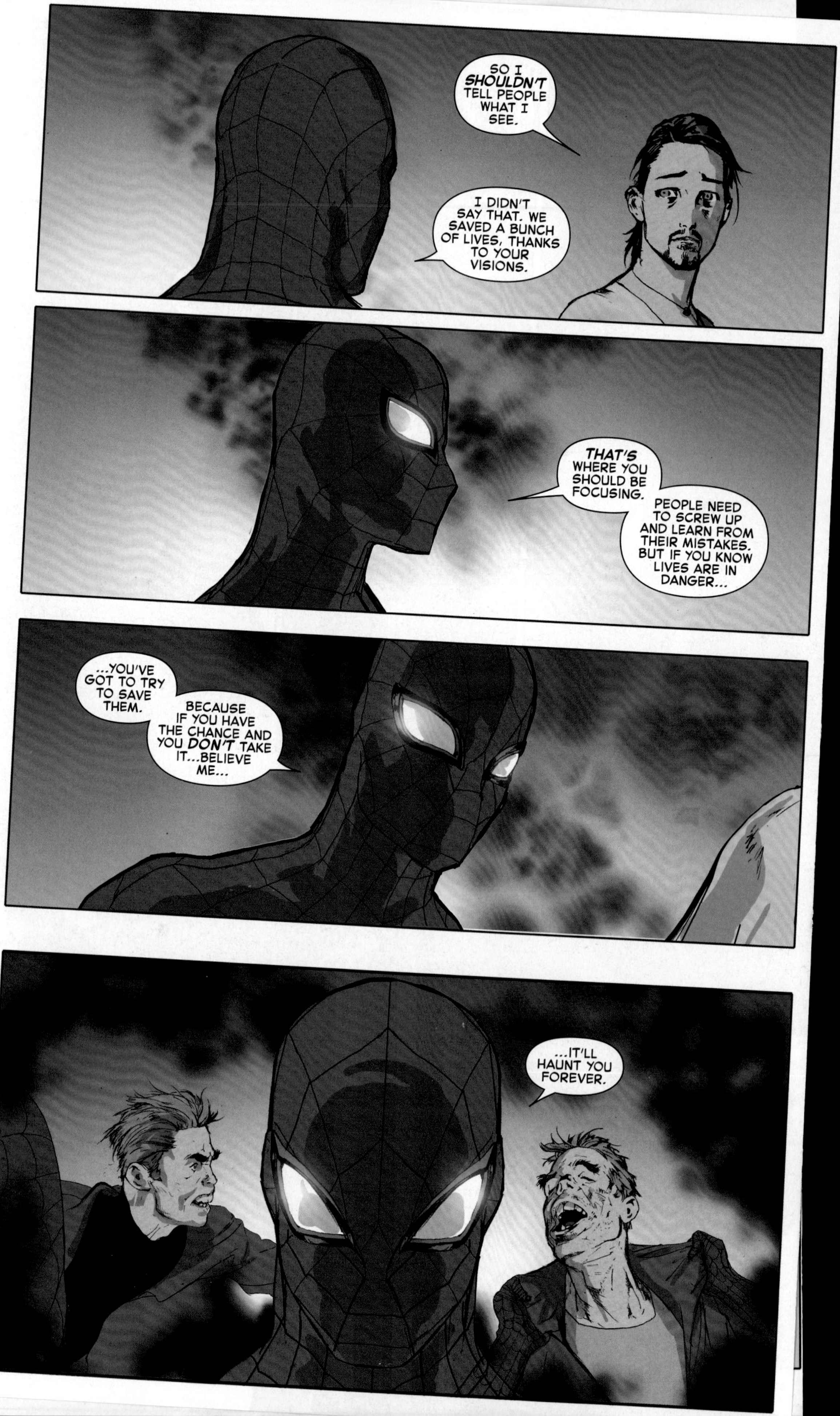
SO I SHOULDN'T TELL PEOPLE WHAT I SEE.
I DIDN'T SAY THAT. WE SAVED A BUNCH OF LIVES, THANKS TO YOUR VISIONS.
THAT'S WHERE YOU SHOULD BE FOCUSING.
PEOPLE NEED TO SCREW UP AND LEARN FROM THEIR MISTAKES. BUT IF YOU KNOW LIVES ARE IN DANGER...
...YOU'VE GOT TO TRY TO SAVE THEM.
BECAUSE IF YOU HAVE THE CHANCE AND YOU DON'T TAKE IT...BELIEVE ME...
...IT'LL HAUNT YOU FOREVER.

AM I MAKING ANY SENSE HERE?

YEAH. IT'S JUST... A LOT. A LOT OF RESPONSIBILITY, TO MAKE SURE THINGS COME OUT RIGHT.

WELL, A SMART GUY ONCE TOLD ME THAT WITH GREAT POWER THERE MUST ALSO COME GREAT RESPONSIBILITY. AND THAT'S TRUE.

BUT IT'S OKAY TO HAVE *HELP.*

HEY, SPIDEY. ULYSSES. HOW WE DOING?

GOOD, I HOPE. I THINK WE BOTH FIGURED SOME STUFF OUT.

THE HUMAN TORCH.

THE INHUMAN ROYAL FAMILY.

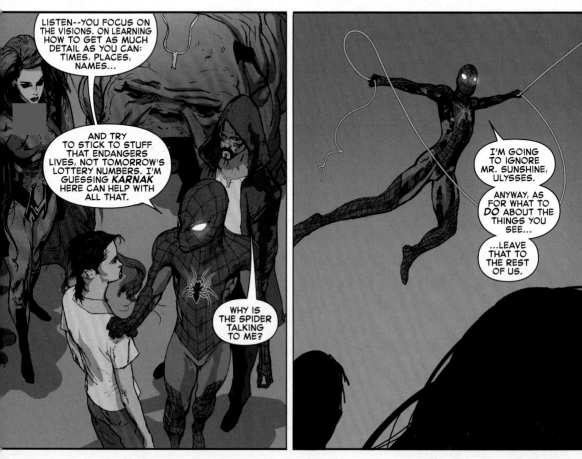

LISTEN--YOU FOCUS ON THE VISIONS. ON LEARNING HOW TO GET AS MUCH DETAIL AS YOU CAN: TIMES, PLACES, NAMES...

AND TRY TO STICK TO STUFF THAT ENDANGERS LIVES, NOT TOMORROW'S LOTTERY NUMBERS. I'M GUESSING *KARNAK* HERE CAN HELP WITH ALL THAT.

WHY IS THE SPIDER TALKING TO ME?

I'M GOING TO IGNORE MR. SUNSHINE, ULYSSES.

ANYWAY, AS FOR WHAT TO *DO* ABOUT THE THINGS YOU SEE...

...LEAVE THAT TO THE REST OF US.

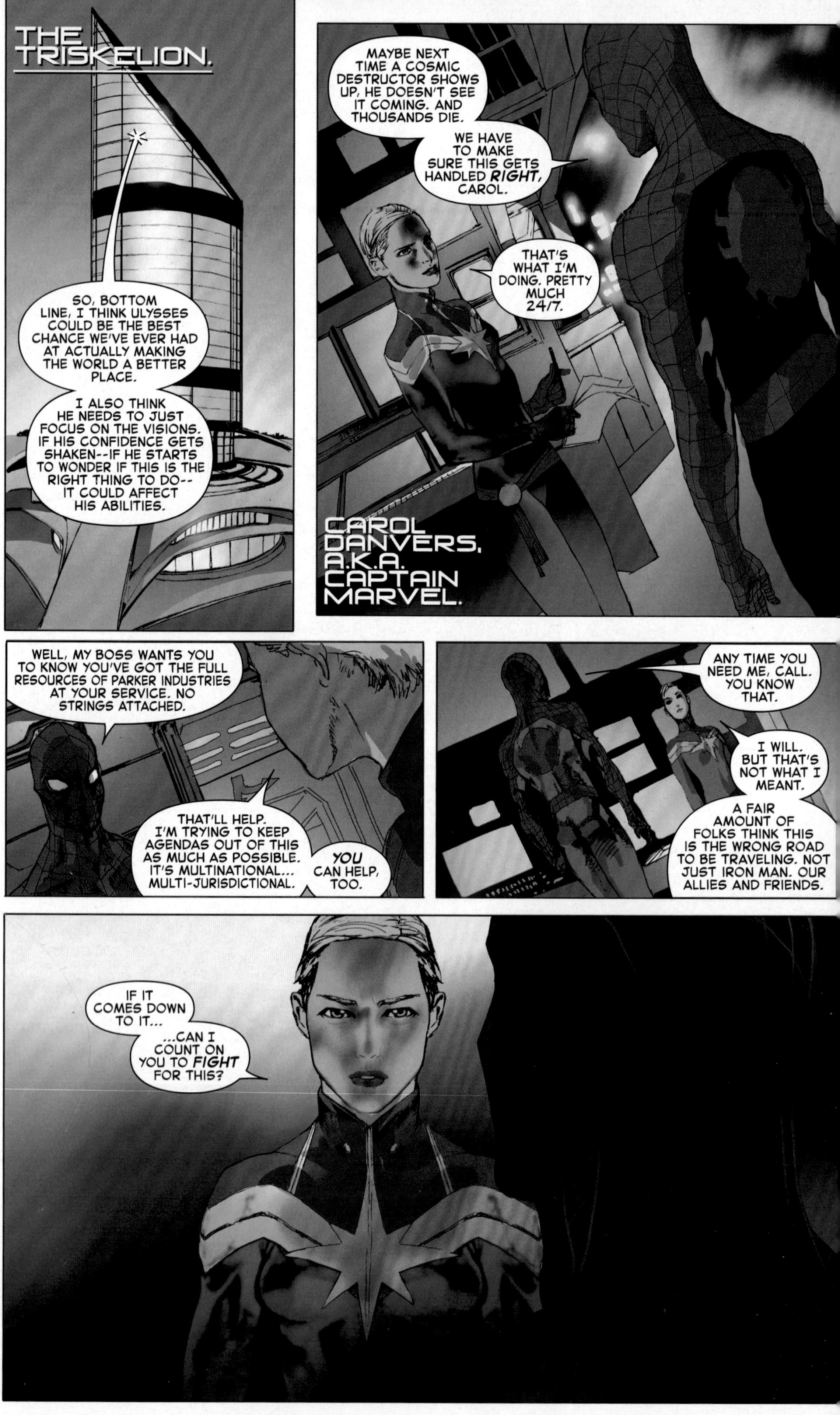

THE TRISKELION.
SO, BOTTOM LINE, I THINK ULYSSES COULD BE THE BEST CHANCE WE'VE EVER HAD AT ACTUALLY MAKING THE WORLD A BETTER PLACE.
I ALSO THINK HE NEEDS TO JUST FOCUS ON THE VISIONS. IF HIS CONFIDENCE GETS SHAKEN--IF HE STARTS TO WONDER IF THIS IS THE RIGHT THING TO DO--IT COULD AFFECT HIS ABILITIES.
MAYBE NEXT TIME A COSMIC DESTRUCTOR SHOWS UP, HE DOESN'T SEE IT COMING. AND THOUSANDS DIE.
WE HAVE TO MAKE SURE THIS GETS HANDLED *RIGHT*, CAROL.
THAT'S WHAT I'M DOING. PRETTY MUCH 24/7.
CAROL DANVERS, A.K.A. CAPTAIN MARVEL.
WELL, MY BOSS WANTS YOU TO KNOW YOU'VE GOT THE FULL RESOURCES OF PARKER INDUSTRIES AT YOUR SERVICE. NO STRINGS ATTACHED.
THAT'LL HELP. I'M TRYING TO KEEP AGENDAS OUT OF THIS AS MUCH AS POSSIBLE. IT'S MULTINATIONAL... MULTI-JURISDICTIONAL.
YOU CAN HELP, TOO.
ANY TIME YOU NEED ME, CALL. YOU KNOW THAT.
I WILL. BUT THAT'S NOT WHAT I MEANT.
A FAIR AMOUNT OF FOLKS THINK THIS IS THE WRONG ROAD TO BE TRAVELING. NOT JUST IRON MAN. OUR ALLIES AND FRIENDS.
IF IT COMES DOWN TO IT...
...CAN I COUNT ON YOU TO *FIGHT* FOR THIS?

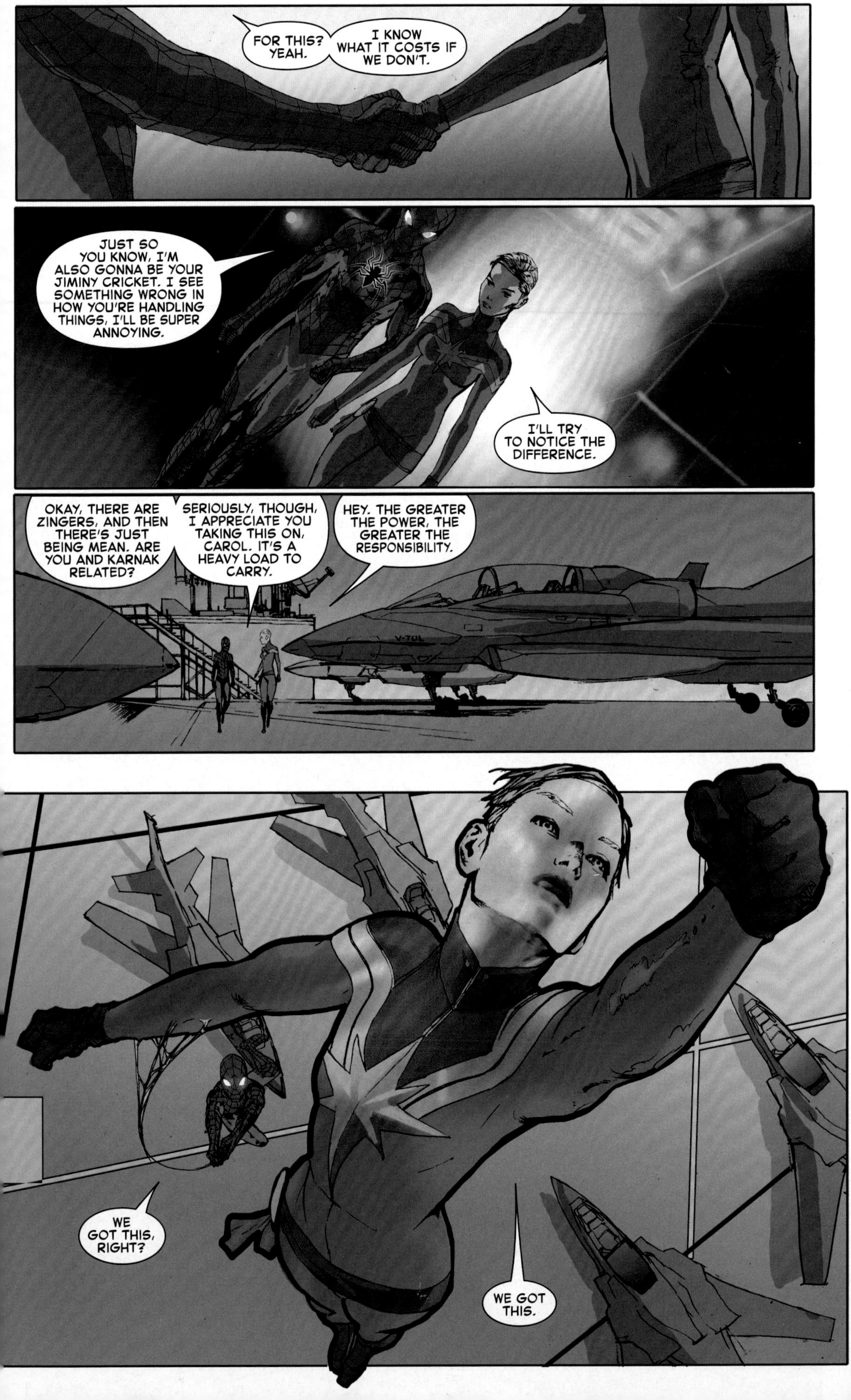
FOR THIS? YEAH.
I KNOW WHAT IT COSTS IF WE DON'T.
JUST SO YOU KNOW, I'M ALSO GONNA BE YOUR JIMINY CRICKET. I SEE SOMETHING WRONG IN HOW YOU'RE HANDLING THINGS, I'LL BE SUPER ANNOYING.
I'LL TRY TO NOTICE THE DIFFERENCE.
OKAY, THERE ARE ZINGERS, AND THEN THERE'S JUST BEING MEAN. ARE YOU AND KARNAK RELATED?
SERIOUSLY, THOUGH, I APPRECIATE YOU TAKING THIS ON, CAROL. IT'S A HEAVY LOAD TO CARRY.
HEY. THE GREATER THE POWER, THE GREATER THE RESPONSIBILITY.
V-TOL
WE GOT THIS, RIGHT?
WE GOT THIS.

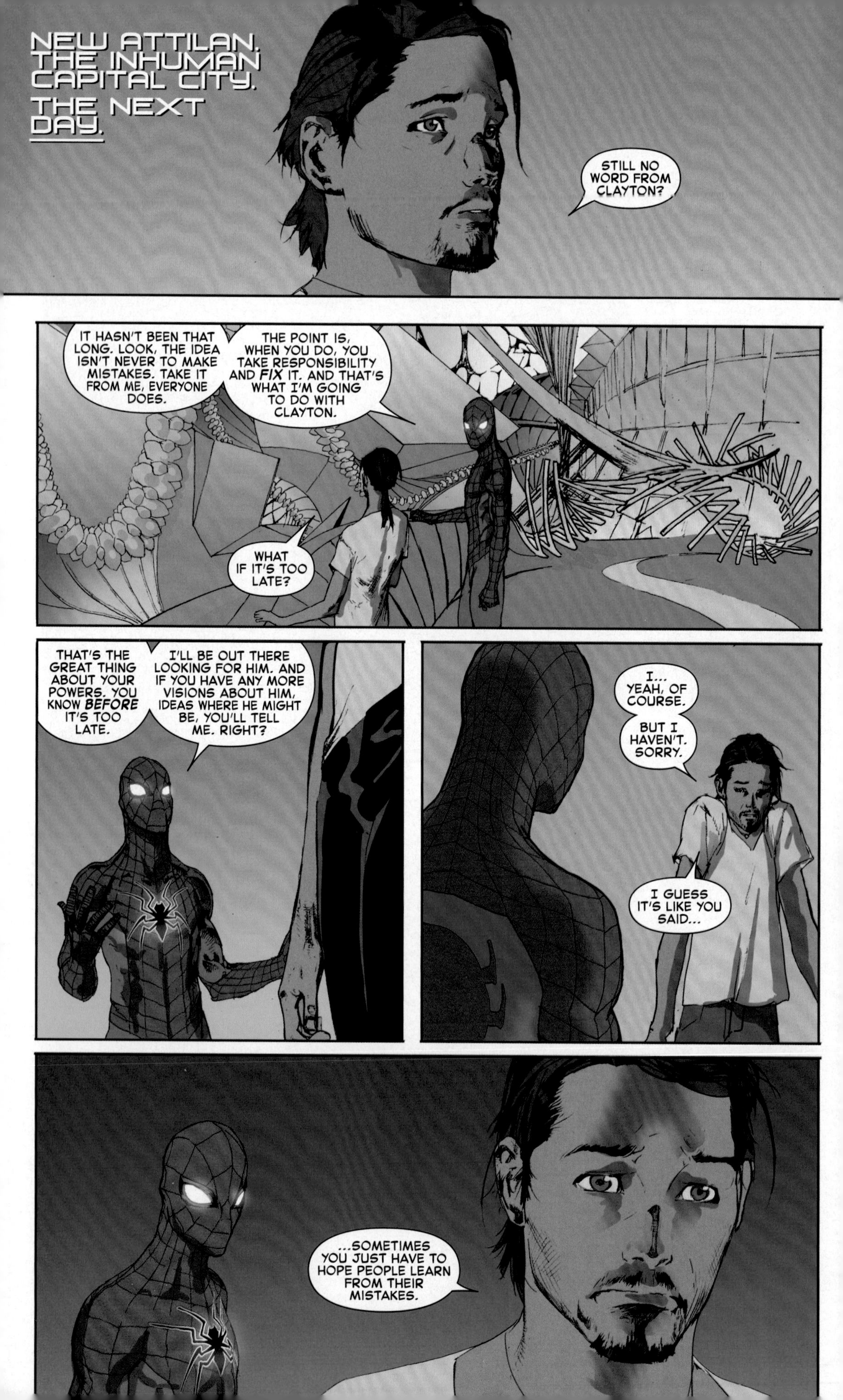
NEW ATTILAN, THE INHUMAN CAPITAL CITY.
THE NEXT DAY.
STILL NO WORD FROM CLAYTON?
IT HASN'T BEEN THAT LONG. LOOK, THE IDEA ISN'T NEVER TO MAKE MISTAKES. TAKE IT FROM ME, EVERYONE DOES.
THE POINT IS, WHEN YOU DO, YOU TAKE RESPONSIBILITY AND FIX IT. AND THAT'S WHAT I'M GOING TO DO WITH CLAYTON.
WHAT IF IT'S TOO LATE?
THAT'S THE GREAT THING ABOUT YOUR POWERS. YOU KNOW BEFORE IT'S TOO LATE.
I'LL BE OUT THERE LOOKING FOR HIM. AND IF YOU HAVE ANY MORE VISIONS ABOUT HIM, IDEAS WHERE HE MIGHT BE, YOU'LL TELL ME. RIGHT?
I... YEAH, OF COURSE.
BUT I HAVEN'T. SORRY.
I GUESS IT'S LIKE YOU SAID...
...SOMETIMES YOU JUST HAVE TO HOPE PEOPLE LEARN FROM THEIR MISTAKES.

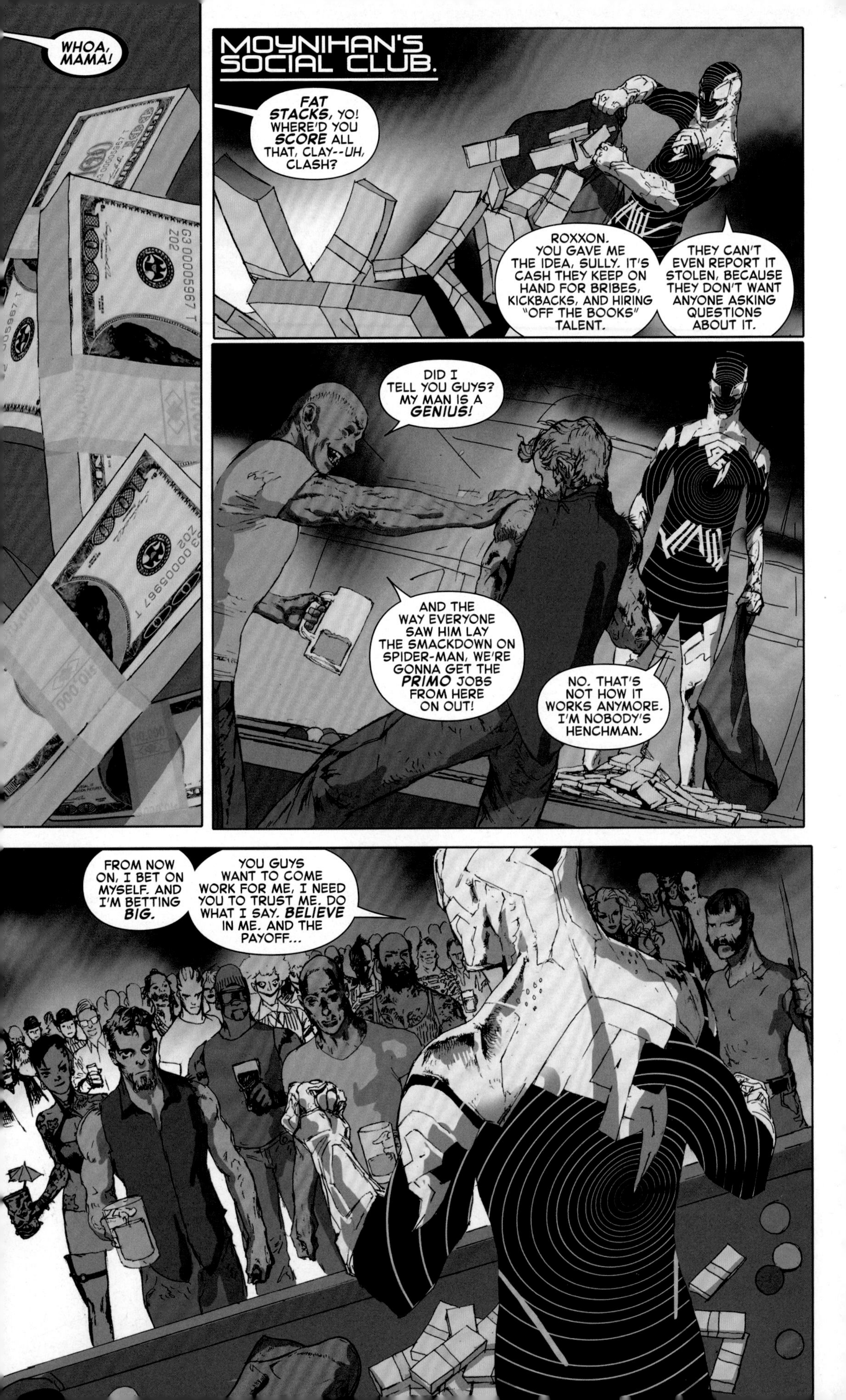
WHOA, MAMA!
MOYNIHAN'S SOCIAL CLUB.
FAT STACKS, YO! WHERE'D YOU SCORE ALL THAT, CLAY--UH, CLASH?
ROXXON. YOU GAVE ME THE IDEA, SULLY. IT'S CASH THEY KEEP ON HAND FOR BRIBES, KICKBACKS, AND HIRING "OFF THE BOOKS" TALENT.
THEY CAN'T EVEN REPORT IT STOLEN, BECAUSE THEY DON'T WANT ANYONE ASKING QUESTIONS ABOUT IT.
DID I TELL YOU GUYS? MY MAN IS A GENIUS!
AND THE WAY EVERYONE SAW HIM LAY THE SMACKDOWN ON SPIDER-MAN, WE'RE GONNA GET THE PRIMO JOBS FROM HERE ON OUT!
NO. THAT'S NOT HOW IT WORKS ANYMORE. I'M NOBODY'S HENCHMAN.
FROM NOW ON, I BET ON MYSELF. AND I'M BETTING BIG.
YOU GUYS WANT TO COME WORK FOR ME, I NEED YOU TO TRUST ME. DO WHAT I SAY. BELIEVE IN ME. AND THE PAYOFF...

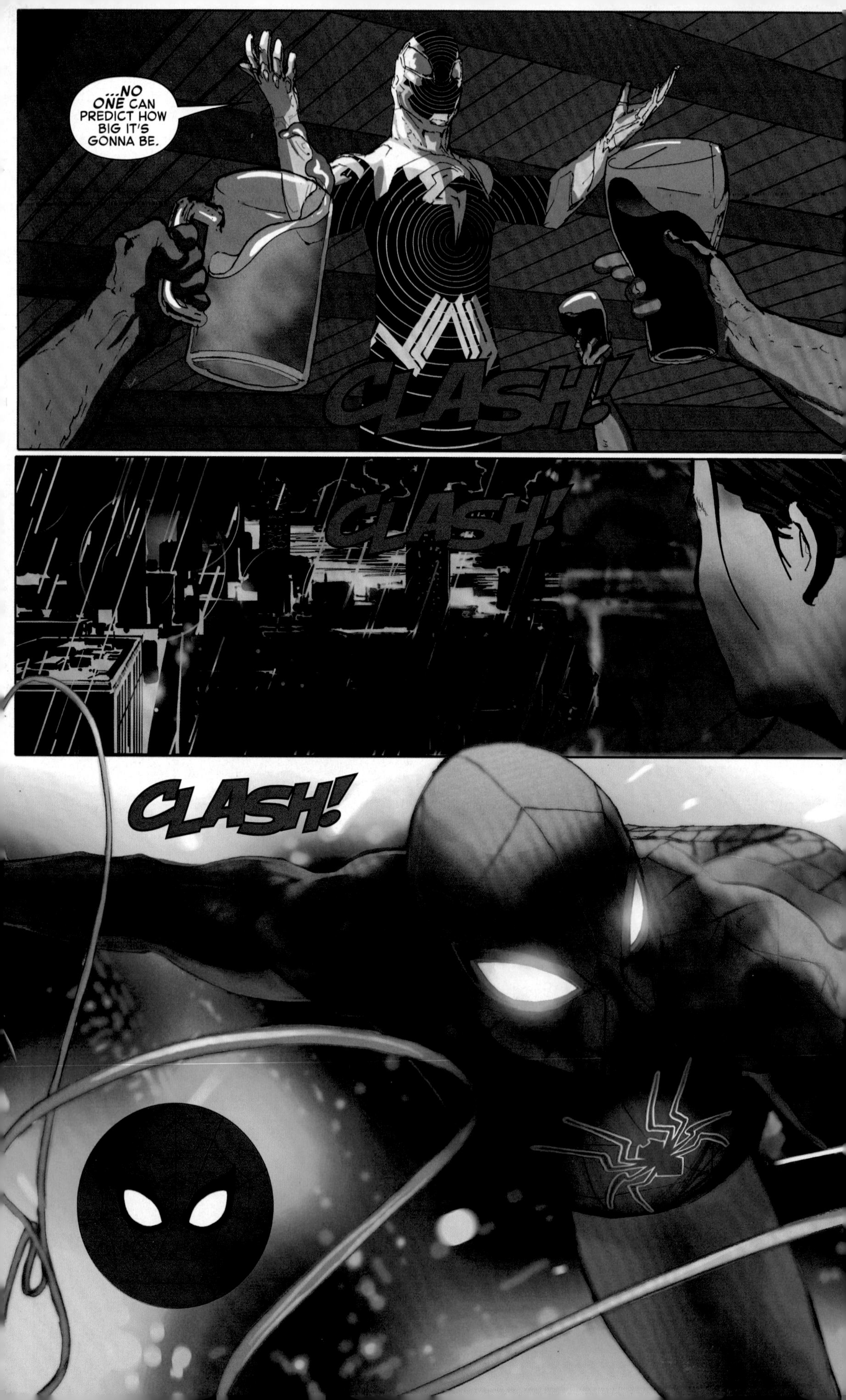
...NO ONE CAN PREDICT HOW BIG IT'S GONNA BE.
CLASH!
CLASH!
CLASH!

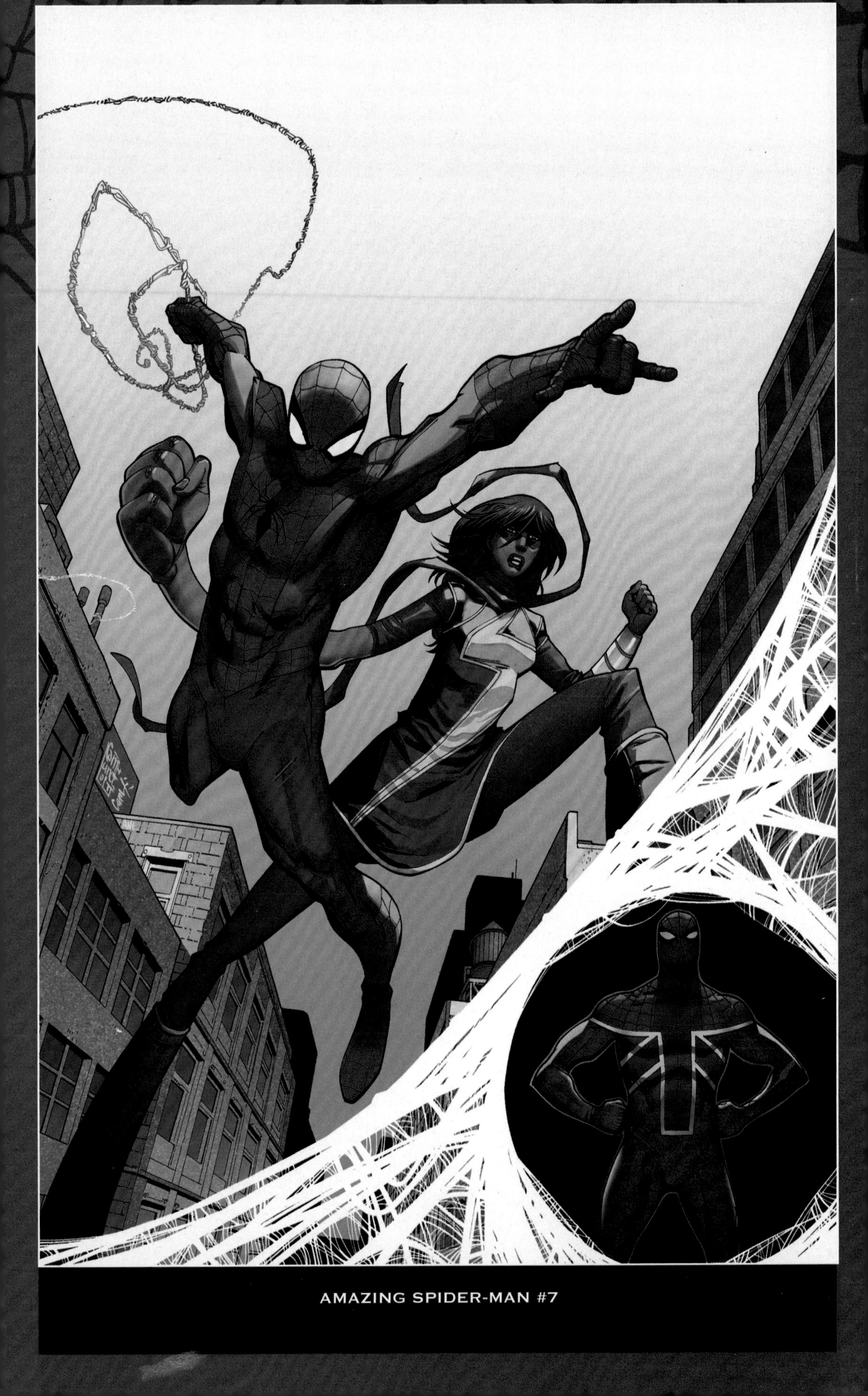

AMAZING SPIDER-MAN #7

AFTER SWAPPING HIS MIND INTO PETER'S BODY, ONE OF SPIDER-MAN'S GREATEST ENEMIES, DOCTOR OCTOPUS, SET OUT TO PROVE HIMSELF THE SUPERIOR SPIDER-MAN. HE ALSO COMPLETED PETER'S DOCTORATE, FELL IN LOVE WITH A WOMAN NAMED ANNA MARIA MARCONI, AND STARTED HIS OWN COMPANY, PARKER INDUSTRIES. BUT IN THE END DOC OCK REALIZED THAT IN ORDER TO BE A TRUE HERO, HE HAD TO SACRIFICE HIMSELF AND GIVE CONTROL OF PETER'S BODY BACK TO PETER.

PETER RECENTLY FOUND OUT THAT SOMEONE ELSE — CINDY MOON A.K.A. SILK — WAS BITTEN BY HIS RADIOACTIVE SPIDER, GIVING HER SIMILAR POWERS TO PETER. AND THAT'S NOT THE ONLY THING THEY HAVE IN COMMON.

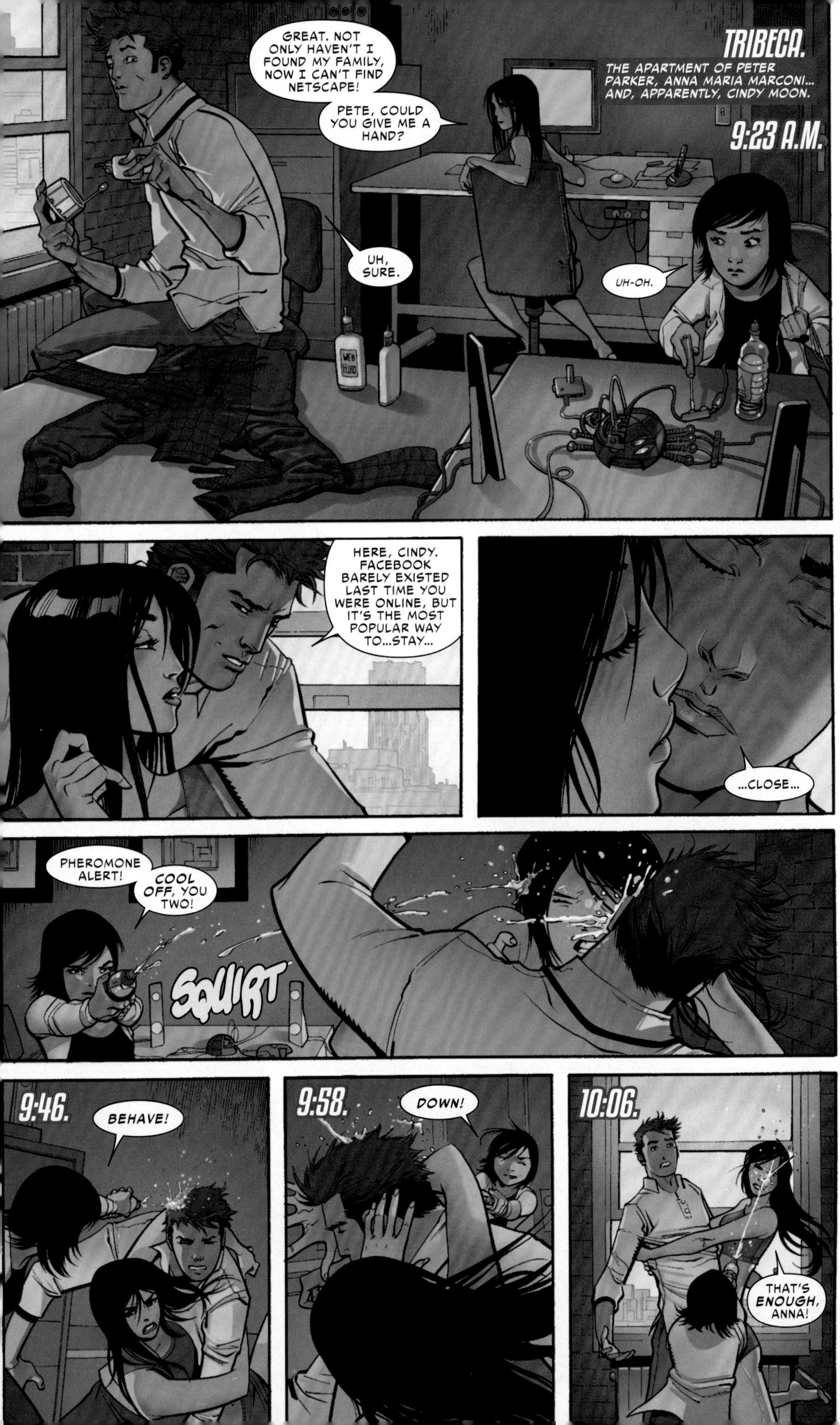
TRIBECA.
THE APARTMENT OF PETER PARKER, ANNA MARIA MARCONI... AND, APPARENTLY, CINDY MOON.
9:23 A.M.
GREAT. NOT ONLY HAVEN'T I FOUND MY FAMILY, NOW I CAN'T FIND NETSCAPE!
PETE, COULD YOU GIVE ME A HAND?
UH, SURE.
UH-OH.
WEB FLUID
HERE, CINDY. FACEBOOK BARELY EXISTED LAST TIME YOU WERE ONLINE, BUT IT'S THE MOST POPULAR WAY TO...STAY...
...CLOSE...
PHEROMONE ALERT!
COOL OFF, YOU TWO!
SQUIRT
9:46.
BEHAVE!
9:58.
DOWN!
10:06.
THAT'S ENOUGH, ANNA!

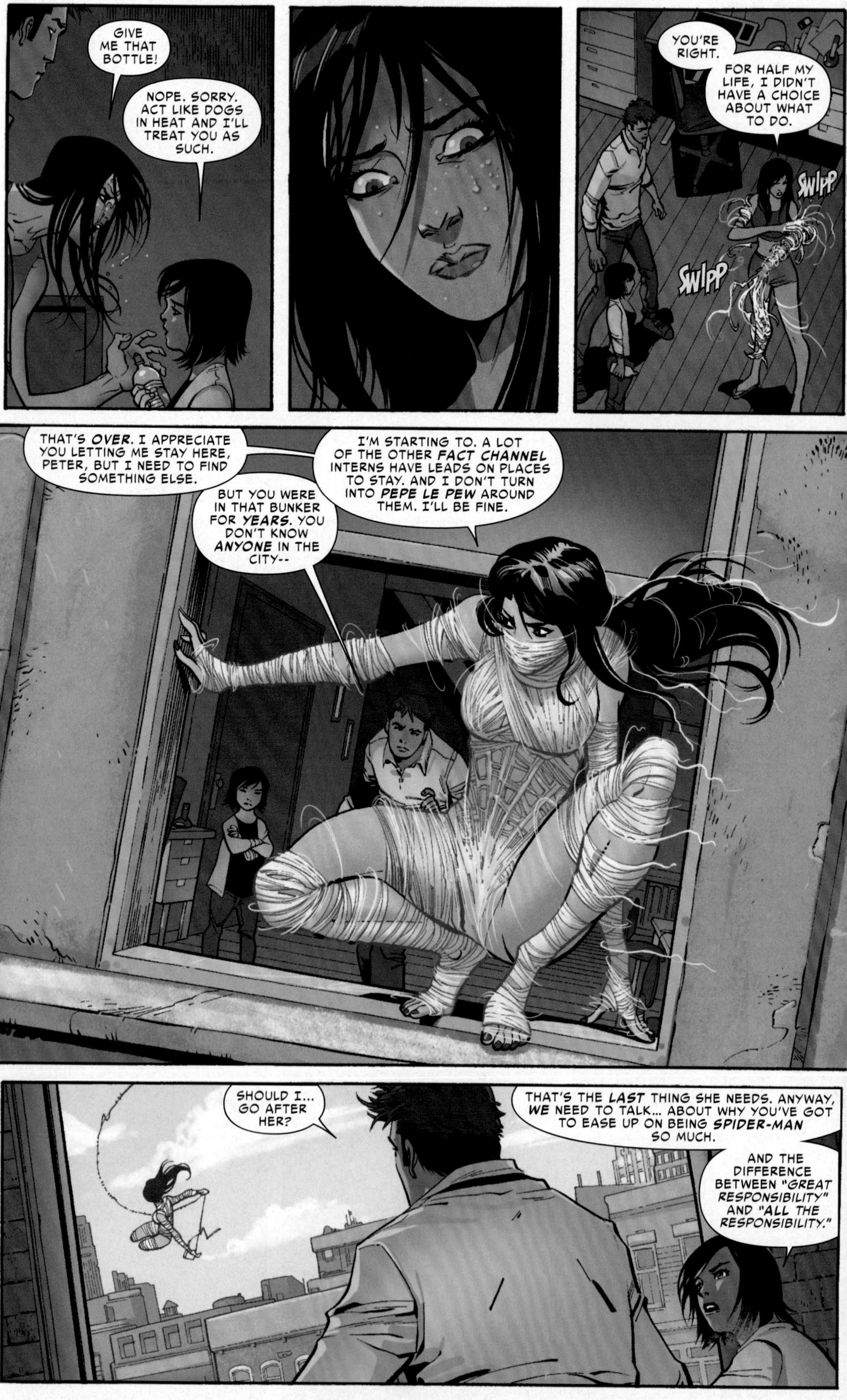
GIVE ME THAT BOTTLE!
NOPE. SORRY. ACT LIKE DOGS IN HEAT AND I'LL TREAT YOU AS SUCH.
YOU'RE RIGHT.
FOR HALF MY LIFE, I DIDN'T HAVE A CHOICE ABOUT WHAT TO DO.
SWIPP
SWIPP
THAT'S OVER. I APPRECIATE YOU LETTING ME STAY HERE, PETER, BUT I NEED TO FIND SOMETHING ELSE.
BUT YOU WERE IN THAT BUNKER FOR YEARS. YOU DON'T KNOW ANYONE IN THE CITY--
I'M STARTING TO. A LOT OF THE OTHER FACT CHANNEL INTERNS HAVE LEADS ON PLACES TO STAY. AND I DON'T TURN INTO PEPE LE PEW AROUND THEM. I'LL BE FINE.
SHOULD I... GO AFTER HER?
THAT'S THE LAST THING SHE NEEDS. ANYWAY, WE NEED TO TALK... ABOUT WHY YOU'VE GOT TO EASE UP ON BEING SPIDER-MAN SO MUCH.
AND THE DIFFERENCE BETWEEN "GREAT RESPONSIBILITY" AND "ALL THE RESPONSIBILITY."

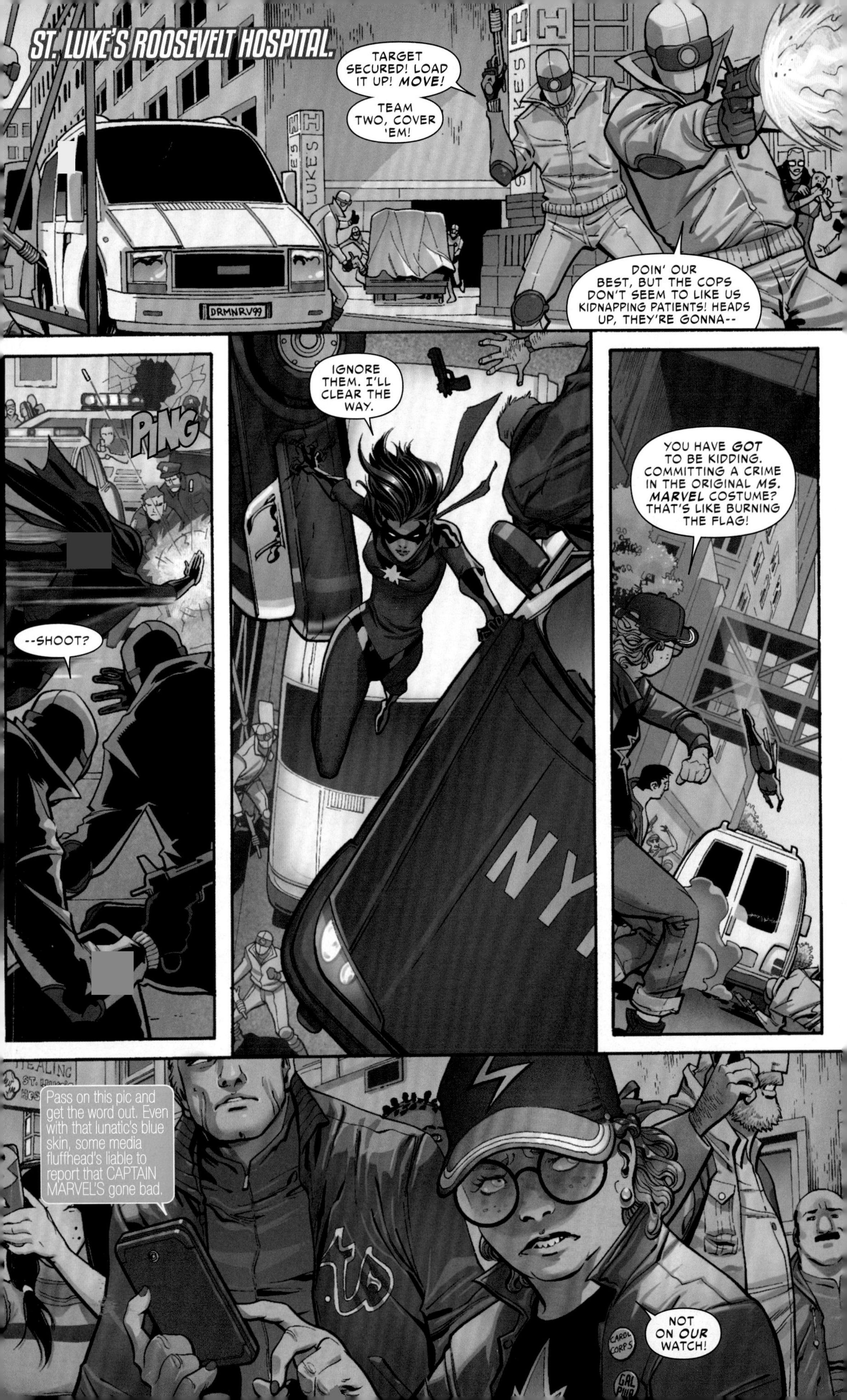

ST. LUKE'S ROOSEVELT HOSPITAL.
TARGET SECURED! LOAD IT UP! *MOVE!*
TEAM TWO, COVER 'EM!
DRMNRV99
DOIN' OUR BEST, BUT THE COPS DON'T SEEM TO LIKE US KIDNAPPING PATIENTS! HEADS UP, THEY'RE GONNA--
PING
--SHOOT?
IGNORE THEM. I'LL CLEAR THE WAY.
NY
YOU HAVE *GOT* TO BE KIDDING. COMMITTING A CRIME IN THE ORIGINAL *MS. MARVEL* COSTUME? THAT'S LIKE BURNING THE FLAG!
Pass on this pic and get the word out. Even with that lunatic's blue skin, some media fluffhead's liable to report that CAPTAIN MARVEL'S gone bad.
NOT ON *OUR* WATCH!
CAROL CORPS

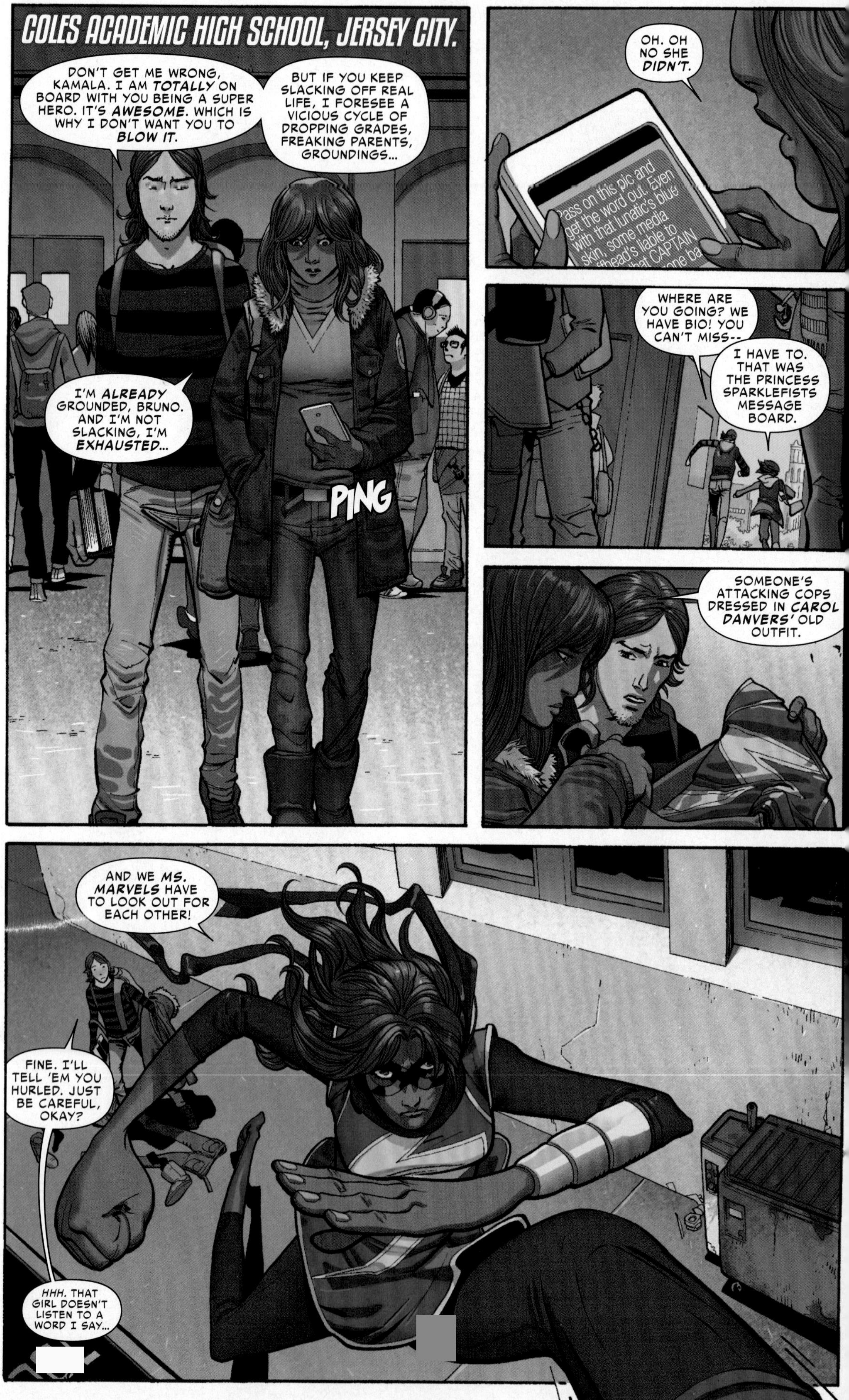
COLES ACADEMIC HIGH SCHOOL, JERSEY CITY.
DON'T GET ME WRONG, KAMALA. I AM TOTALLY ON BOARD WITH YOU BEING A SUPER HERO. IT'S AWESOME. WHICH IS WHY I DON'T WANT YOU TO BLOW IT.
BUT IF YOU KEEP SLACKING OFF REAL LIFE, I FORESEE A VICIOUS CYCLE OF DROPPING GRADES, FREAKING PARENTS, GROUNDINGS...
I'M ALREADY GROUNDED, BRUNO. AND I'M NOT SLACKING, I'M EXHAUSTED...
PING
OH. OH NO SHE DIDN'T.
Pass on this pic and get the word out. Even with that lunatic's blue skin, some media
WHERE ARE YOU GOING? WE HAVE BIO! YOU CAN'T MISS--
I HAVE TO. THAT WAS THE PRINCESS SPARKLEFISTS MESSAGE BOARD.
SOMEONE'S ATTACKING COPS DRESSED IN CAROL DANVERS' OLD OUTFIT.
AND WE MS. MARVELS HAVE TO LOOK OUT FOR EACH OTHER!
FINE. I'LL TELL 'EM YOU HURLED. JUST BE CAREFUL, OKAY?
HHH. THAT GIRL DOESN'T LISTEN TO A WORD I SAY...

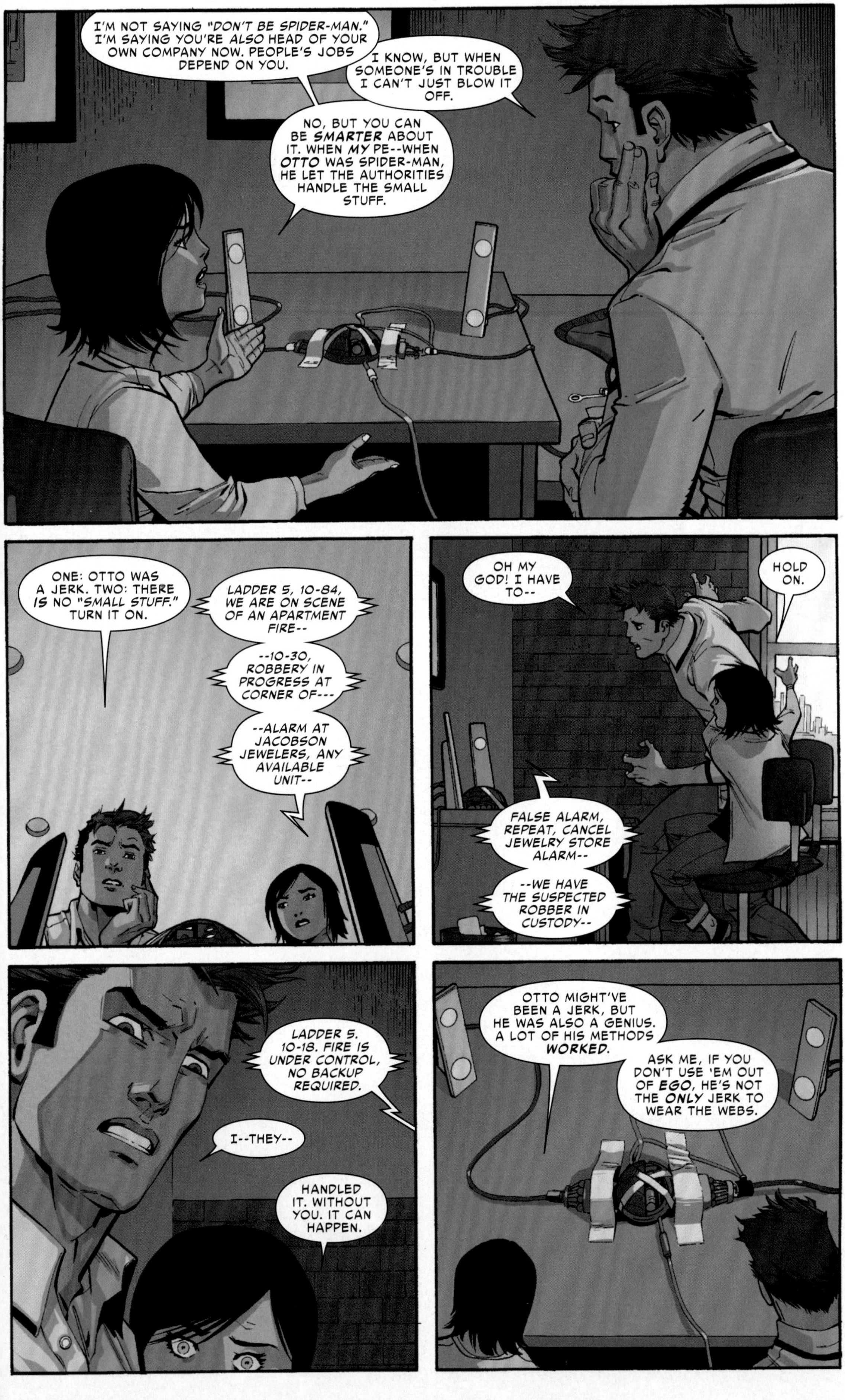
I'M NOT SAYING "DON'T BE SPIDER-MAN." I'M SAYING YOU'RE ALSO HEAD OF YOUR OWN COMPANY NOW. PEOPLE'S JOBS DEPEND ON YOU.
I KNOW, BUT WHEN SOMEONE'S IN TROUBLE I CAN'T JUST BLOW IT OFF.
NO, BUT YOU CAN BE SMARTER ABOUT IT. WHEN MY PE--WHEN OTTO WAS SPIDER-MAN, HE LET THE AUTHORITIES HANDLE THE SMALL STUFF.
ONE: OTTO WAS A JERK. TWO: THERE IS NO "SMALL STUFF." TURN IT ON.
LADDER 5, 10-84, WE ARE ON SCENE OF AN APARTMENT FIRE--
--10-30, ROBBERY IN PROGRESS AT CORNER OF---
--ALARM AT JACOBSON JEWELERS, ANY AVAILABLE UNIT--
OH MY GOD! I HAVE TO--
HOLD ON.
FALSE ALARM, REPEAT, CANCEL JEWELRY STORE ALARM--
--WE HAVE THE SUSPECTED ROBBER IN CUSTODY--
LADDER 5. 10-18. FIRE IS UNDER CONTROL, NO BACKUP REQUIRED.
I--THEY--
HANDLED IT. WITHOUT YOU. IT CAN HAPPEN.
OTTO MIGHT'VE BEEN A JERK, BUT HE WAS ALSO A GENIUS. A LOT OF HIS METHODS WORKED.
ASK ME, IF YOU DON'T USE 'EM OUT OF EGO, HE'S NOT THE ONLY JERK TO WEAR THE WEBS.

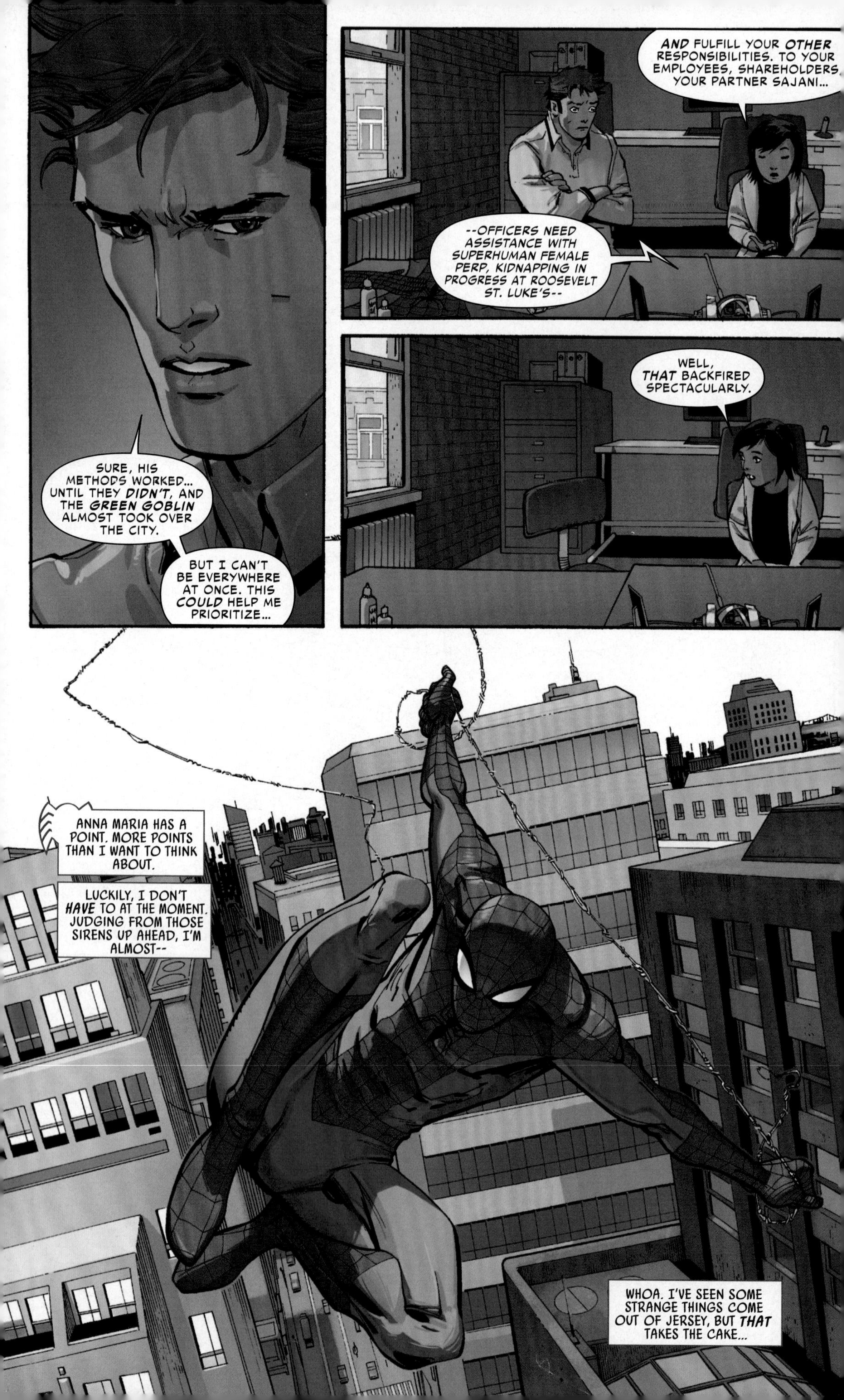
SURE, HIS METHODS WORKED... UNTIL THEY DIDN'T, AND THE GREEN GOBLIN ALMOST TOOK OVER THE CITY.
BUT I CAN'T BE EVERYWHERE AT ONCE. THIS COULD HELP ME PRIORITIZE...
AND FULFILL YOUR OTHER RESPONSIBILITIES. TO YOUR EMPLOYEES, SHAREHOLDERS, YOUR PARTNER SAJANI...
--OFFICERS NEED ASSISTANCE WITH SUPERHUMAN FEMALE PERP, KIDNAPPING IN PROGRESS AT ROOSEVELT ST. LUKE'S--
WELL, THAT BACKFIRED SPECTACULARLY.
ANNA MARIA HAS A POINT. MORE POINTS THAN I WANT TO THINK ABOUT.
LUCKILY, I DON'T HAVE TO AT THE MOMENT. JUDGING FROM THOSE SIRENS UP AHEAD, I'M ALMOST--
WHOA. I'VE SEEN SOME STRANGE THINGS COME OUT OF JERSEY, BUT THAT TAKES THE CAKE...

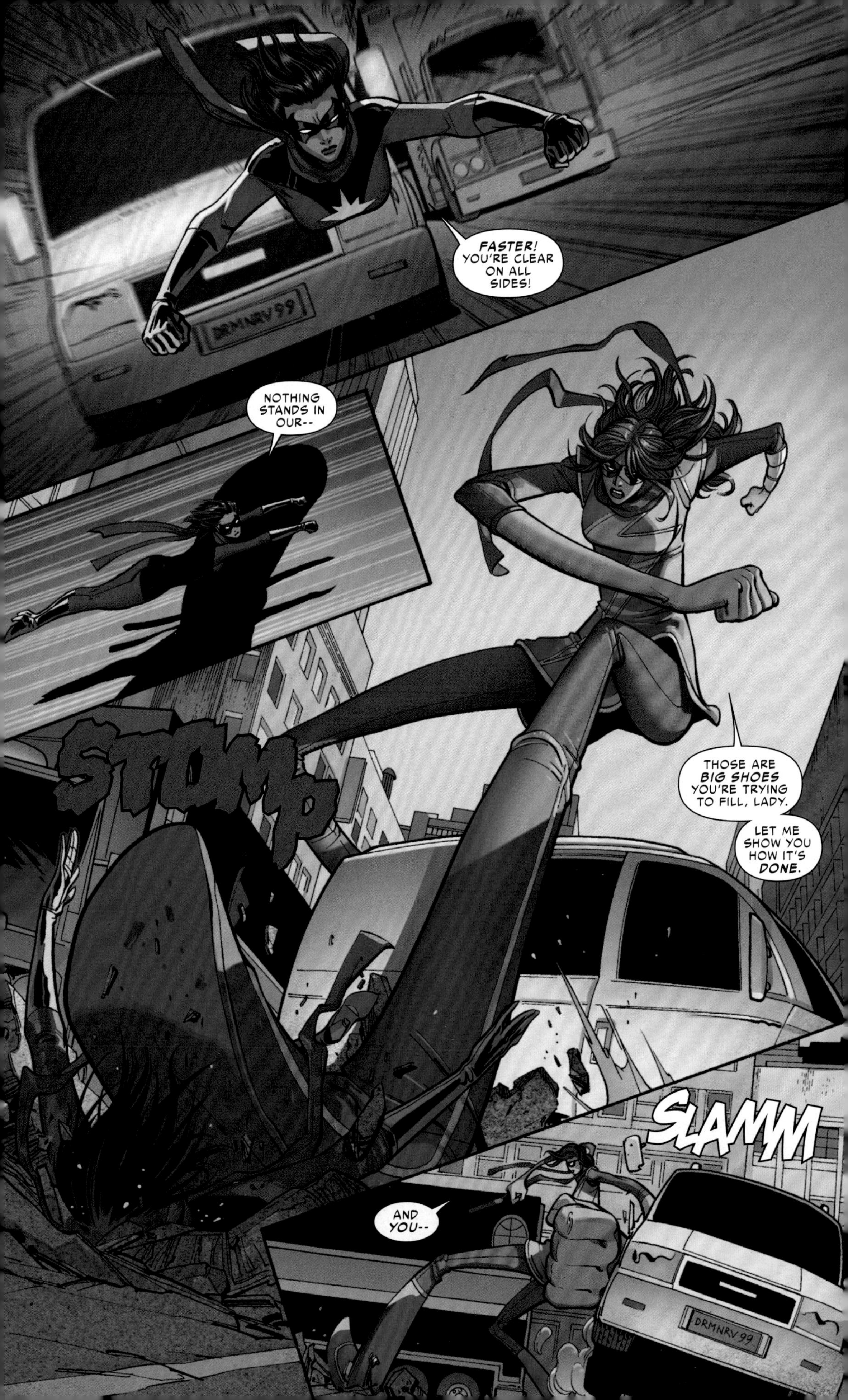
FASTER! YOU'RE CLEAR ON ALL SIDES!
NOTHING STANDS IN OUR--
STOMP
THOSE ARE BIG SHOES YOU'RE TRYING TO FILL, LADY.
LET ME SHOW YOU HOW IT'S DONE.
SLAMM
AND YOU--

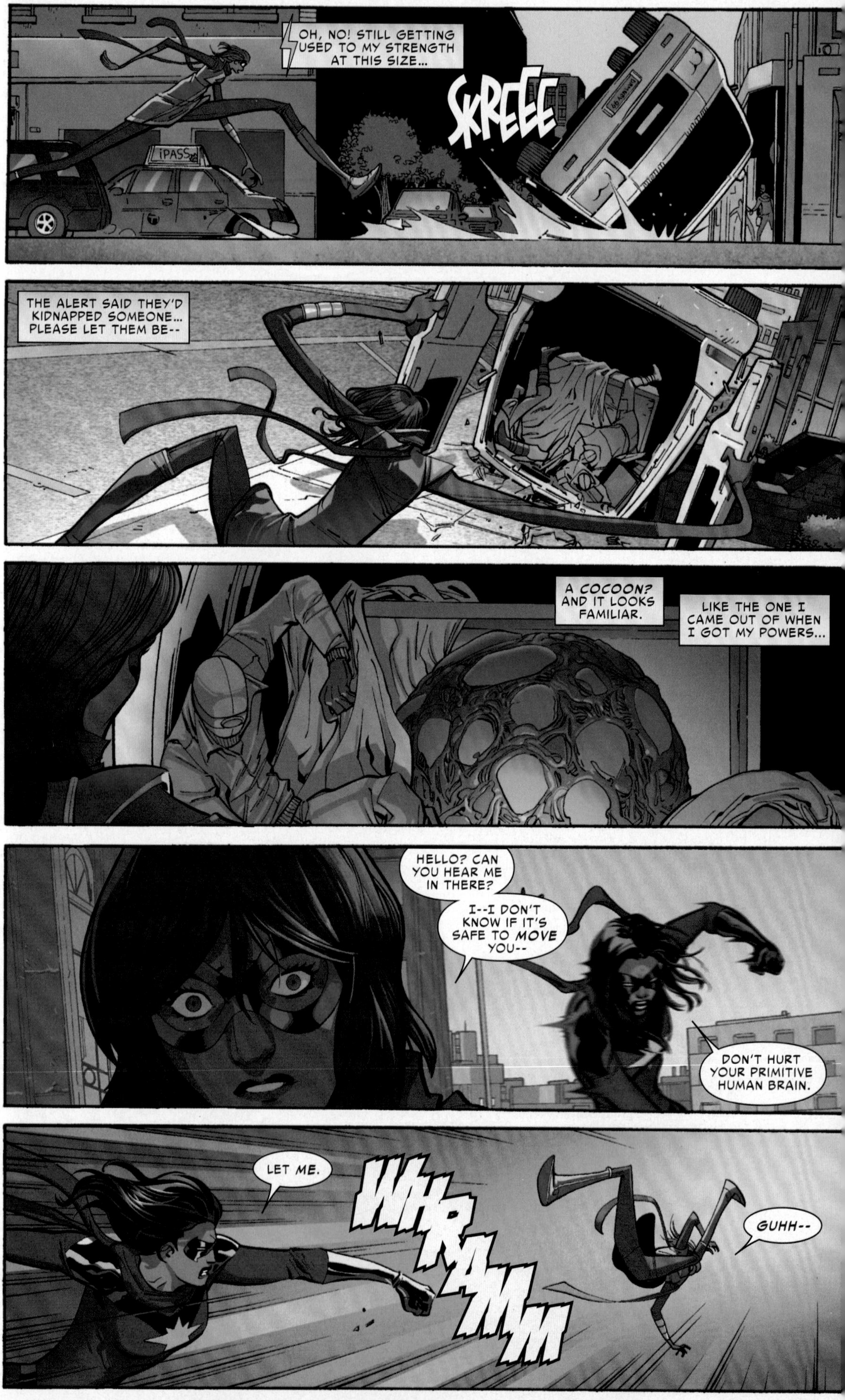

OH, NO! STILL GETTING USED TO MY STRENGTH AT THIS SIZE...
SKREEEE
THE ALERT SAID THEY'D KIDNAPPED SOMEONE... PLEASE LET THEM BE--
A COCOON? AND IT LOOKS FAMILIAR.
LIKE THE ONE I CAME OUT OF WHEN I GOT MY POWERS...
HELLO? CAN YOU HEAR ME IN THERE?
I--I DON'T KNOW IF IT'S SAFE TO MOVE YOU--
DON'T HURT YOUR PRIMITIVE HUMAN BRAIN.
LET ME.
WHRAMMM
GUHH--

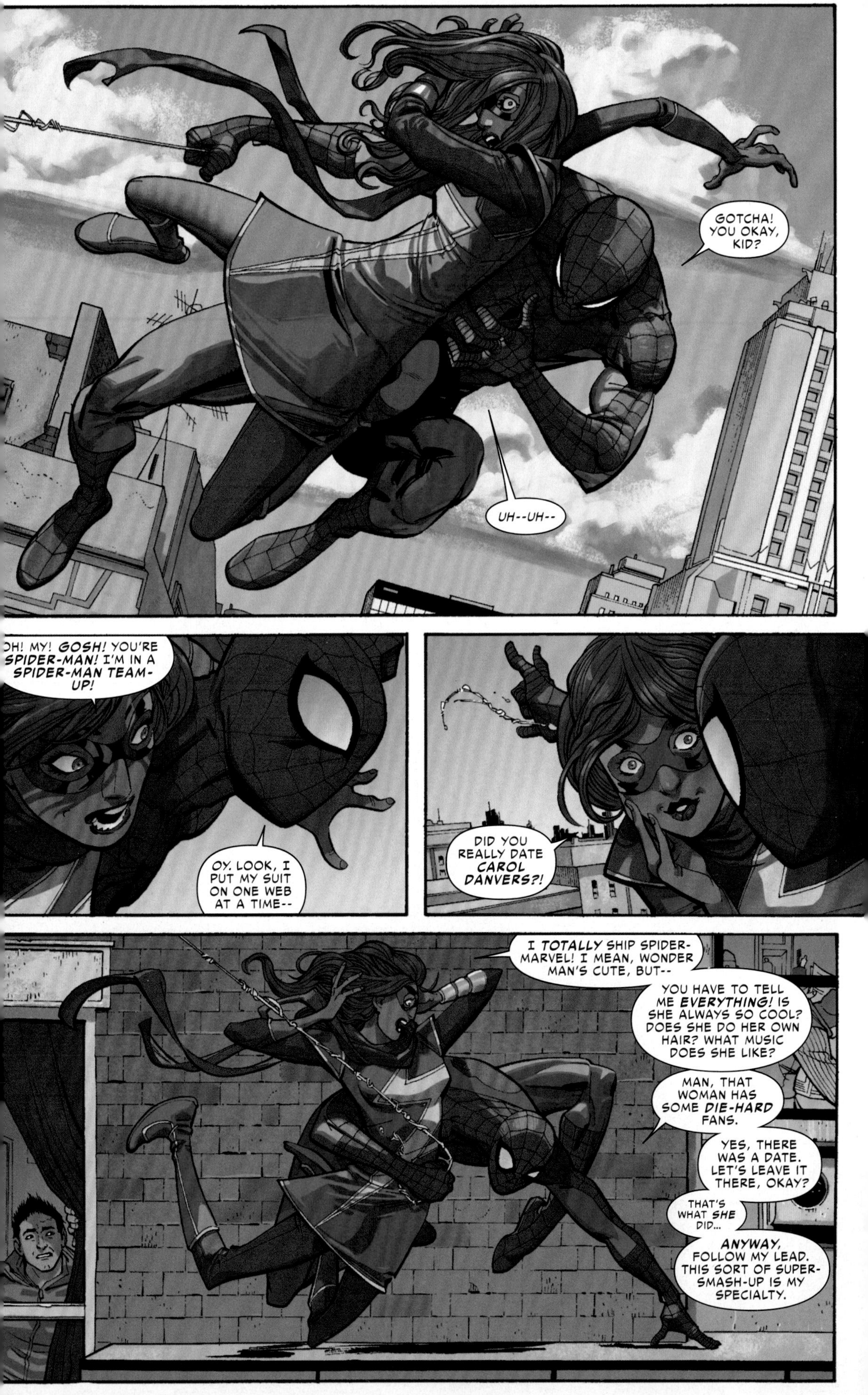
GOTCHA! YOU OKAY, KID?
UH--UH--
OH! MY! GOSH! YOU'RE SPIDER-MAN! I'M IN A SPIDER-MAN TEAM-UP!
OY. LOOK, I PUT MY SUIT ON ONE WEB AT A TIME--
DID YOU REALLY DATE CAROL DANVERS?!
I TOTALLY SHIP SPIDER-MARVEL! I MEAN, WONDER MAN'S CUTE, BUT--
YOU HAVE TO TELL ME EVERYTHING! IS SHE ALWAYS SO COOL? DOES SHE DO HER OWN HAIR? WHAT MUSIC DOES SHE LIKE?
MAN, THAT WOMAN HAS SOME DIE-HARD FANS.
YES, THERE WAS A DATE. LET'S LEAVE IT THERE, OKAY?
THAT'S WHAT SHE DID...
ANYWAY, FOLLOW MY LEAD. THIS SORT OF SUPER-SMASH-UP IS MY SPECIALTY.

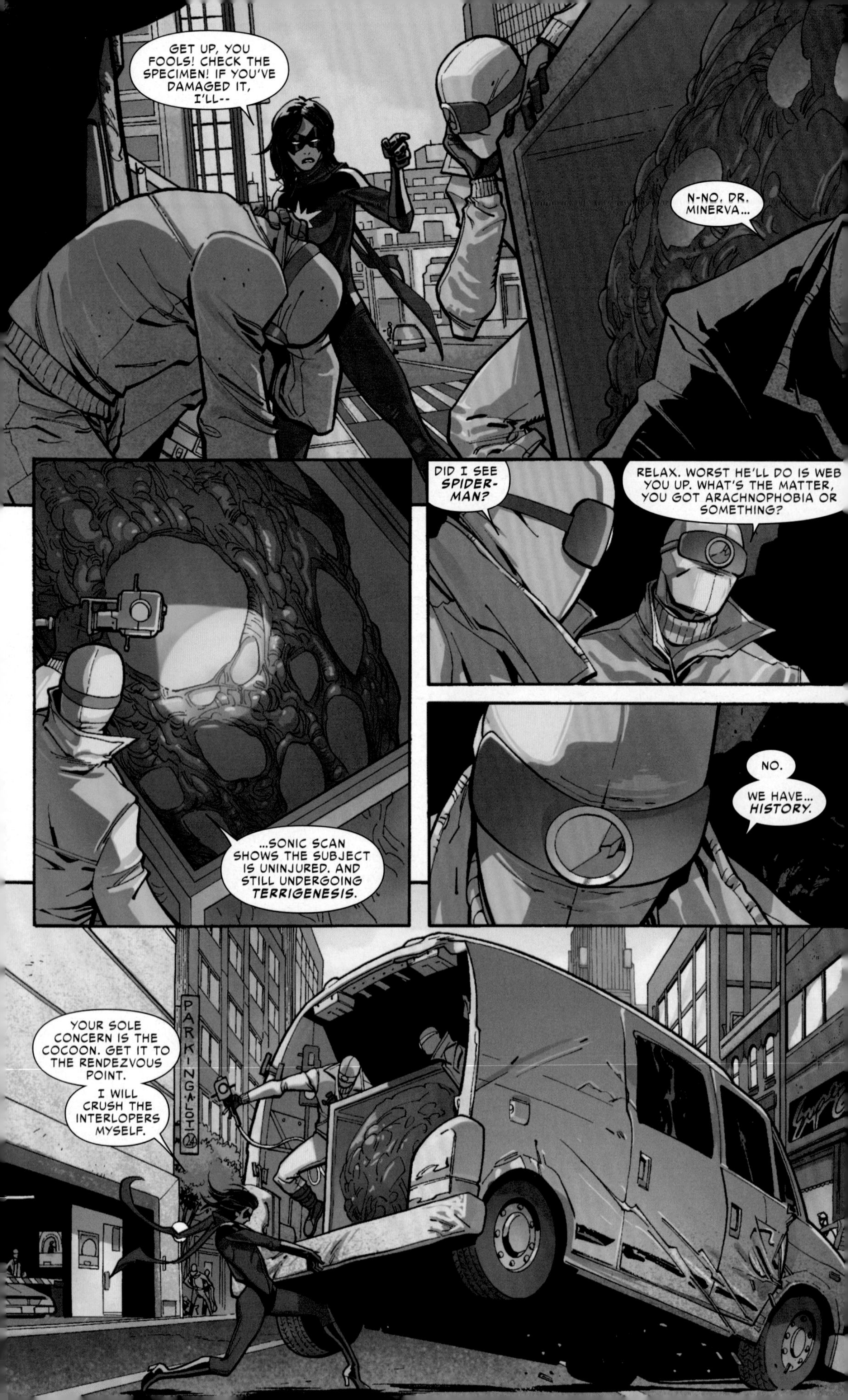
GET UP, YOU FOOLS! CHECK THE SPECIMEN! IF YOU'VE DAMAGED IT, I'LL--
N-NO, DR. MINERVA...
...SONIC SCAN SHOWS THE SUBJECT IS UNINJURED. AND STILL UNDERGOING *TERRIGENESIS*.
DID I SEE *SPIDER-MAN?*
RELAX. WORST HE'LL DO IS WEB YOU UP. WHAT'S THE MATTER, YOU GOT ARACHNOPHOBIA OR SOMETHING?
NO.
WE HAVE... *HISTORY.*
PARKING-A-LOT 24
YOUR SOLE CONCERN IS THE COCOON. GET IT TO THE RENDEZVOUS POINT.
I WILL CRUSH THE INTERLOPERS MYSELF.

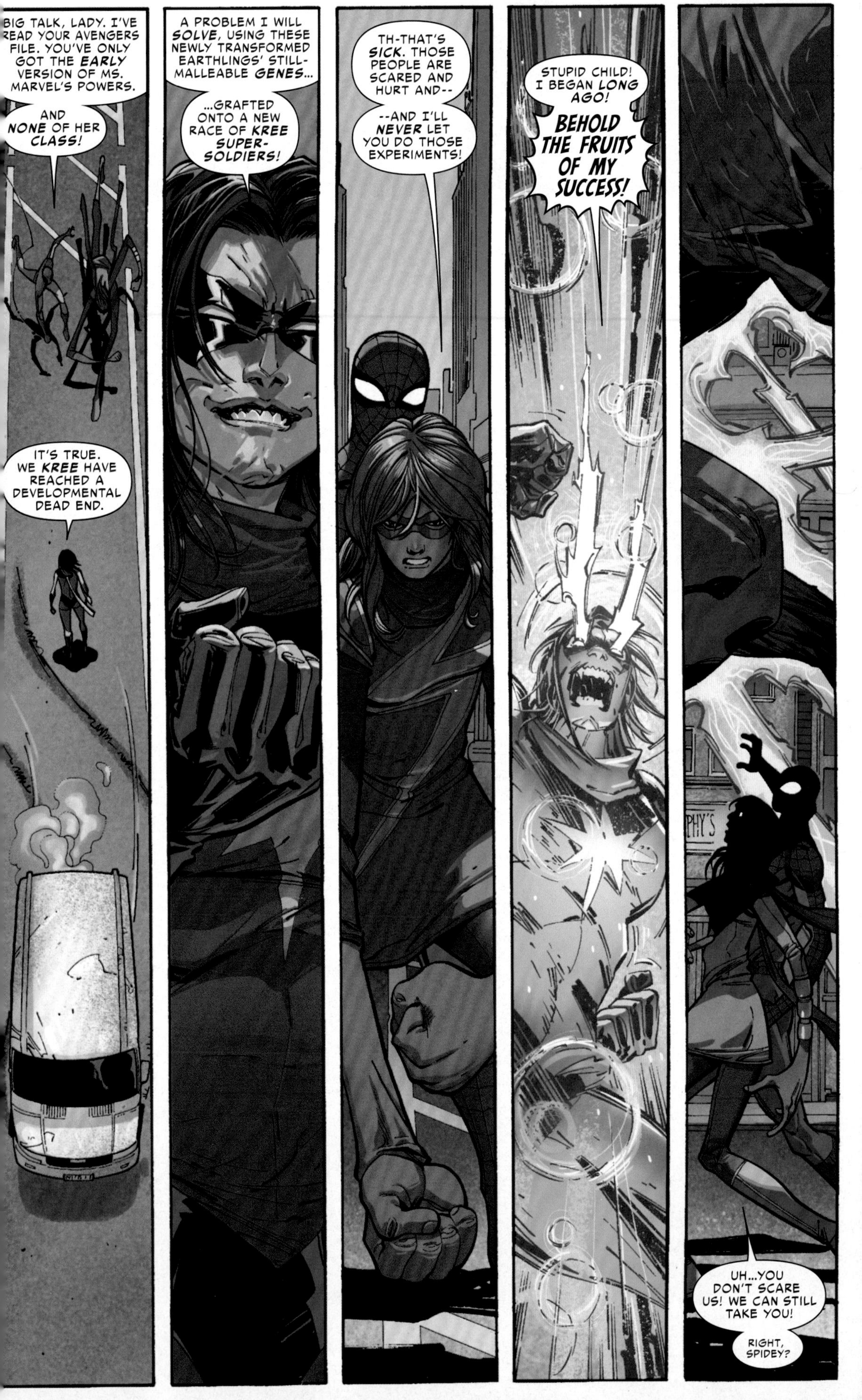
BIG TALK, LADY. I'VE READ YOUR AVENGERS FILE. YOU'VE ONLY GOT THE EARLY VERSION OF MS. MARVEL'S POWERS.
AND NONE OF HER CLASS!
IT'S TRUE. WE KREE HAVE REACHED A DEVELOPMENTAL DEAD END.
A PROBLEM I WILL SOLVE, USING THESE NEWLY TRANSFORMED EARTHLINGS' STILL-MALLEABLE GENES...
...GRAFTED ONTO A NEW RACE OF KREE SUPER-SOLDIERS!
TH-THAT'S SICK. THOSE PEOPLE ARE SCARED AND HURT AND--
--AND I'LL NEVER LET YOU DO THOSE EXPERIMENTS!
STUPID CHILD! I BEGAN LONG AGO!
BEHOLD THE FRUITS OF MY SUCCESS!
UH...YOU DON'T SCARE US! WE CAN STILL TAKE YOU!
RIGHT, SPIDEY?

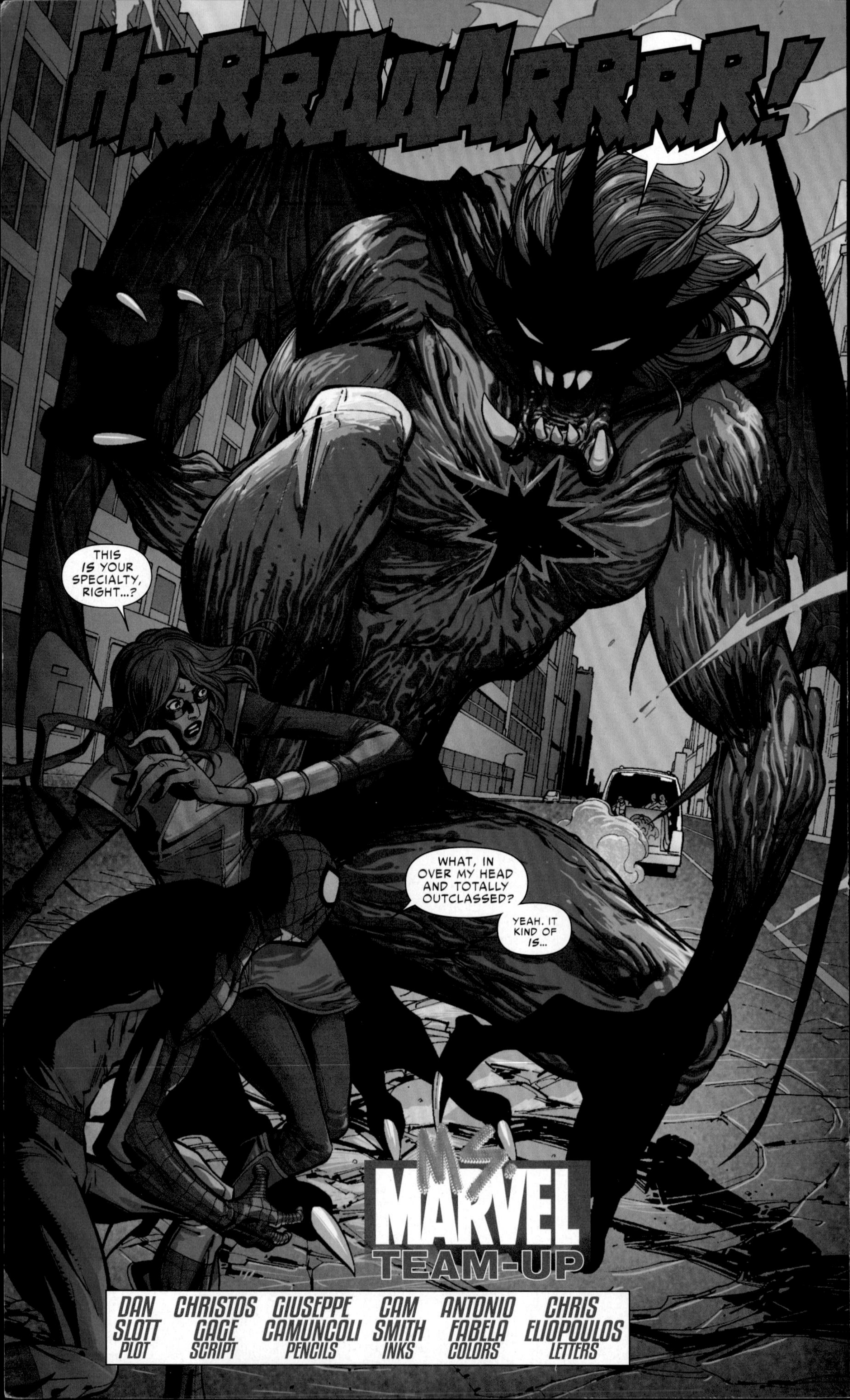
HRRRAAARRRR!
THIS IS YOUR SPECIALTY, RIGHT...?
WHAT, IN OVER MY HEAD AND TOTALLY OUTCLASSED?
YEAH. IT KIND OF IS...
MS. MARVEL TEAM-UP
DAN SLOTT PLOT
CHRISTOS GAGE SCRIPT
GIUSEPPE CAMUNCOLI PENCILS
CAM SMITH INKS
ANTONIO FABELA COLORS
CHRIS ELIOPOULOS LETTERS

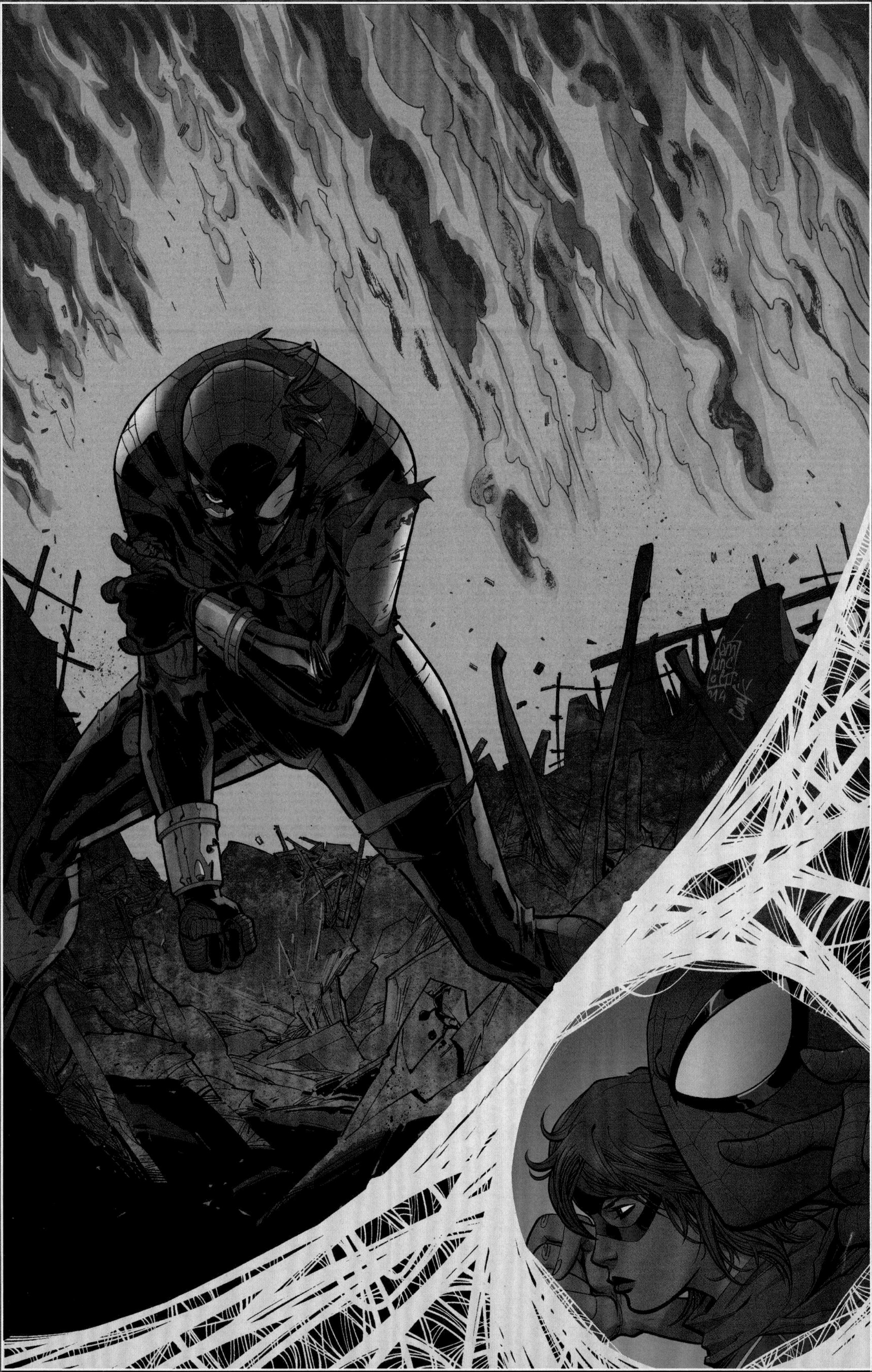

AMAZING SPIDER-MAN #8

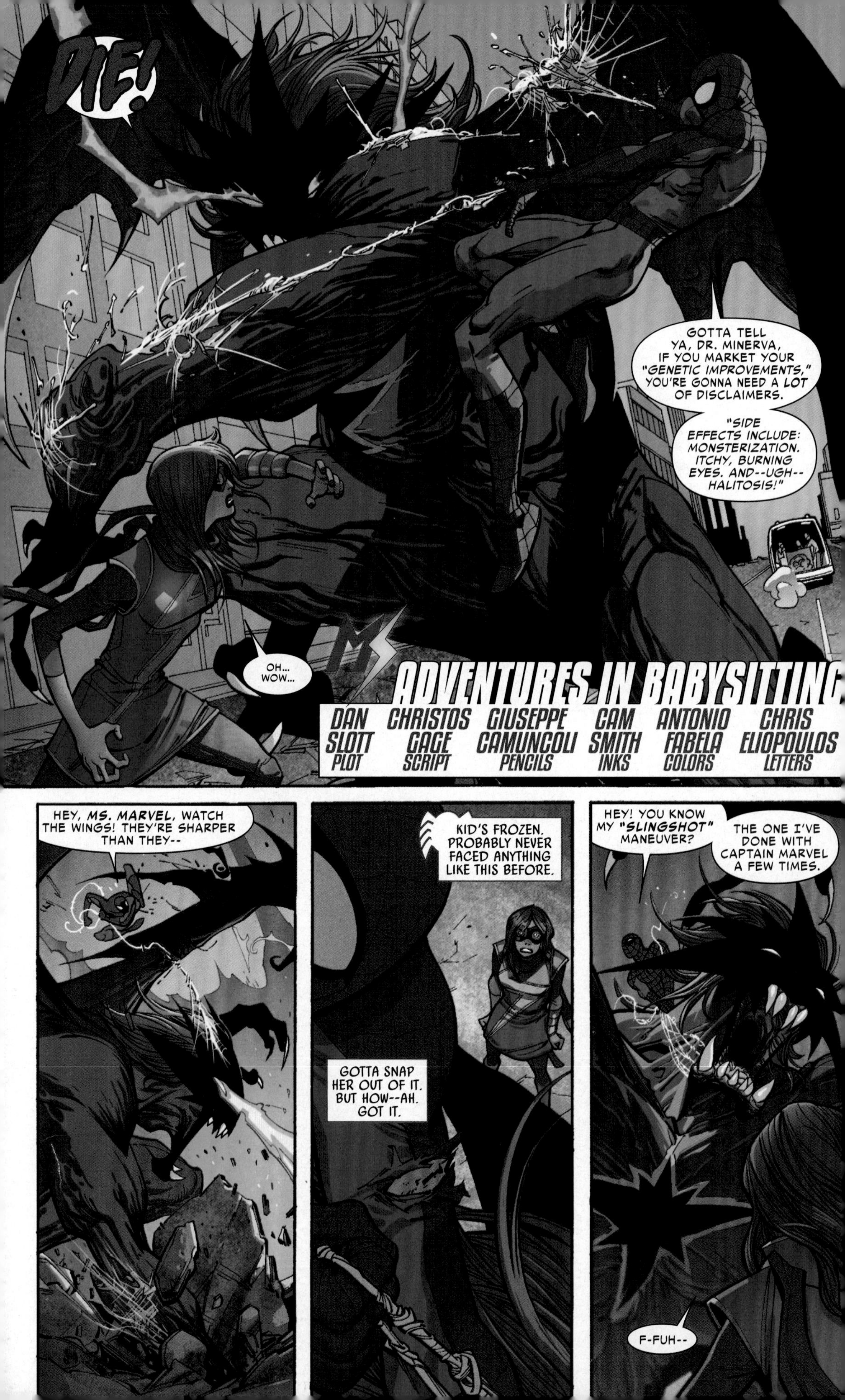

DIE!
GOTTA TELL YA, DR. MINERVA, IF YOU MARKET YOUR "GENETIC IMPROVEMENTS," YOU'RE GONNA NEED A LOT OF DISCLAIMERS.
"SIDE EFFECTS INCLUDE: MONSTERIZATION. ITCHY, BURNING EYES. AND--UGH--HALITOSIS!"
OH... WOW...
ADVENTURES IN BABYSITTING
DAN SLOTT PLOT
CHRISTOS GAGE SCRIPT
GIUSEPPE CAMUNCOLI PENCILS
CAM SMITH INKS
ANTONIO FABELA COLORS
CHRIS ELIOPOULOS LETTERS
HEY, MS. MARVEL, WATCH THE WINGS! THEY'RE SHARPER THAN THEY--
KID'S FROZEN. PROBABLY NEVER FACED ANYTHING LIKE THIS BEFORE.
GOTTA SNAP HER OUT OF IT. BUT HOW--AH. GOT IT.
HEY! YOU KNOW MY "SLINGSHOT" MANEUVER?
THE ONE I'VE DONE WITH CAPTAIN MARVEL A FEW TIMES.
F-FUH--

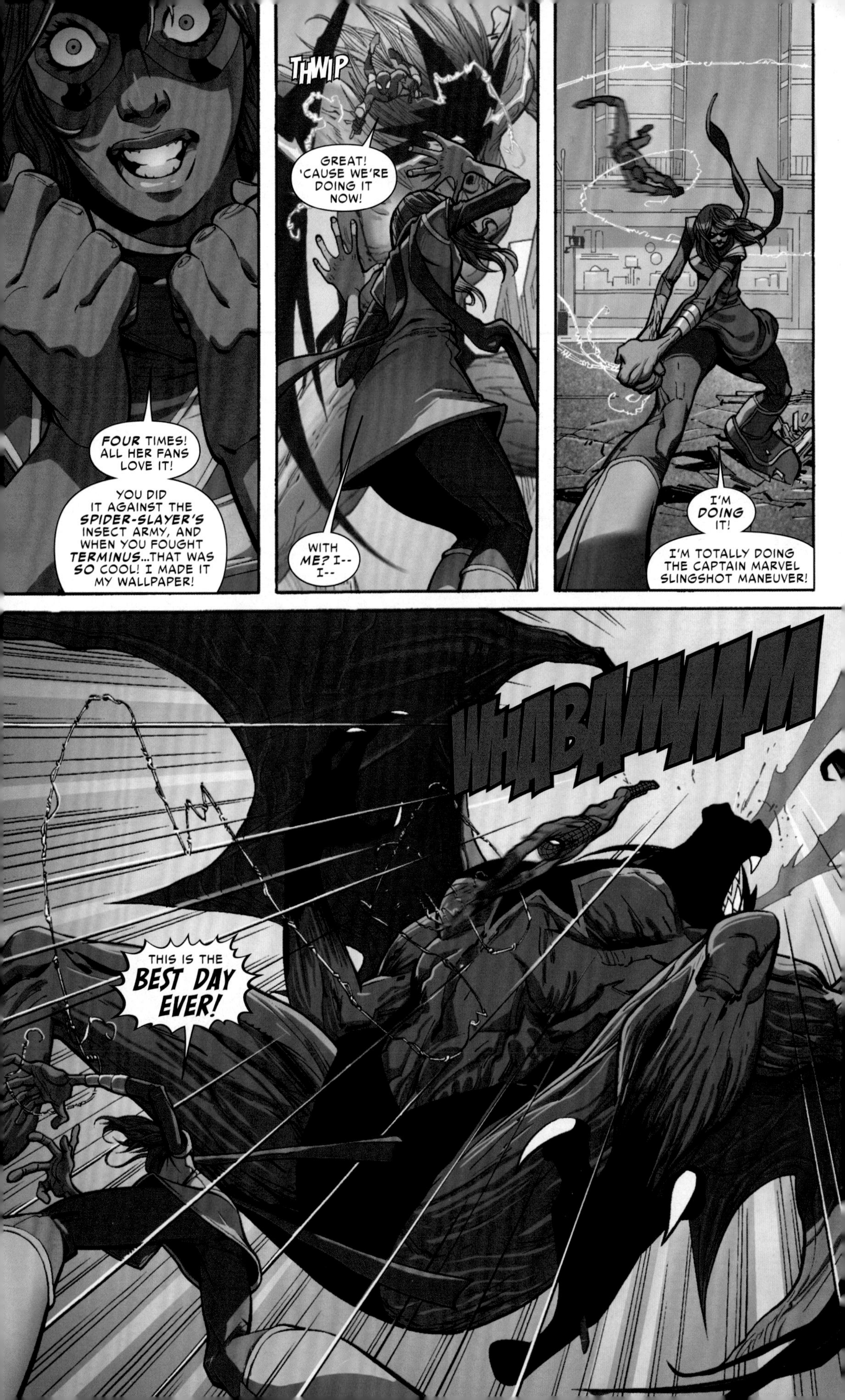
FOUR TIMES! ALL HER FANS LOVE IT!
YOU DID IT AGAINST THE SPIDER-SLAYER'S INSECT ARMY, AND WHEN YOU FOUGHT TERMINUS...THAT WAS SO COOL! I MADE IT MY WALLPAPER!
THWIP
GREAT! 'CAUSE WE'RE DOING IT NOW!
WITH ME? I-- I--
I'M DOING IT!
I'M TOTALLY DOING THE CAPTAIN MARVEL SLINGSHOT MANEUVER!
WHABAMMM
THIS IS THE BEST DAY EVER!

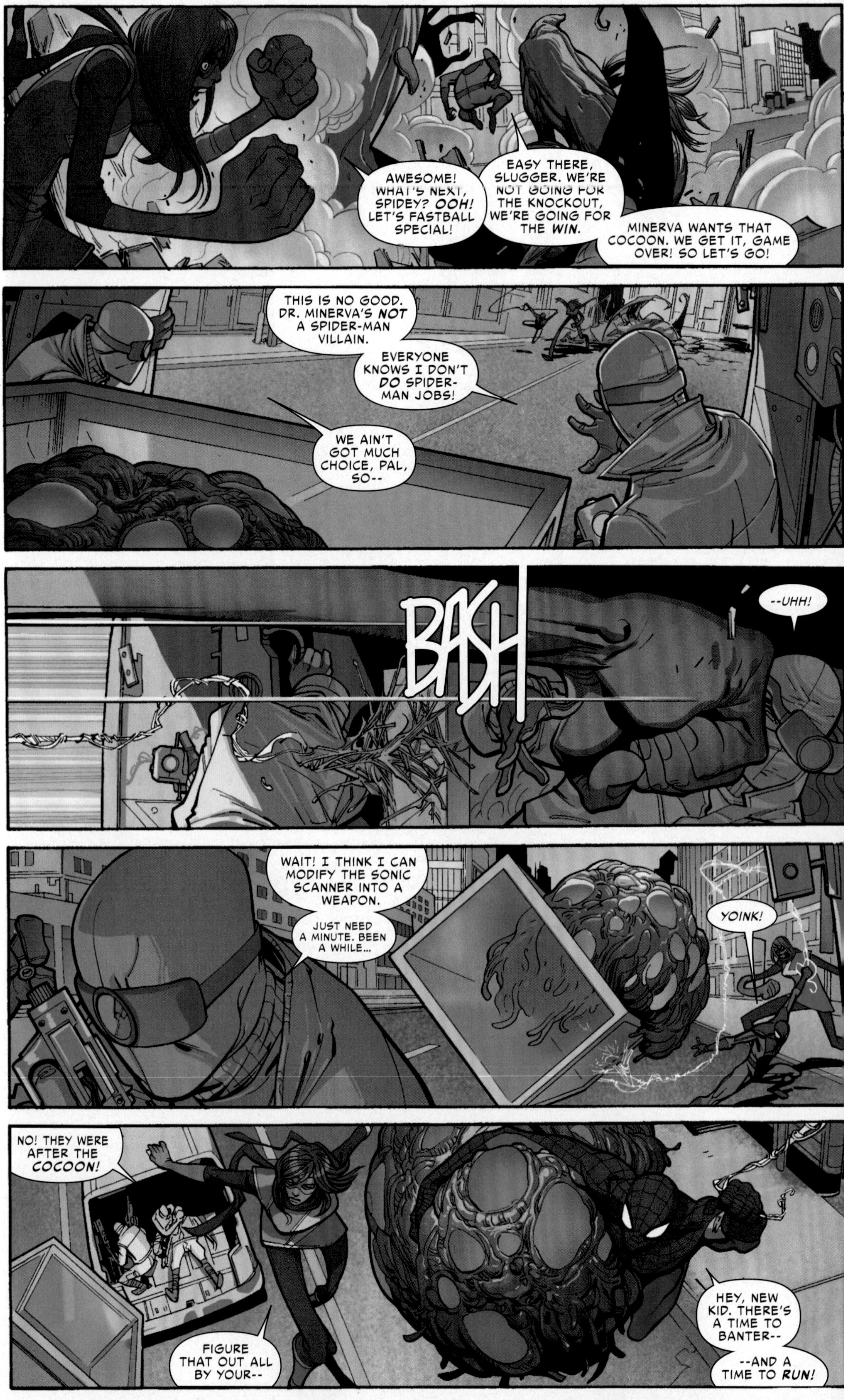
AWESOME! WHAT'S NEXT, SPIDEY? OOH! LET'S FASTBALL SPECIAL!
EASY THERE, SLUGGER. WE'RE NOT GOING FOR THE KNOCKOUT, WE'RE GOING FOR THE WIN.
MINERVA WANTS THAT COCOON. WE GET IT, GAME OVER! SO LET'S GO!
THIS IS NO GOOD. DR. MINERVA'S NOT A SPIDER-MAN VILLAIN.
EVERYONE KNOWS I DON'T DO SPIDER-MAN JOBS!
WE AIN'T GOT MUCH CHOICE, PAL, SO--
BASH
--UHH!
WAIT! I THINK I CAN MODIFY THE SONIC SCANNER INTO A WEAPON.
JUST NEED A MINUTE. BEEN A WHILE...
YOINK!
NO! THEY WERE AFTER THE COCOON!
FIGURE THAT OUT ALL BY YOUR--
HEY, NEW KID. THERE'S A TIME TO BANTER--
--AND A TIME TO RUN!

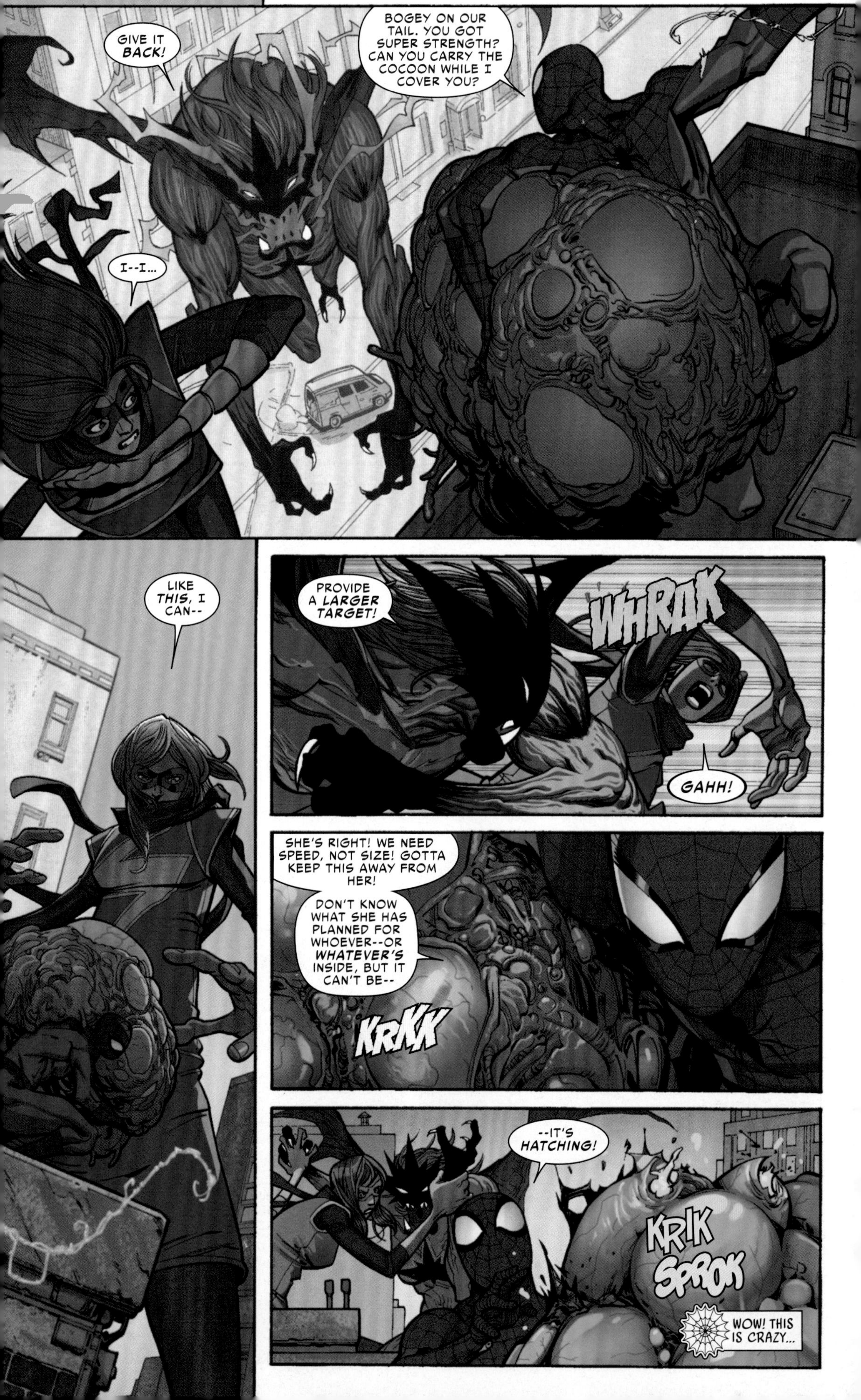
GIVE IT BACK!
BOGEY ON OUR TAIL. YOU GOT SUPER STRENGTH? CAN YOU CARRY THE COCOON WHILE I COVER YOU?
I--I...
LIKE THIS, I CAN--
PROVIDE A LARGER TARGET!
WHRAK
GAHH!
SHE'S RIGHT! WE NEED SPEED, NOT SIZE! GOTTA KEEP THIS AWAY FROM HER!
DON'T KNOW WHAT SHE HAS PLANNED FOR WHOEVER--OR WHATEVER'S INSIDE, BUT IT CAN'T BE--
KRKK
--IT'S HATCHING!
KRIK
SPROK
WOW! THIS IS CRAZY...

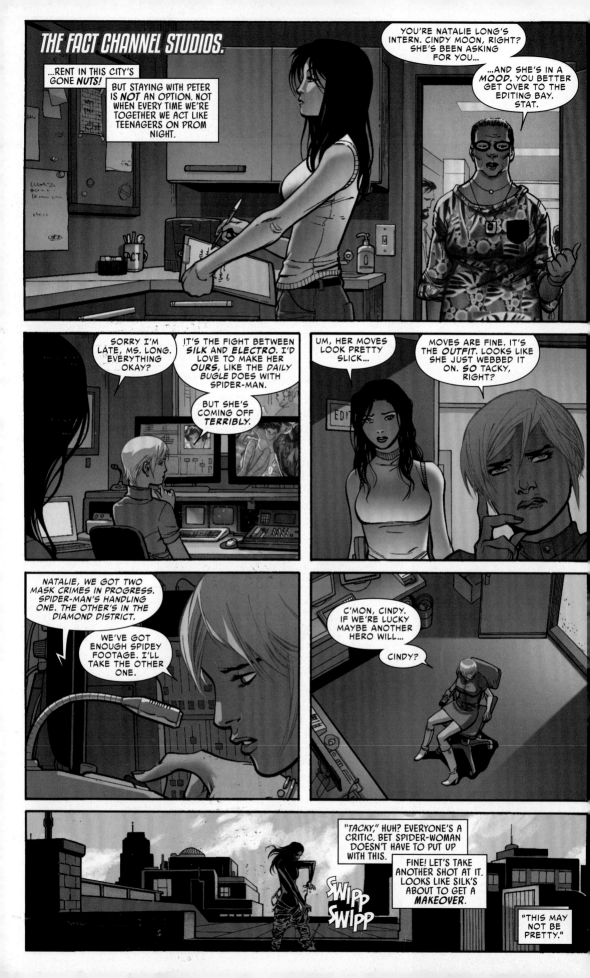

THE FACT CHANNEL STUDIOS.

...RENT IN THIS CITY'S GONE *NUTS!*

BUT STAYING WITH PETER IS *NOT* AN OPTION. NOT WHEN EVERY TIME WE'RE TOGETHER WE ACT LIKE TEENAGERS ON PROM NIGHT.

YOU'RE NATALIE LONG'S INTERN. CINDY MOON, RIGHT? SHE'S BEEN ASKING FOR YOU...

...AND SHE'S IN A *MOOD.* YOU BETTER GET OVER TO THE EDITING BAY. STAT.

SORRY I'M LATE, MS. LONG. EVERYTHING OKAY?

IT'S THE FIGHT BETWEEN *SILK* AND *ELECTRO.* I'D LOVE TO MAKE HER *OURS,* LIKE THE *DAILY BUGLE* DOES WITH SPIDER-MAN.

BUT SHE'S COMING OFF *TERRIBLY.*

UM, HER MOVES LOOK PRETTY SLICK...

MOVES ARE FINE. IT'S THE *OUTFIT.* LOOKS LIKE SHE JUST WEBBED IT ON. SO TACKY, RIGHT?

NATALIE, WE GOT TWO MASK CRIMES IN PROGRESS. SPIDER-MAN'S HANDLING ONE. THE OTHER'S IN THE DIAMOND DISTRICT.

WE'VE GOT ENOUGH SPIDEY FOOTAGE. I'LL TAKE THE OTHER ONE.

C'MON, CINDY. IF WE'RE LUCKY MAYBE ANOTHER HERO WILL...

CINDY?

"TACKY," HUH? EVERYONE'S A CRITIC. BET SPIDER-WOMAN DOESN'T HAVE TO PUT UP WITH THIS.

FINE! LET'S TAKE ANOTHER SHOT AT IT. LOOKS LIKE SILK'S ABOUT TO GET A *MAKEOVER.*

"THIS MAY NOT BE PRETTY."

SWIPP SWIPP

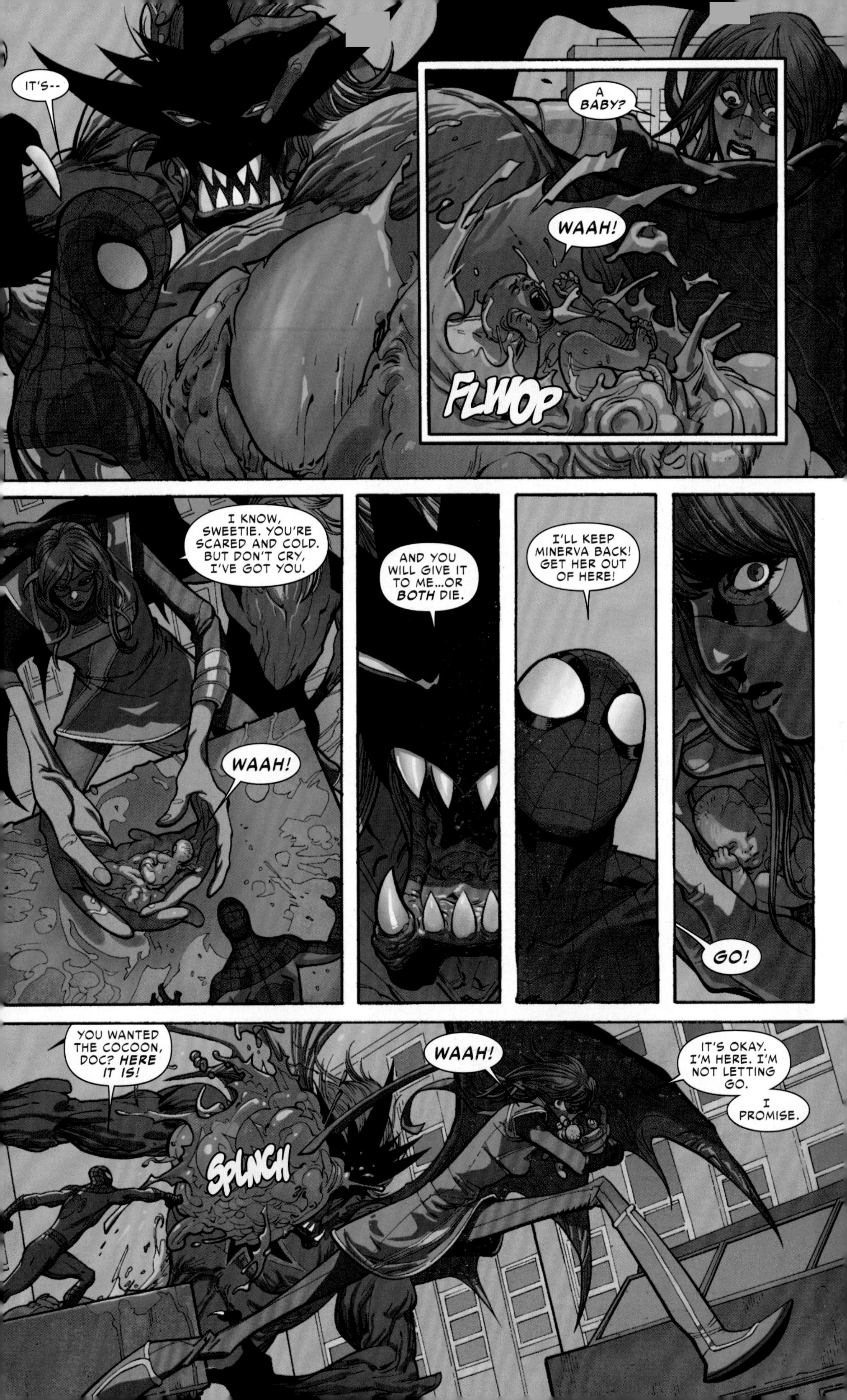
IT'S--
A BABY?
WAAH!
FLWOP
I KNOW, SWEETIE. YOU'RE SCARED AND COLD. BUT DON'T CRY, I'VE GOT YOU.
WAAH!
AND YOU WILL GIVE IT TO ME...OR BOTH DIE.
I'LL KEEP MINERVA BACK! GET HER OUT OF HERE!
GO!
YOU WANTED THE COCOON, DOC? HERE IT IS!
SPLNCH
WAAH!
IT'S OKAY. I'M HERE. I'M NOT LETTING GO.
I PROMISE.

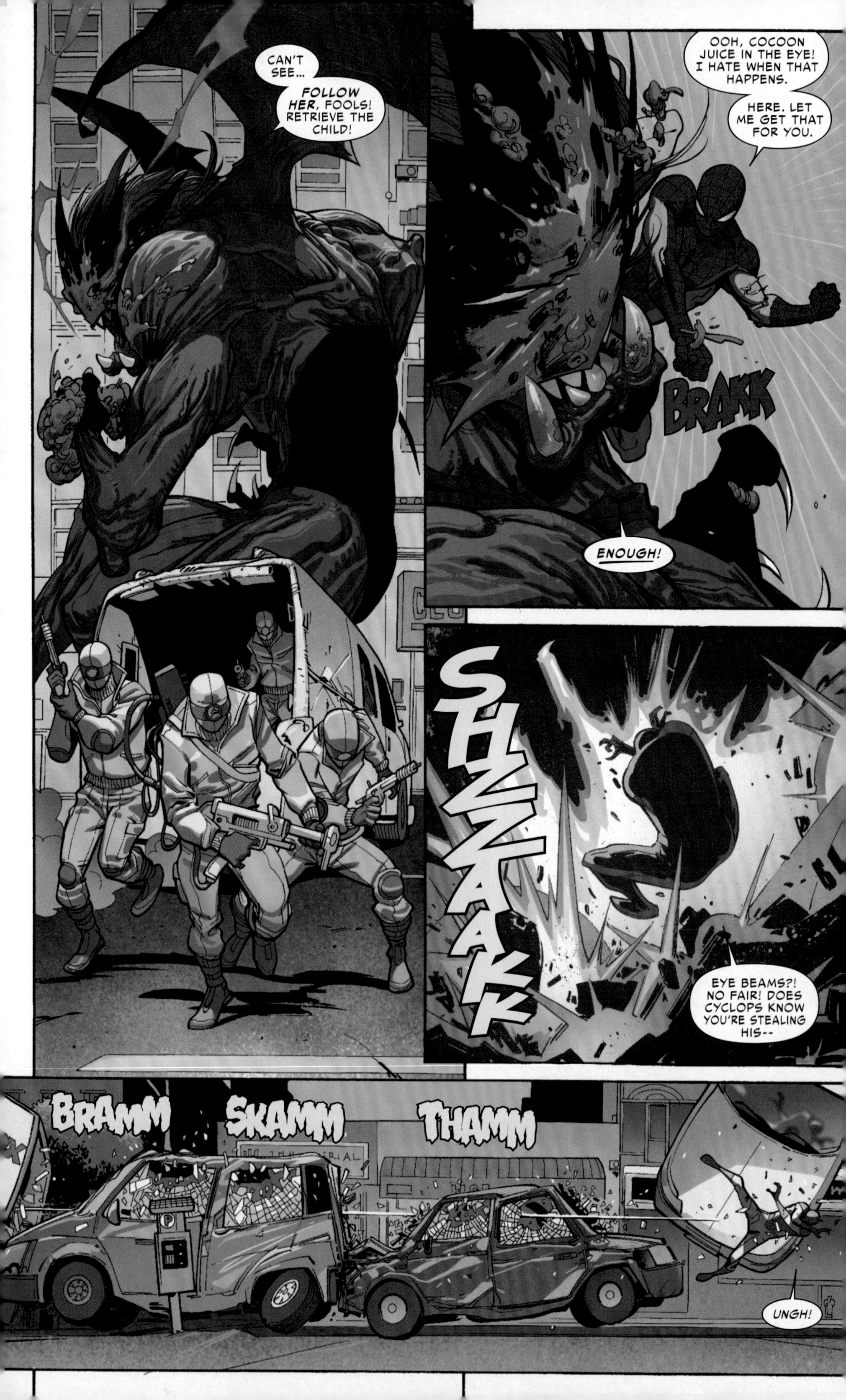

CAN'T SEE... FOLLOW HER, FOOLS! RETRIEVE THE CHILD!
OOH, COCOON JUICE IN THE EYE! I HATE WHEN THAT HAPPENS.
HERE. LET ME GET THAT FOR YOU.
BRAKK
ENOUGH!
SHZZAKK
EYE BEAMS?! NO FAIR! DOES CYCLOPS KNOW YOU'RE STEALING HIS--
BRAMM
SKAMM
THAMM
UNGH!

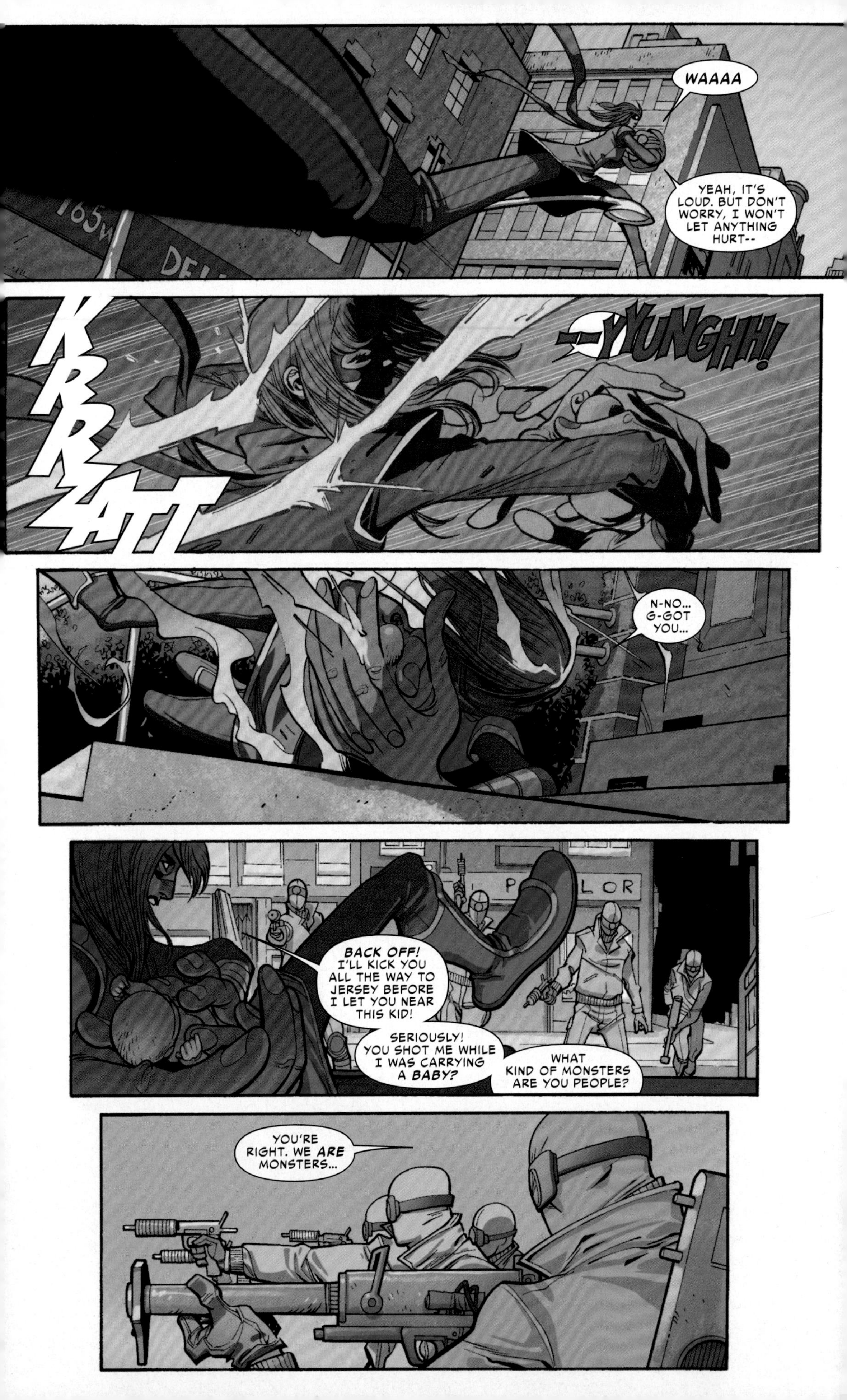
WAAAA
YEAH, IT'S LOUD. BUT DON'T WORRY, I WON'T LET ANYTHING HURT--
KRRZATT
--YYUNGHH!
N-NO... G-GOT YOU...
BACK OFF! I'LL KICK YOU ALL THE WAY TO JERSEY BEFORE I LET YOU NEAR THIS KID!
SERIOUSLY! YOU SHOT ME WHILE I WAS CARRYING A BABY?
WHAT KIND OF MONSTERS ARE YOU PEOPLE?
YOU'RE RIGHT. WE ARE MONSTERS...

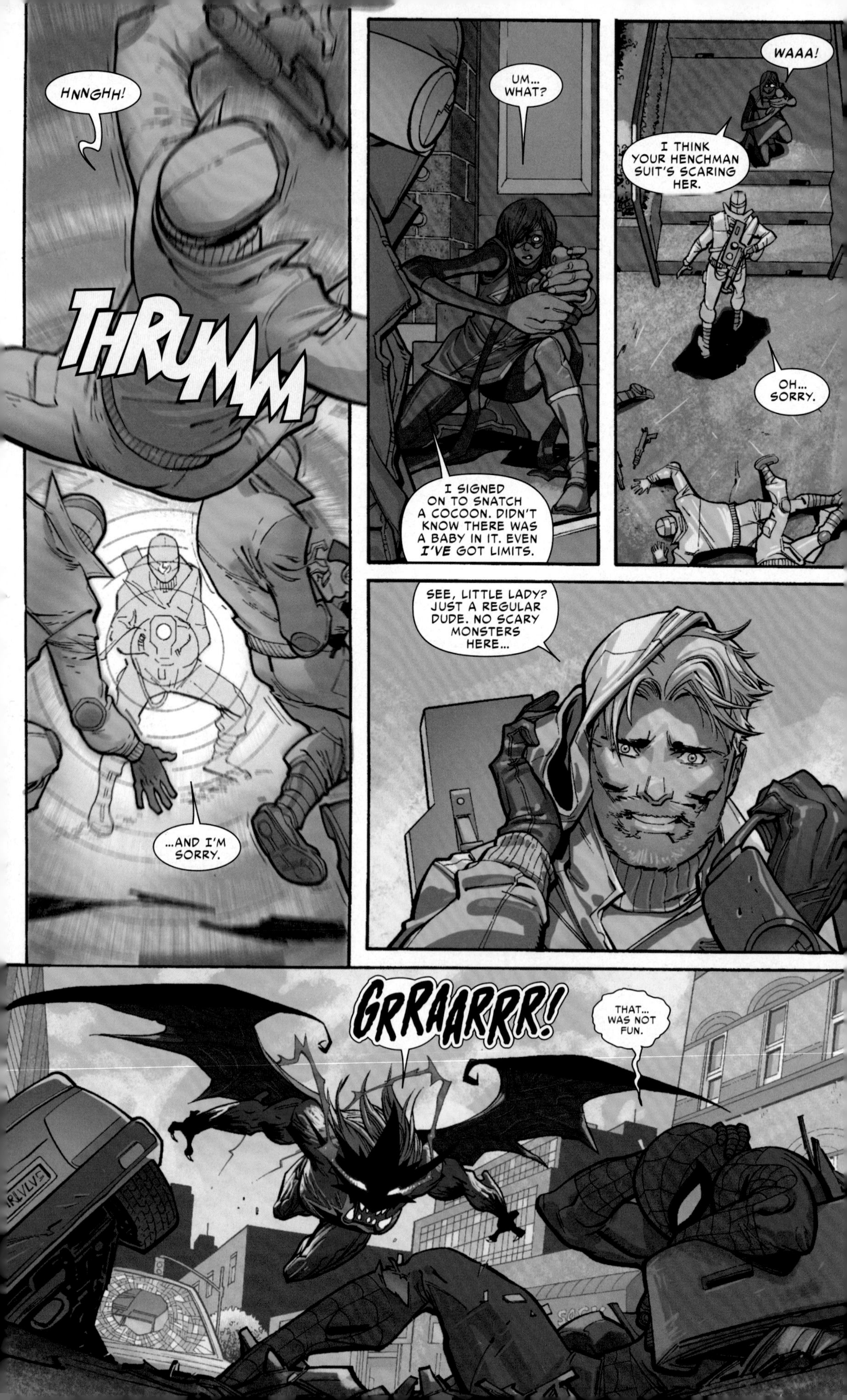
HNNGHH!
THRUMM
...AND I'M SORRY.
UM... WHAT?
I SIGNED ON TO SNATCH A COCOON. DIDN'T KNOW THERE WAS A BABY IN IT. EVEN I'VE GOT LIMITS.
WAAA!
I THINK YOUR HENCHMAN SUIT'S SCARING HER.
OH... SORRY.
SEE, LITTLE LADY? JUST A REGULAR DUDE. NO SCARY MONSTERS HERE...
GRRAARRR!
THAT... WAS NOT FUN.

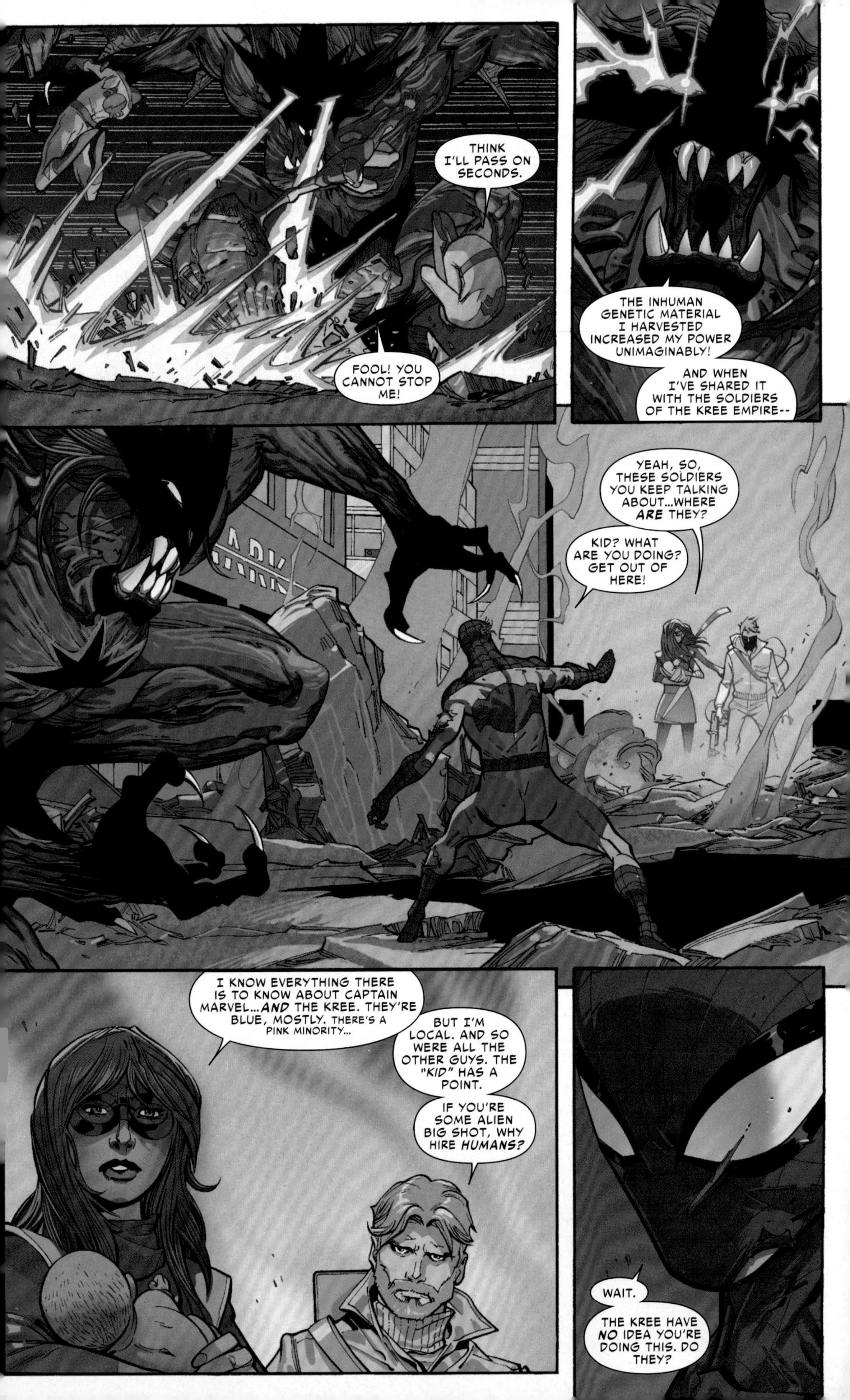
THINK I'LL PASS ON SECONDS.
FOOL! YOU CANNOT STOP ME!
THE INHUMAN GENETIC MATERIAL I HARVESTED INCREASED MY POWER UNIMAGINABLY!
AND WHEN I'VE SHARED IT WITH THE SOLDIERS OF THE KREE EMPIRE--
YEAH, SO, THESE SOLDIERS YOU KEEP TALKING ABOUT...WHERE *ARE* THEY?
KID? WHAT ARE YOU DOING? GET OUT OF HERE!
I KNOW EVERYTHING THERE IS TO KNOW ABOUT CAPTAIN MARVEL...*AND* THE KREE. THEY'RE BLUE, MOSTLY. THERE'S A PINK MINORITY...
BUT I'M LOCAL. AND SO WERE ALL THE OTHER GUYS. THE "*KID*" HAS A POINT.
IF YOU'RE SOME ALIEN BIG SHOT, WHY HIRE *HUMANS?*
WAIT.
THE KREE HAVE *NO* IDEA YOU'RE DOING THIS. DO THEY?

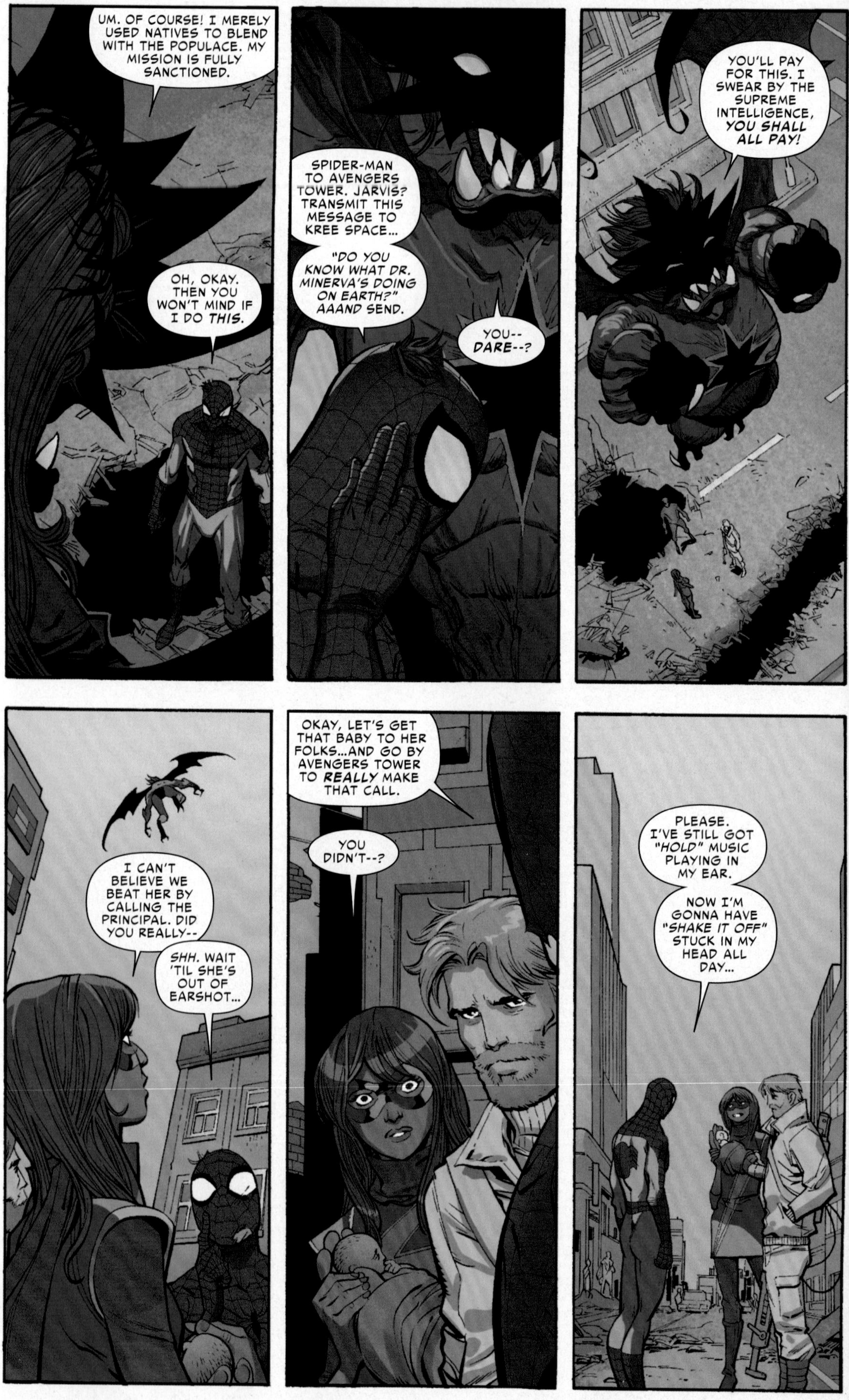
UM. OF COURSE! I MERELY USED NATIVES TO BLEND WITH THE POPULACE. MY MISSION IS FULLY SANCTIONED.
OH, OKAY. THEN YOU WON'T MIND IF I DO *THIS*.
SPIDER-MAN TO AVENGERS TOWER. JARVIS? TRANSMIT THIS MESSAGE TO KREE SPACE...
"DO YOU KNOW WHAT DR. MINERVA'S DOING ON EARTH?" AAAND SEND.
YOU-- *DARE*--?
YOU'LL PAY FOR THIS. I SWEAR BY THE SUPREME INTELLIGENCE, ***YOU SHALL ALL PAY!***
I CAN'T BELIEVE WE BEAT HER BY CALLING THE PRINCIPAL. DID YOU REALLY--
SHH. WAIT 'TIL SHE'S OUT OF EARSHOT...
OKAY, LET'S GET THAT BABY TO HER FOLKS...AND GO BY AVENGERS TOWER TO ***REALLY*** MAKE THAT CALL.
YOU DIDN'T--?
PLEASE. I'VE STILL GOT *"HOLD"* MUSIC PLAYING IN MY EAR.
NOW I'M GONNA HAVE *"SHAKE IT OFF"* STUCK IN MY HEAD ALL DAY...

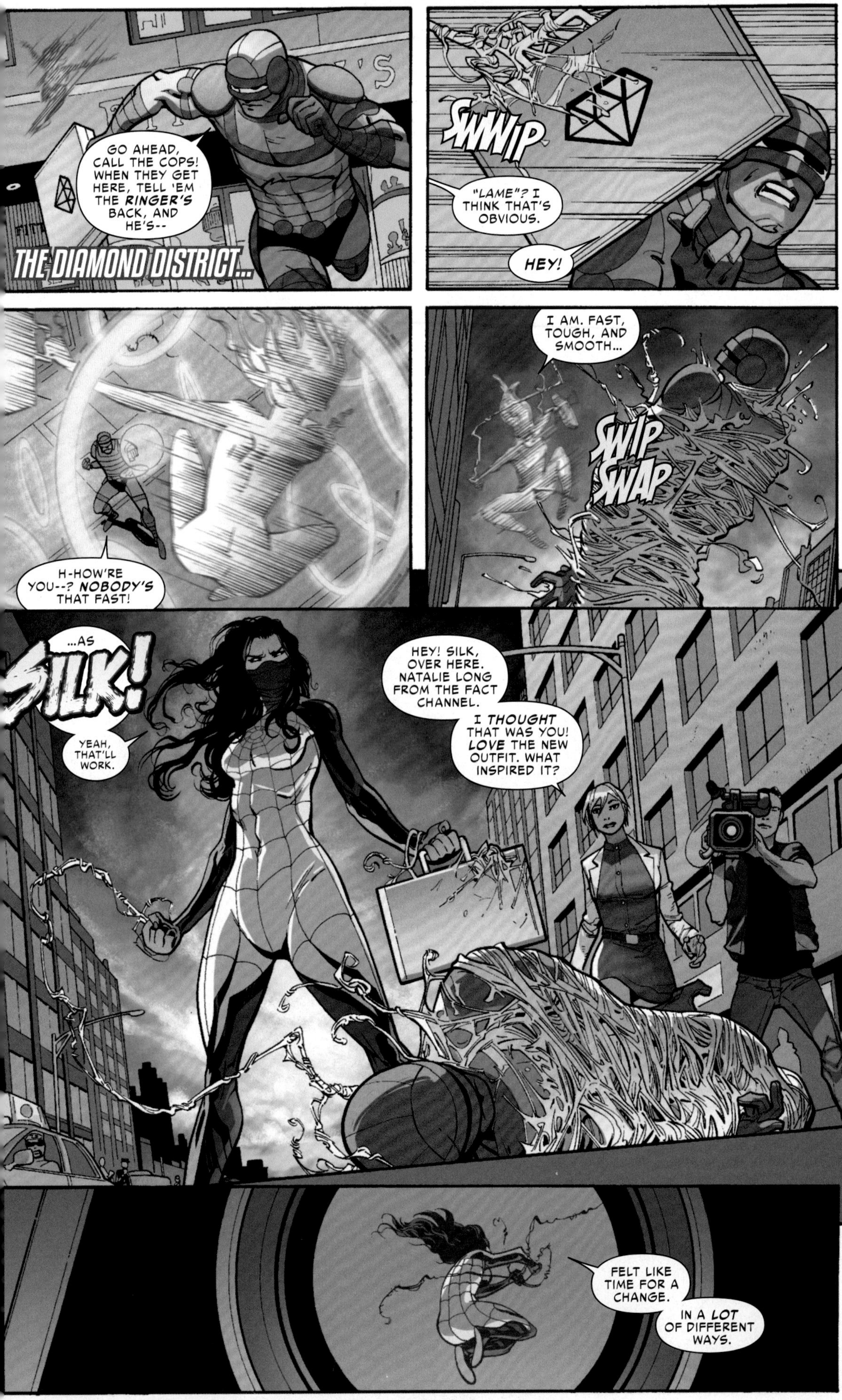

GO AHEAD, CALL THE COPS! WHEN THEY GET HERE, TELL 'EM THE RINGER'S BACK, AND HE'S--
THE DIAMOND DISTRICT...
SWWIP
"LAME"? I THINK THAT'S OBVIOUS.
HEY!
H-HOW'RE YOU--? NOBODY'S THAT FAST!
I AM. FAST, TOUGH, AND SMOOTH...
SWIP SWAP
...AS SILK!
YEAH, THAT'LL WORK.
HEY! SILK, OVER HERE. NATALIE LONG FROM THE FACT CHANNEL.
I THOUGHT THAT WAS YOU! LOVE THE NEW OUTFIT. WHAT INSPIRED IT?
FELT LIKE TIME FOR A CHANGE.
IN A LOT OF DIFFERENT WAYS.

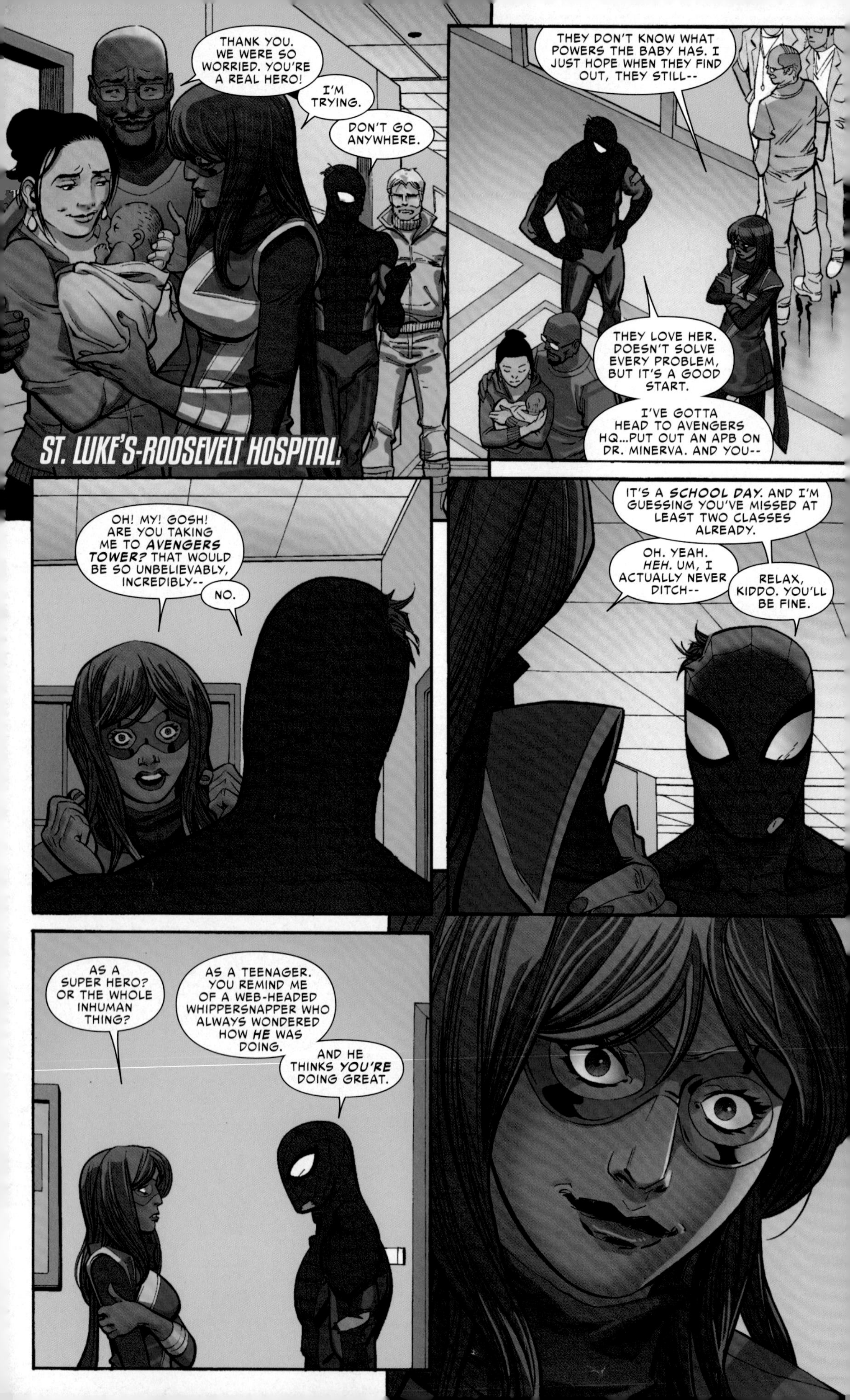
THANK YOU. WE WERE SO WORRIED. YOU'RE A REAL HERO!
I'M TRYING.
DON'T GO ANYWHERE.
ST. LUKE'S-ROOSEVELT HOSPITAL.
THEY DON'T KNOW WHAT POWERS THE BABY HAS. I JUST HOPE WHEN THEY FIND OUT, THEY STILL--
THEY LOVE HER. DOESN'T SOLVE EVERY PROBLEM, BUT IT'S A GOOD START.
I'VE GOTTA HEAD TO AVENGERS HQ...PUT OUT AN APB ON DR. MINERVA. AND YOU--
OH! MY! GOSH! ARE YOU TAKING ME TO AVENGERS TOWER? THAT WOULD BE SO UNBELIEVABLY, INCREDIBLY--
NO.
IT'S A SCHOOL DAY. AND I'M GUESSING YOU'VE MISSED AT LEAST TWO CLASSES ALREADY.
OH. YEAH. HEH. UM, I ACTUALLY NEVER DITCH--
RELAX, KIDDO. YOU'LL BE FINE.
AS A SUPER HERO? OR THE WHOLE INHUMAN THING?
AS A TEENAGER. YOU REMIND ME OF A WEB-HEADED WHIPPERSNAPPER WHO ALWAYS WONDERED HOW HE WAS DOING.
AND HE THINKS YOU'RE DOING GREAT.

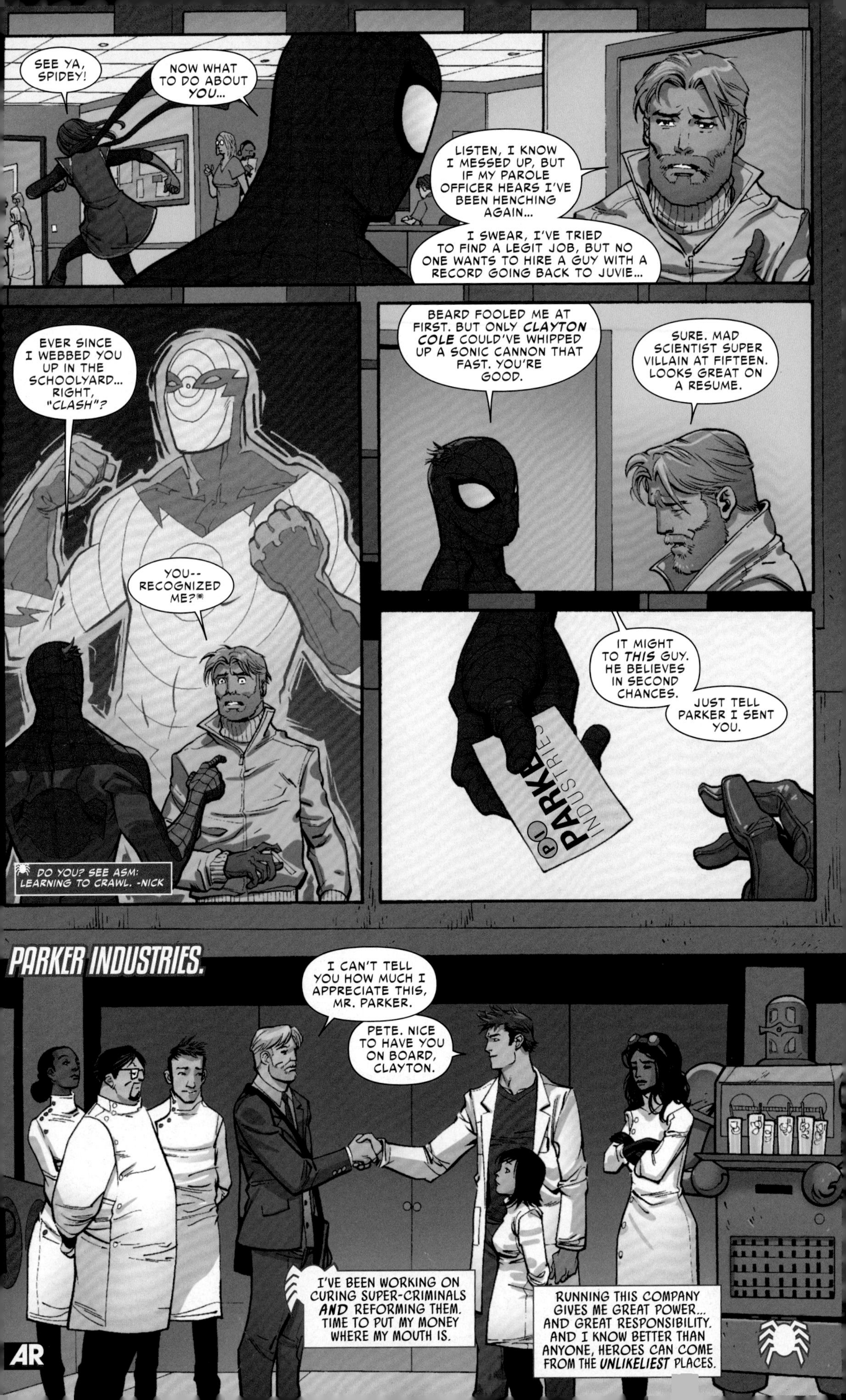
SEE YA, SPIDEY!
NOW WHAT TO DO ABOUT YOU...
LISTEN, I KNOW I MESSED UP, BUT IF MY PAROLE OFFICER HEARS I'VE BEEN HENCHING AGAIN...
I SWEAR, I'VE TRIED TO FIND A LEGIT JOB, BUT NO ONE WANTS TO HIRE A GUY WITH A RECORD GOING BACK TO JUVIE...
EVER SINCE I WEBBED YOU UP IN THE SCHOOLYARD... RIGHT, "CLASH"?
YOU-- RECOGNIZED ME?
DO YOU? SEE ASM: LEARNING TO CRAWL. -NICK
BEARD FOOLED ME AT FIRST. BUT ONLY CLAYTON COLE COULD'VE WHIPPED UP A SONIC CANNON THAT FAST. YOU'RE GOOD.
SURE. MAD SCIENTIST SUPER VILLAIN AT FIFTEEN. LOOKS GREAT ON A RESUME.
IT MIGHT TO THIS GUY. HE BELIEVES IN SECOND CHANCES.
JUST TELL PARKER I SENT YOU.
PARKER INDUSTRIES
PARKER INDUSTRIES.
I CAN'T TELL YOU HOW MUCH I APPRECIATE THIS, MR. PARKER.
PETE. NICE TO HAVE YOU ON BOARD, CLAYTON.
I'VE BEEN WORKING ON CURING SUPER-CRIMINALS AND REFORMING THEM. TIME TO PUT MY MONEY WHERE MY MOUTH IS.
RUNNING THIS COMPANY GIVES ME GREAT POWER... AND GREAT RESPONSIBILITY. AND I KNOW BETTER THAN ANYONE, HEROES CAN COME FROM THE UNLIKELIEST PLACES.
AR

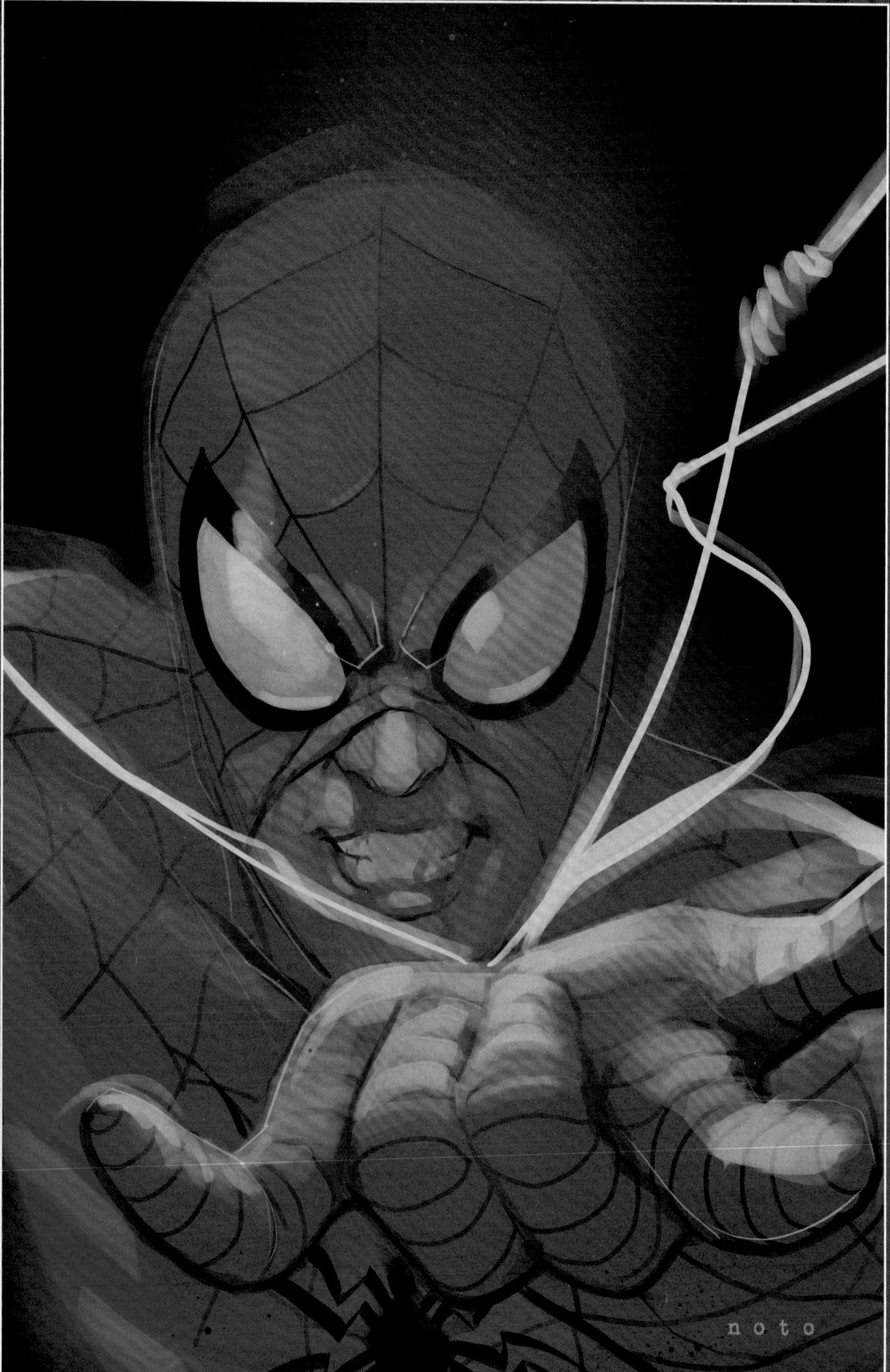
noto

#1 VARIANT BY PHIL NOTO

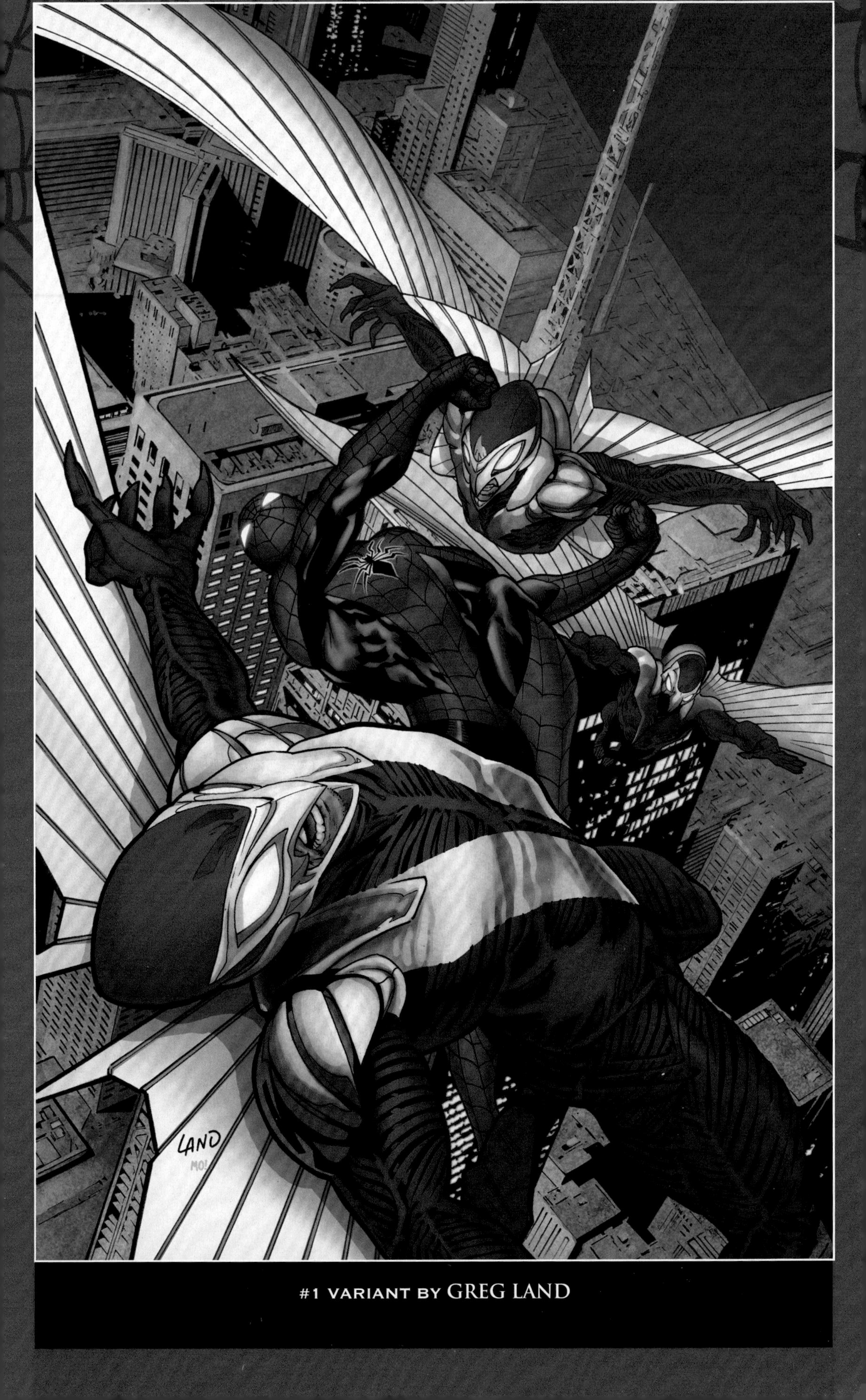
LAND
MO!

#1 VARIANT BY GREG LAND

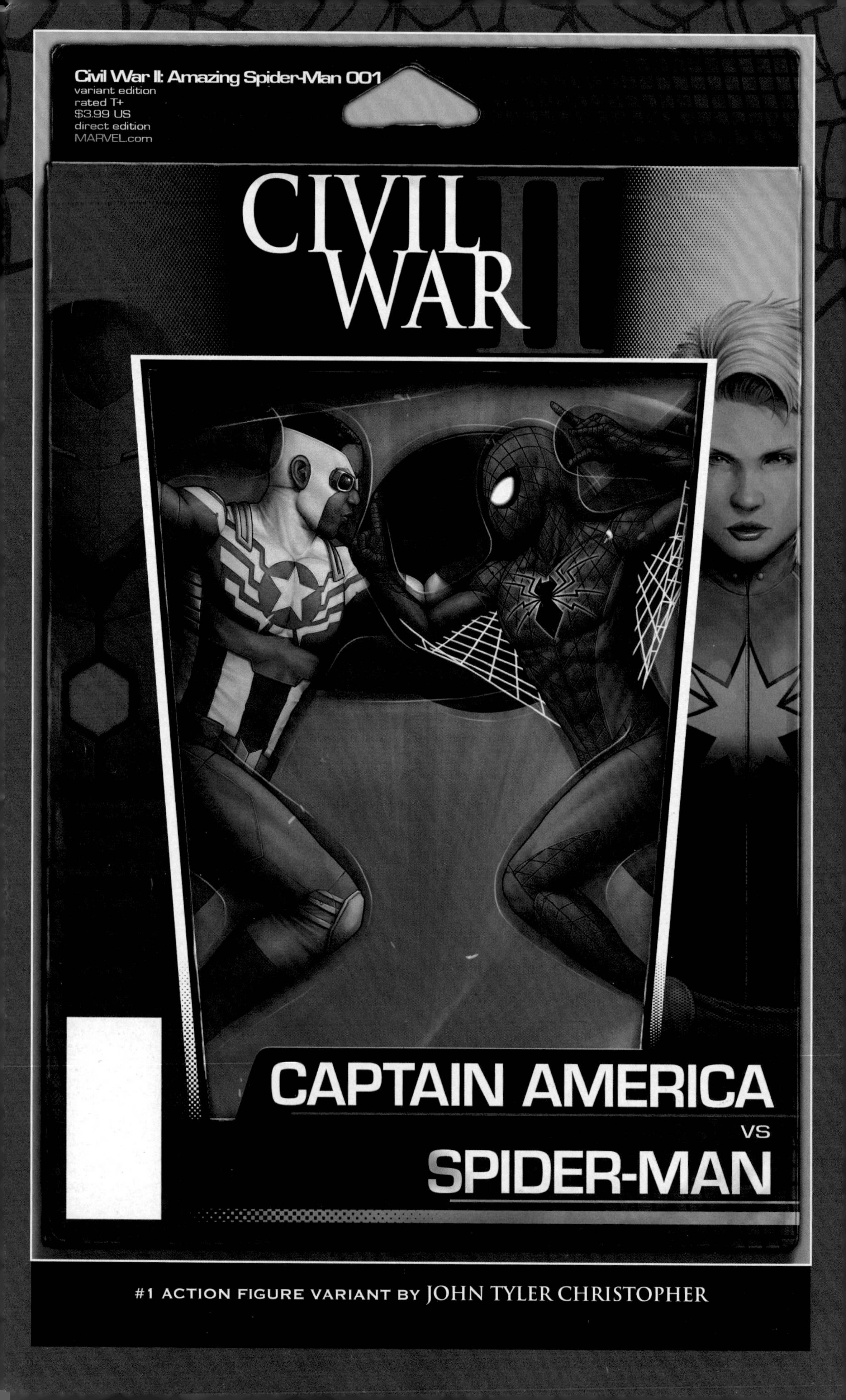
Civil War II: Amazing Spider-Man 001
variant edition
rated T+
$3.99 US
direct edition
MARVEL.com
CIVIL WAR II
CAPTAIN AMERICA
VS
SPIDER-MAN
#1 ACTION FIGURE VARIANT BY JOHN TYLER CHRISTOPHER

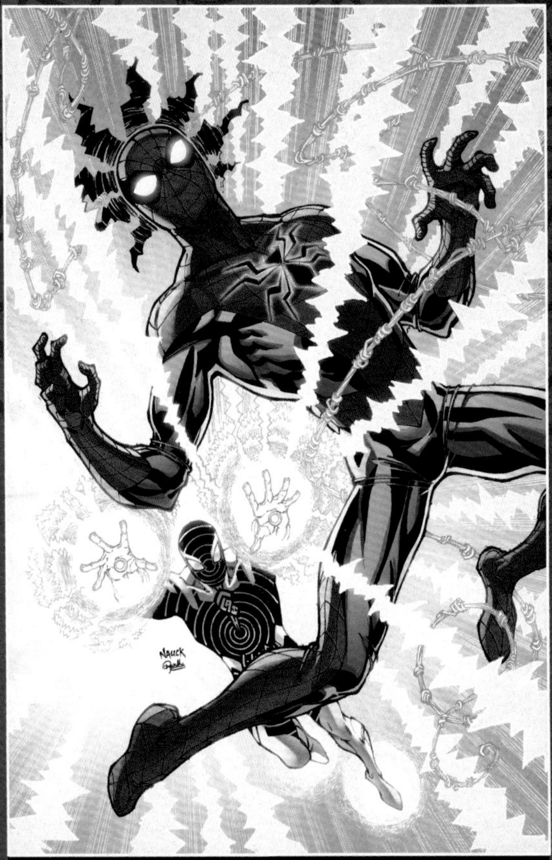
NAUCK

#2 VARIANT BY
TODD NAUCK &
RACHELLE ROSEBERG

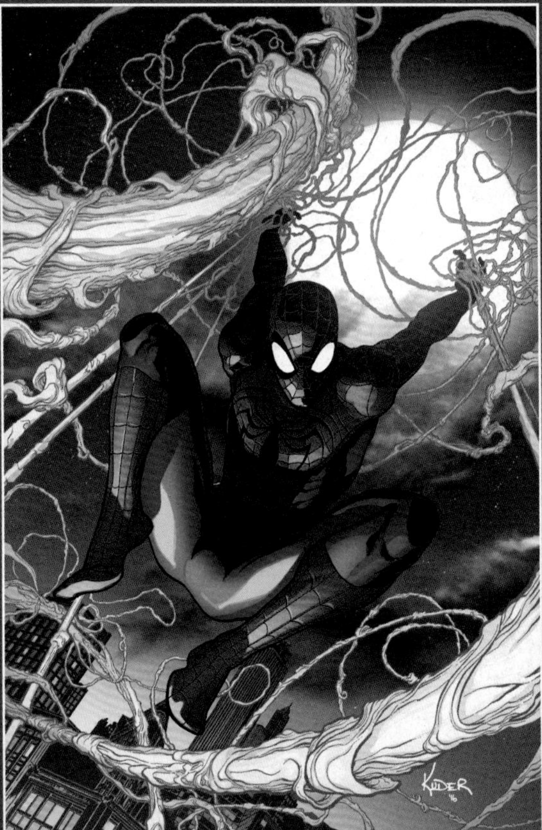
KUDER

#3 VARIANT BY
AARON KUDER &
MORRY HOLLWELL

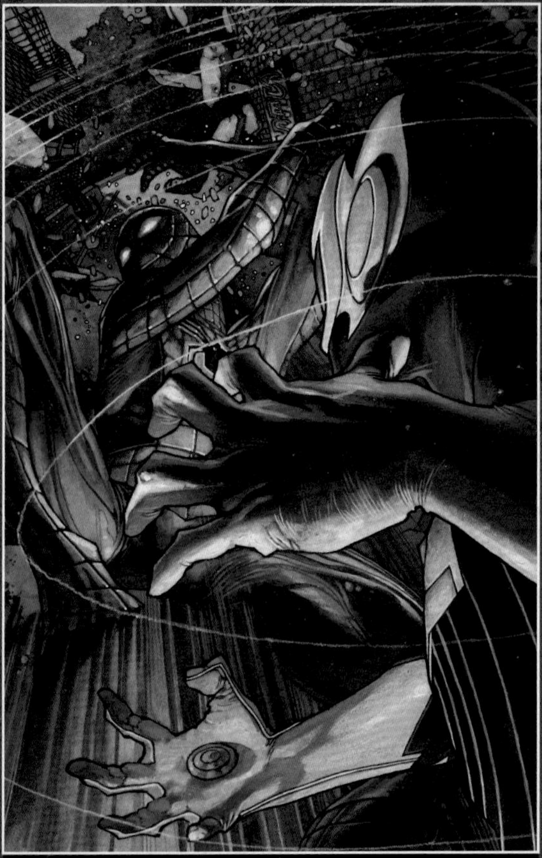

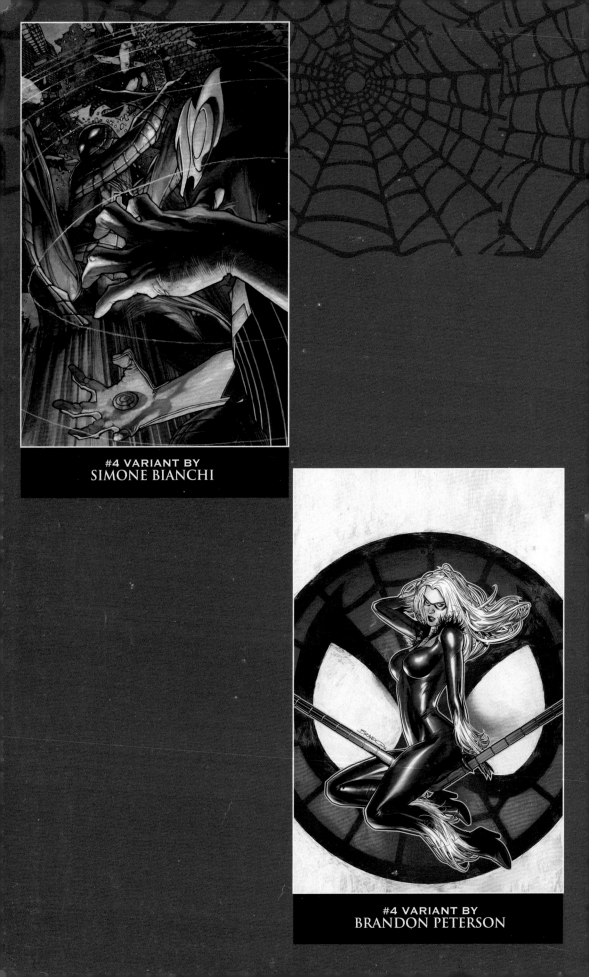

#4 VARIANT BY
SIMONE BIANCHI

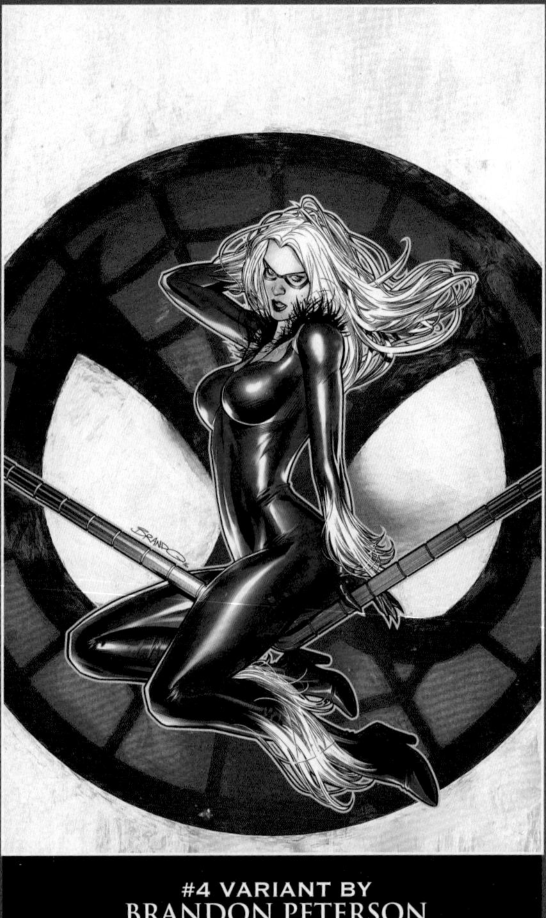

#4 VARIANT BY
BRANDON PETERSON